OVER THE COUNTER
AND ON THE SHELF

OVER THE COUNTER
AND ON THE SHELF

COUNTRY STOREKEEPING
IN AMERICA, 1620-1920

by

LAURENCE A. JOHNSON

edited by

MARCIA RAY

BONANZA BOOKS · New York

CONTENTS

LIST OF ILLUSTRATIONS

PREFACE

FROM THE TIME Laurence Johnson first flattened his stubby little boy nose against the glass case filled with Jackson balls and chocolate drops in the country store at South Butler, New York—and watched big eyed while the grocer turned a flat piece of paper into a poke to hold a penny's worth of goodies, he wanted to be a storekeeper.

His opportunity came in 1906 when he hired out to clerk in Mr. Edward Farrell's grocery in Clyde, New York, at the princely wage of six dollars a week. After he had learned the stock he was entrusted to "take out the team," calling on customers for their orders, then delivering them—a customary accommodation in days when phones were few. When he was raised to seven-fifty, he was, he says, never happier in his life. But he'd had hardly more than a six-month's taste of merchandising when emergency called him back to the farm. Not until 1918, when he helped set up and later managed the National Economy Store at Solvay, New York, was he back in the store business again In a year's time he had bought a small store and set up for himself. In 1931, with two other Syracusans, he organized the Associated Foods, Inc., and started the second large self-service operation in the East. Shortly he resigned to open the first of his own Johnson Supermarkets. He was a Charter member of Supermarket Institute, and its secretary for

many years, a member of the National Association of Chain Stores Operation, Inc., of the National Association of Retail Grocers, and other grocer's organizations.

Though his own stores were operated by the most modern and progressive methods, he never forgot the fascination of the little general store in Wayne County. In 1940, he united his interest in bygone ways with a shrewd sense of advertising display when he set up a replica of an old country store in his South Salina Street supermarket.

As he poked through the backrooms and attics of "closed-up" stores in the locality, seeking out fixtures and old merchandise, talking to men who had owned or clerked in country stores, he came across many old-time products once familiar to country store shelves, now seen no more, or conversely, as familiar today as they were a hundred years ago. He became intrigued in ferretting out the stories back of the stores, and back of the products. Within a fifty mile radius of his Syracuse home, he discovered many old store account books, day-books and ledgers—some as early as 1809—old catalogues, trade cards, bills and receipts—all uniting to draw an exact picture of what was bought and sold, and when and for how much.

His curiosity about times and things past was attended by a passion for accuracy. In following through on Bath brick, for instance, the only commercial scouring abrasive known in this country for years, he visited the plant at Bridgewater in Somersetshire in England, and saw Bath brick being made today, by almost the same process as was used before the Napoleonic Wars.

From his desire to pass on to others the pleasure he himself has found in knowing more about America's storekeeping past, this book was born. There has been no effort made to produce a "profound" work, rather, a readable, factual, and accurate background story of General Merchandising, from earliest trading posts to the shopping centers of today.

It might be mentioned in passing that many of the early storekeepers who appear in these pages, and whose experiences are noted are among Mr. Johnson's forebears. Thomas Stanton, John Jeffrey and S. B. Ayers, all furnished "family store talk"

around the Johnson farm. Country storekeeping was quite literally in his blood. The local stores and storekeepers who fanned his boyhood ambition to follow their steps were Wilson Brothers and John Hough of South Butler, and George Van De Water and Judson Green of Spring Lake.

In recent years, Mr. Johnson has disposed of his supermarkets and has retired into the country store business that has always been his love. His spare time now goes into collecting old store items and assembling complete establishments for museums and restorations. His latest "stores" are at the Tweetsie Railroad Station near Boone, North Carolina, and at the Bayliss' Cracker Barrel Store at Phoenix, Arizona.

FOREWORD

THIS IS a book to hold the interest of everyone who is curious about the history and development of America. Its appeal is in no way limited to those engaged in the business of "store-keeping."

Over the Counter and On the Shelf is truly an entertaining and informative treatise on the development of a national enterprise that has contributed vitally to the survival and growth of this country.

Without the trading centers, early settlers could not have endured the rigors of colonization and expansion described in this story of early American storekeeping. These pioneer "stores" were oases in a vast and frightening wilderness.

Well documented for accuracy, but avoiding heavy historical treatment of the facts, the book is much more than an interesting review of early trade operations. Its obvious intention is to focus on the whole structure of trade in the New World, closing with references to today's over $50 billion dollar food distribution business, the nation's largest, and to the wonderful world of tomorrow.

One follows the fascinating story of pioneer storekeeping, noting that in 1634, the Indians decreed the basis for the country store to come as well as the 20th Century shopping center—"Plenty of Everything, and All in One Spot."

Storekeeping in the early days was not for the faint hearted, the author points out, and we know that the same qualities of persistence and hard work are required of today's merchants. The frontier's merchants were men of courage and resourcefulness, and today's enterprising retailer also must persevere in his business with ceaseless energy and relentless supervision, using imagination to survive in a keenly competitive industry.

As we read of the physical hazards in the olden days and the axe-swinging, rugged competition among the fur traders, we appreciate, but do not minimize today's methods of meeting competition which demand the greatest ingenuity, if not the scalp, of the modern businessman.

National Association of Retail Grocers of the United States was founded in 1893 to establish an organization that would operate in the interests of community food store owners and the consuming public. From 213 members, NARGUS has grown to the largest trade association in the world, representing a total membership of over 112,000 stores, handling nearly $45 billion in annual sales. To assist its members in meeting contstantly growing domestic demands and marketing challenges, NARGUS continually expands its programs of education and research and increases its services and activities, ranging from the handling and promotion of merchandise to the selection and training of personnel. Its monthly magazine, NARGUS BULLETIN, publishes the latest information on modern retailing.

I am delighted that in this book the development of such a vital industry has been so thoroughly and interestingly recorded. The reader is made aware that we have completed a cycle that began with the "everything-under-one roof" country store and has returned, full circle, to the modern food store that provides one-stop shopping for the busy American homemaker.

ROSE KIEFER, *Secretary*
National Association of
Retail Grocers of the
United States.

July 15, 1960

IN THE past decade, interest in the country store as a means for historical and social study has been steadily mounting. Far-sighted individuals and museums, recognizing the importance of preserving tangible evidence of a past way of life, have, for an even longer time, been quietly gathering and preserving country store fixtures and merchandise. Some of these collections have been made open to the public as museums; others, in private hands, are still in the building stage, providing their owners with a collecting hobby of serious intent and of considerable enjoyment. Evidence of the growing number of such collections is witnessed by the frequency with which "store" items are appearing in today's antiques shops.

An early collector of "country store stuff" was Laurence Johnson, a storekeeper himself, who demonstrated its appeal to public fancy through attention-getting displays in his own stores. His wider contribution has been the assembling of complete country stores for folk museums and other restorations throughout the country. An able organizer and diligent student and researcher, he has constantly concerned himself with the "why" and "how" as well as the "what" of country store merchandise. As a result, the studies assembled in this volume depict not only the growth and development of the country store as a merchandising effort, but broaden to include the progress of American industry as illustrated by the progression of manufactured goods available over the counter.

He traces the advancements of the manufactured necessities of home and farm, as well as of food stuffs, from the first patent issued by the U.S. Patent Bureau on July 31, 1760, granted to one Samuel Hopkins of Philadelphia on an "Improved method of making pot or pearl ashes" through patents granted and tools used by numerous industries as they developed, down to modern manufactures and present day merchandising.

Today there are still a few general stores in rural districts, and accommodation stores in resort areas; but the country store of the open cracker barrel has become Americana.

To antiquarians and other students of our country's development, this volume will answer many questions pertaining to the social, commercial, and industrial life we have passed through in our first three hundred years of growth.

FRED C. SABIN, *M.D*
Early American Indus-
tries Association

Little Falls, New York
July 26, 1960

OVER THE COUNTER
AND ON THE SHELF

CHAPTER ONE

MONEY, MONEY

The Dutch Traded for Furs

THE TRADING post was the first mercantile establishment in America —indeed, it was the first European establishment of any kind. Trading houses had been built, and a brisk trade in furs and tobacco inaugurated with the Indians, long before any settlers had come to these shores.

Even in 1609 when Henry Hudson sailed the *Half Moon* up the Hudson to establish a fur trade that would give basis to the Dutch claim to sovereignty—and to get acquainted with his future customers and suppliers by a sample trading of baubles and spirits for Indian corn, beans, grapes, pumpkins, and tobacco—he found the French had been before him. The Indians were already acquainted with kettles and axes, beads and awls. They were in contact with the French at Montreal, and had done business some ninety years earlier at a French trading house on Castle Island, just opposite the present site of Albany.

The French might have maintained their early advantage—and New York State and most of Canada might have been under French dominion today—had not Samuel de Champlain misjudged the strength of the Iroquois. With an eye on their rich lands, he supported the Hurons and Algonquins against them in a surprise attack in 1609—

the year of Hudson's first up-river visit. Though the powerful Iroquois suffered considerable loss in this attack, they were far from beaten. They rallied to swear eternal hatred for the French—and turned their trading allegiance toward the Dutch.

For the first four years after Hudson's visit, trade with the Indians was carried on without any permanent posts. In 1612–1613, Adrian Block built the cabins on Manhattan Island that became the nucleus for New Netherlands, and in 1614, with Hendrick Christiansen, agent for the Holland Fur Traffickers, and Cornelius Jacobsen Mey, he erected a 36 by 26 foot trading house a short distance below present-day Albany. They enclosed it with a stockade 50 feet square, encircled by a ditch 18 feet wide. This was defended by two pieces of cannon and eleven stone guns, and garrisoned by twelve men under Jacobsen Elkens.

The following year the Dutch repaired and occupied the trading house abandoned by the French on Castle Island, and called it Fort Nassau. In 1617, they built another fort on the banks of Norman's Kill. Here was made the treaty with the Five Nations by which the Dutch obtained quiet possession of the coveted Indian trade, and the Five Nations obtained the means to continue the supremacy they had long maintained over neighboring tribes.

In 1623, the year before Peter Minuet, as first director of New Netherlands,

PLATE 1. Champlain's attack on the Indian Fort. From the original in the New York State Library.

brought a colony to settle on Manhattan Island, Fort Orange was erected at the present site of Albany.

The French in the meantime had withdrawn from the picture. Champlain, seeking to repeat his earlier success had, in 1615, with his own troops and four hundred Indian allies, invaded the country of the Iroquois, and laid siege to their village south of Oneida Lake. The village was fortified by four rows of interlaid palisades 30 feet high, inside galleries protected by ball proof parapets, and a very workable fire extinguishing system. The siege did not go well for the French, and on the sixth day, Champlain was twice wounded. With Iroquoian arrows imbedded in his person, he had been carried ignominiously from the field "doubled up in a basket on the back of one of his Canadian Indians." With him went any hopes for a New France in that section.

The Dutch reigned supreme and the Indians liked trading with them. For trinkets and ornaments, strong water to drink, powder and guns, knives and hatchets, they had only to follow their favorite pursuit of hunting, and deliver their spoils to the Dutch at Fort Orange. These amounted to some twenty-five to thirty-five thousand pelts each year.

A sample cargo from New Netherlands was one carried to Holland by *The Arms of Amsterdam* in October 1626. It consisted of 7,246 beaver, 853 otter, 81 mink, 36 wildcat, and 24 muskrat skins; also "samples

of summer grain such as wheat, rye, barley, oats, buckwheat, caraway seed, beans and flax."

As Dutch settlers became established on Manhattan, the ships from Holland included more sophisticated goods in their assorted invoices for they now traded with settlers as well as with Indians. In 1643, *The Arms of Rensellerwick,* a patroon's ship, brought in woolen, linen, and cotton goods, ready made clothing, silks, glass, crockery, leather, fruit, cheese, spices, brandy, gin, wines, cordials, tobacco, pipes, nets, looking glasses, beads, axes, adzes, razors, knives, scissors, bells, nails, spoons, kettles, thimbles, pins, needles, threads, rings, shoes, stockings, gloves, combs, buttons, muskets, pistols, swords, shot, lead, canvas, pitch and tar, candles, stationery, and various other commodities, valued at 12, 870 guilders.

To insure success to this venture, the skipper, the supercargo, and other members of the ship were allowed a direct pecuniary interest in the proceeds of the voyage.

For all their friendship with the Dutch, the Indians did not hesitate to trade elsewhere if the profits were greater, and into this Dutch idyl of happy Iroquois and easy wealth, there crept the dread shadow of competition.

Competition

THE PILGRIMS, under the British flag, had moved into Plimoth Plantation in 1620, and in 1627 had established a trading post

PLATE 2. Fort Orange, 1624.

at Aptucxet on the south side of Cape Cod, about twenty miles from Plimoth. The Dutch West Indian Company considered this a threat to their trade with the Indians of Long Island Sound, and sent Isaack de Rasiers, Peter Minuit's secretary, up to Aptucxet to look over the situation. He found the Pilgrims, with a shallop built, about to set off for Sloup's Bay to look for trade in sewan, the shell beads the New York and New England Indians used for money.

"This," de Rasiers wrote in his report of the trip, "I have prevented for this year by selling them fifty fathoms of sewan, because the seeking after sewan by them is prejudicial to us, inasmuch as they would, by so doing, discover the trade in furs; which if they were to find out, it would be a great trouble for us to maintain, for they already dare to threaten if we will not leave off dealing with that people, [the Indians] they will be obliged to use other means; if they do that now, while they are yet ignorant how the case stands, what will they do when they get a notion of it!"

(When the Bourne, Massachusetts, Historical Society recently reconstructed the Aptucxet trading post near Buzzards Bay, the records of de Rasiers, so carefully detailed, along with Governor Bradford's thorough description, made it possible to erect a replica of the trading post on its exact site.)

The trading post at Aptucxet consisted of a house, occupied by servants, who planted corn, reared swine, and were always ready to go out with the barque when occasion arose. The Dutch were bringing rum, molasses, sugar, and other products to the post and thought the English were content.

But even then skirmishes between Dutch and English traders were taking place in other parts. English and Dutch fortified posts were posed against each other in Connecticut. English traders had sailed up the Hudson in *The William of London,* pitched a tent near Fort Orange and laid out their stock of trade goods for the Indians, pretending to a security by reason of English claims to the whole territory. The Dutch from Fort Orange bore down upon them with half-pikes, swords, muskets, and pistols, forbade the agent and his assistants to trade any more, commanded them to leave, and pulled down their tent. When *The William* returned to its home port, a complaint was lodged with the English government.

The Dutch were also having trade difficulties from another direction. Marten Gerritsen, the factor at Fort Orange, was watching the number of pelts brought in decrease, and hearing rumors that the French were out-trading them in the "upper Mohawk."

To try to regain some of their lost trade, he sent Herman Meyndertsz van den Boegaert, a surgeon at Fort Orange and an educated man, with Jeronimus de la Croix and William Thomassen, accompanied by five Mohawk guides, into the "wilden," on what might be called a Good Will Tour.

Van den Boegaert's 32-page diary of that trip, found by James Grant Wilson two hundred and sixty years later, in 1895, in a Dutch garret at Amsterdam, New York, gave a full account of the trip, surely as difficult as any "travelling man" ever made.

PLATE 3.   Rear View of the Restored Trading Post.

PLATE 4.   Trader and Indian.

The journal began and ended, as well it might, "Praise the Lord above all."

The party started out on December 11, 1634, armed with vague knowledge of the route—a Figurative Map had been drawn up some twenty years earlier by two men who explored the fur country from Fort Orange down the Susquehanna into Pennsylvania—and the more certain knowledge that the Mohawks, through whose territory they would pass, were notorious people eaters—only ten years before they had broiled and consumed one Tymen Bouwensen of the Dutch army.

At every Indian village they contacted—they stopped at them all—they left sugar, salt, tobacco, awls, scissors, trinkets, and bits of cloth. Van den Boegaert took notes all along the line. In the Mohawk Valley near Schenectady, he saw iron chains, hoops and nails, "houses full of corn and maize, yes, in some of the houses more than 300 bushels," and inside doors of hewn boards, finished with iron hinges. In a 16-house settlement near Canahoharie Creek, he checked off 120 pieces of saleable beaver skins.

On December 20, they arrived at Schandisee Castel, a village of 32 houses, soaked to the waist, their clothes frozen on them. The curious Indians crowded so close to look at them, they pushed each other into the fire. Van den Boegaert was finally bedded down with the chief's "lionskin" for a cover, and stated "in the morning I had more than a hundred lice." At the community called Hulled-Corn Soup, he learned there were French Indians with the Oneidans; two days before Christmas, he had an opportunity to buy bear meat, half a bushel of beans, and a quantity of dried strawberries. He was also given loaves of bread to take with him, "some baked with nuts and cherries and dry blueberries and grains of the sunflower."

The party reached its destination, Oneida Castel, (near present day Munnsville in Madison County), after Christmas, and saw from the shirts, razors, and "very good axes to cut the underwood" which the French had been giving out, that the Dutch were up against real competition. They spent New Year's haggling over prices with the Oneidans and the Onondagan chieftains who had been called to sit in.

The Indians were reasonable traders, and pointed out several ways in which the Dutch had fallen down. Finally they set their own price. They would receive four hands of sewan and four hand-breadths of cloth for every beaver skin, and they expected sewan and cloth, as well as axes and kettles and other articles of trade—enough for everyone—to be waiting for them. They had no inclination to carry their skins such a distance only to find the Dutch had nothing to trade. They had no time to shop around.

Thus in 1634, the Indians laid on the line the basis for the country stores to come and the 20th century shopping center—Plenty of Everything, and All in One Spot.

The aggressive character of the English, who surrounded the Dutch on the east, west, and south, was the underlying factor for the Dutch withdrawal from the New World. When the Dutch flag came down and the British flag went up over Fort Orange around 1664, the Iroquois transferred their allegiance to the English. They traded with them, protected them from hostile tribes, fought for them against the French, and during the Revolution. Until their castels were destroyed under General John Sullivan of the Revolutionary Army, they furnished a good part of the food supplies used by British forces.

Indian Money

THE DELIGHT the Indians took in awls, which they used to pierce shell beads for stringing, quickly made clear to early traders that beads were a welcome item of exchange. The Indians had no use for coins, but shell beads, or wampum, as a convenient form of barter, they understood. They could use these for ornamentation, trade them for other desirable goods, or store them without fear of deterioration. So pressing was the need for wampum that enterprising traders produced many types of beads.

This "Indian money" was a factor in early merchandising with both New York and New England Indians. Pacific Coast Indians used shell money, too.

One advantage of wampum as money was that anybody could make it. Housewives in Manhattan and Fort Orange, utilizing fresh water shells as well as salt water quahogs, winkles, and welks, made it at a shilling a string, or passed it as money at mercantile houses.

Wampum was not difficult to make, though it did require a certain skill—the Indians would not accept poor wampum. It was wrought from the thick blue portions of the shell. Drills were made from an untempered handsaw, ground into proper shape, and tempered in the flame of a candle. Placed against a steel plate on the operator's chest and nicely adjusted to the center of the shell, the drill was rotated by means of a common hand-bow. The beads were polished by a flat piece of wood held in the right hand, then strung on hempen strings about a foot in length. Five to ten such strings could be made in a day.

The New Amsterdam government validated wampum beads at various rates, but usually two white beads equalled one purple or black. Four loose white beads and six darks passed for a stiver, or penny. The English later changed this to six white beads and three black.

During the last half of the 17th century, church contributions were made in wampum, and the first church "on the Jersey shore" was paid for by wampum funds. Even as late as 1683 the Flatbush school-

master was paid his wages in wampum. New England towns collected their taxes in these shell beads, and the ferry rate from New York to Brooklyn was two pennies worth of wampum.

Long after the American Revolution, wampum remained important to the Indians. Wampum supplies had almost vanished from Iroquoian villages burned by the French and in Sullivan's invasion. Only a few belts were left of the hundreds they had once owned. Such lack of wampum seriously hampered their usual inter-tribe trading with Western Indians.

Turning this unhappy situation to advantage, John Campbell, a Scotsman, established a wampum factory in Pasack, New Jersey (now Park Ridge), in 1775. Later he branched out into "shell pipes" a sort of elongated shell bead with a large opening, which the Indians prized highly. These could be worn as hair ornaments, strung as necklaces, or used to trim breastplates. An especially good one, worth maybe a few cents, would purchase a beaver skin. John Jacob Astor in his early fur trading in the West used many a "hair pipe," purchased from the Campbell factory, as currency.

No Money At All

THE PILGRIMS had come upon the Massachusetts coast by mistake. Their patent had been granted within the Virginia Company. But stormy weather had landed them in a region where they had no permission to be. Some of the "lesser" men, faced with the hardships of what looked like a cold and barren land, threatened to sail back with the *Mayflower* unless concessions were made them. And so, in Provincetown Harbor, before anyone landed at all, the Mayflower Compact was drawn up and signed. Forty-one adult males did "solemnly and mutually convenant and combine themselves together into a civil Body Politic to enact, constitute, and frame, such just and equal Laws, Ordinances, Acts, Constitutions, and Offices as should be thought most meet and convenient for the General good of the Colony." This democratic compact of government is accounted the earliest written Constitution in history.

Because it was organized as a communal enterprise, Plimoth Plantation had no independent storekeepers, nor did the Massachusetts Bay Colony, which operated under a Governor and Central Court.

As to the distribution of the much needed supplies that arrived spasmodically from England, Capt. Roger Clap, a passenger on the *Mary and John,* putting in at Boston in 1630, wrote in his Memoirs—

When People's Wants were great, not only in one Town but in divers Towns, such was the godly Wisdom, Care and Prudence of our Governour, Captain Winthrop and his Assistants, that when a ship came laden with Provisions, they did Order that the whole Cargo should be bought for a General Stock; and so accordingly it was, and Distribution was made in every Town and to every person in each Town as every man had need. Thus God was pleased to care for his People in Times of Straits, and to fill his Servants with Food & Gladness.

Though the Pilgrims began to abandon the socialistic system as impractical after the first three years, their early trading posts, such as the one at Aptucxet, remained group ventures. Some of these did not do well, bound to failure by the high cost of outfitting ships, as well as a paucity of things to trade; they had only fish and furs—and furs were being fast exhausted on the Eastern seaboard. Whatever monies they had brought with them were soon expended.

The settlers of the Massachusetts Colony were more affluent, but they, too, had difficulty in holding onto cash. Most of theirs went for the purchase of manufactured articles from England.

Although values were reckoned in English money, grain and wampum came to be the ordinary means of exchange. Inventories of estates seldom mentioned gold or silver. Even Thomas Newberry's Dorchester estate, inventoried at £1520. 4s. 7d, contained only £ 1.1s. in cash.

This dearth of coin was most inconvenient in transacting business, and when in 1642 the Civil Wars broke out in England and the flow of emigrants and exports was cut off, Winthrop wrote sadly: "These straits set our people on work to provide fish, clapboards, plank &c . . . and to look out to the W. Indies for a trade."

From this West Indies trade, embarked on as a necessity, evolved a very satisfactory "triangular" trade, in which little or no cash was needed. The Colonists utilized the plentiful lumber of the forests to build ships which they loaded with clapboards, hogsheads, and pipes (about twice the size of hogsheads), and set sail for the West Indies. The hogsheads and pipes, made from staves bound together with spliced hoops, were assembled, numbered, then knocked down for economy in shipping.

In the West Indies they traded their plank and clapboards for rum, molasses, and sugar. These they carried home in their reassembled casks and pipes, to trade with whatever English ships were in port for farm and building equipment, bolts of cloth, gunpowder, leather goods, pots and pans, or other cargo available.

Such three-cornered trading in which no money changed hands, but bills of credit, due bills, and store orders were the usual thing, set the pattern for trading in commodities instead of cash which continued in use in many general country stores until the late 19th century. Even today many country grocers are not averse to a little moneyless trading in local farm produce.

PLATE 5. Handmade hogsheads bound with spliced hoops, filled with tobacco, at Aptuxcet Trading Post Restoration. For fear of fire, social smoking in early New England settlements was discouraged.

"What Do You Pay In," Says The Merchant

PERHAPS the best available account of country store trading in the early 1700s was written for her contemporaries by Madam Knight in 1704. With her kinsman Robert Loos as guide, she had ridden horseback from Boston to New York, following what was later the Boston Post Road route. In her diary of this exceptional adventure, which was later published, she noted all she saw— and she was extremely observant. As a gentlewoman, accustomed to as elegant society as the New World afforded, some of her experiences in the back country must have seemed as bizarre to her as they do to those who read them today. The country store in New Haven, Connecticut, which she described so vividly, was undoubtedly a far cry from the English-styled shops she had known in Boston and New York—

They give the title of merchant to every trader; who Rate their Goods according to the time and spetia they pay in: viz. Pay, mony, Pay as mony, and trusting. Pay is Grain, Pork, Beef, &c at the prices sett by the General Court that Year; mony is pieces of Eight, Ryalls, or Boston or

Bay shillings (as they call them), or Good hard money, as sometimes silver coin is termed by them; also Wampum, viz. Indian beads wch serves for change. Pay as mony is provisions, as aforesd one Third cheaper than as the Assembly of Generl Court sets its; and Trust as they and the mercht agree for time.

Now, when the buyer comes to ask for a comodity, sometimes before the merchants answers that he has it, he sais, is Your pay redy? Perhaps the Chap Reply's Yes: what do you pay in? say's the merchant. The buyer having answered, then the price is set; as suppose he wants a six-penny knife, in pay it is 12d; in pay as money, eight pence, and hard money it's own price, viz. 6d. It seems a very Intricate way of trade and what Lex Mercatoria had not thought of.

Being at a merchant's house, in comes a tall

PLATE 6.   Earliest known advertisements of oldest tobacco company in the U.S., House of Lorillard, dated May 27, 1789, indicates types of tobacco available. "Ladies Twist Tobacco" and scented snuffs suggest men were not the only "chewers and spitters."

Tobacco & Snuff of the best quality & flavor,
At the Manufactory, No. 4, Chatham street, near the Gaol
By Peter and George Lorillard,
Where may be had as follows :

Cut tobacco,	Prig or carrot do.
Common kitefoot do.	Maccuba snuff,
Common smoaking do.	Rappee do.
Segars do.	Strasburgh do.
Ladies twist do.	Common rappee do.
Pigtail do. in small rolls,	Scented rappee do. of different kinds,
Plug do.	
Hogtail do.	Scotch do.

The above Tobacco and Snuff will be sold reasonable, and warranted as good as any on the continent. If not found to prove good, any part of it may be returned, if not damaged.

N. B. Proper allowance will be made to those that purchase a quantity.   May 27—tm.

country fellow, with his alfogeos [cheeks] full of Tobacco; for they seldom loose their Cudd, but keep Chewing and Spitting as long as they'r eyes are open, —he avanc't to the middle of the Room, makes and Awkward Nodd, and spitting a Large deal of Aromatick Tincture, he gave a scrape with his shovel-like shoo, leaving a small shovel full of dirt on the floor, made a full stop, Hugging his own pretty Body with his hands under his arms, Stood staring rewn'd him, like a Catt let out of a Baskett. At last, like the creature Balaam Rode on, he opened his mouth and said: have You any Ribinen for Hatbands to sell I pray? The Questions and Answers about the pay being past, the Ribin is bro't and opened. Bumpkin Simpers cryies, Its confounded Gay I vow; and beckning to the door, in comes Jone Tawdry dropping about 50 curtsees, and stands by him: he shows her the Ribin. Law You, sais shee, its right. Gent, do You take it, tis dreadfull pretty. Then she enquires, have You any hood silk I pray? wch being brought and bought, Have you any thred silk to sew it wth says she, wch being accomodated with they Departed.

They Generaly stand after they come in a great while speachless, and some times dont say a word till they are askt what they want, which I Impute to the Awe they stand in of the merchants, who they are constantly almost Indebted too; and must take what they bring without Liberty to choose for themselves; but they serve as well, making the

PLATE 7. Advertisement in early Boston newspaper shows merchants Gridley and Nolan willing to exchange merchandise for "brown tow and other country cloth."

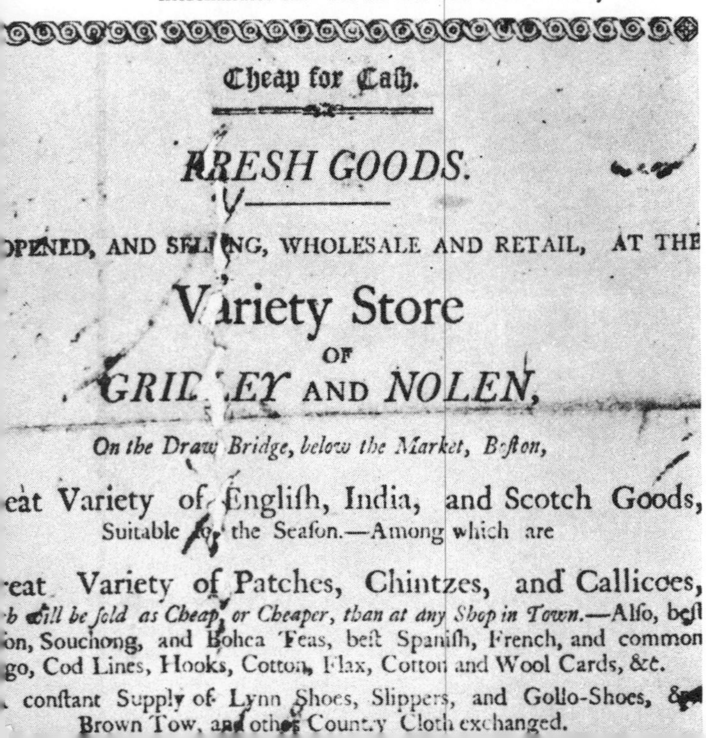

merchants stay long enough for their pay.

We may Observe here the great necessity and benefit both of Education and Conversation; for these people have as Large a portion of mother witt; and sometimes a Larger, than those who hav been brought up in Cities; But for want of emprovements, Render themselves almost Ridicules, as above. I should be glad if they would leave off such follies, and am sure all that Love Clean Houses (at least) would be glad on't too.

In spite of Madam Knight's expressed—and published—disapproval of "Chewing & Spitting," chewing tobacco ever remained a chief item on country store shelves. The fussy females who Loved Clean Houses had to wait nearly a hundred years for their first "boughten" soap.

Money To Burn

OF TIMBER, settlers in the New World found aplenty, and clearing the land of forests and trees was the immediate and mighty project. "Burning over" was the first step toward cultivation of the land, and fire attended the pioneers in their steady westward push.

Samuel Hayden, an eye witness to the clearing of 400 acres of land near Howland's Island in New York State in 1804, left a written account of this necessary act of destruction:—

The job of clearing 400 acres of land was let to John A. Taylor, Crandall Giles, Adam Crykendall, Z. Wachman, James Hamilton, Johnathan Vaugh, Martin Harker, Daniel Walling and his father Jeremiah Walling. These men took the job by contract, clearing from ten to fifty acres each. This was a great enterprise for this part of the country at that time, but the echoing click of a hundred axes told that the island instead of being a haunt for game, must soon be covered with fields of waving grain. The next year found the work of clearing off well done. Great elms and maples and mighty oaks had been felled and piled in windrows; none were spared for any purpose. The whole mass was as dry as tinder and a suffi-

cient number of men were employed to fire it at one time.

During the day the smoke was seen for fifty miles around and at night the blaze lit up the country for the same distance. The sight was magnificent and grand beyond description. The heat was so intense that men and cattle were driven into the swamps and into the river even, and it ruined fields of green oats a great distance away.

The first crop of grain on this 400 told of the richness of the soil. Ten thousand bushels of wheat were taken from the first clearing the first season.

This fiery spectacle, in greater or lesser degree, with proportionate results in wheat and other grain was taking place wherever settlers moved in.

In Wayne County, New York, in the early 1800s, Thomas Johnson, as an individual, contracted to clear thirty acres of heavy timber land and "fit it for the plow," at $14 an acre. This was not easy labor.

His son, Dr. Laurence Johnson, writing of his father's recollections of this work, spoke of the impoverishment of the virgin soil by the fires used in consuming the trees:—

The burning was, of course, done in as dry weather as possible, and as a consequence the vegetable mold accumulated under the trees during the ages, was consumed with the wood. I remember father pointing to certain low ridges in our neighborhood and remarking that they were burned over in a very dry time, and consequently had been poor lands ever since. After burning the more inflam-

PLATE 9. The Virgin Forest in the Adirondacks. Photo by U.S. Forest Service.

mable material, there remained a residue of charred logs which had to be hauled together in heaps, seasoned, and fired again.

Though forests were destroyed by these clearing fires, the end results—the wood ashes and potash—were of immediate cash value, and as a medium of exchange for barter and trade, supplied much of the early settlers' "money."

Charcoal, Too

EVERY blacksmith used charcoal in his furnaces, and the settler with woodland to clear and time to kill could turn an honest penny—even though he took it in trade—by building a little kiln for charcoal burning.

Jared Van Wagenen, Jr. in *The Golden Age of Homespun* described how this was done—

Wood for charcoal burning was commonly cut about four feet long. Any kind of wood might be used, but elm was considered especially desirable. The man who made the kiln began with a pile of light, dry kindling wood in the center. Around this kindling, the wood was set on end, and leaning towards the center; this was continued until there was a circle of wood about twenty feet in diameter. On top of this lower pile another pile was constructed, the wood being set on end as before.

A pit generally contained 25 to 30 cords of four-foot wood. When complete, the pile was thickly covered with earth and sod, and in general shape

PLATE 8. Newly cleared land in New York. From an etching by Basil Hall, 1829.

PLATE 10. Charcoal kilns. Photo by U.S. Forest Service.

might have suggested an old-fashioned straw bee-hive. Openings were left in the earth and collaring so as to give some draft at the beginning. When all was ready, the pile was fired by thrusting burning poles into it, and as soon as it was well started, all openings were closed with earth.

This charcoal burning took a long time, and the pyre needed careful attention. Usually the burner built a little shelter where he could rest as he watched his fire. If he were ambitious, and had wood enough, he could have two pits, with the shelter between, and guard two fires at the same time. A cord of four-foot wood usually made about 30 bushels of charcoal, and sold when finished for about 14¢ a bushel.

The charcoal burner would net, for time, labor, and wood, about $4.20 a cord. Though this seems little enough today, store accounts show that whiskey was then selling for 31¢ a quart; pigtail tobacco at 3¢ a yard, and tea—well, tea was a luxury, at $1.50 a pound.

Pigtail for Ashes

POTASH is the crude potassium carbonate obtained by leaching wood ashes and evaporating the solution to dryness. As this ancient operation, was performed in iron pots, the name derived from "pots" and "ashes."

Used in the making of soaps, the washing of woolens, and to some extent in glassmaking, potash was dearly needed in seventeenth century England, where more than a million people were engaged in the processing of wool, and a considerable number in

chandlering. The new source of potash offered by the American Colonies was welcome, for hitherto England had been entirely dependent on the low countries of Europe for their necessary supply.

Wood ashes were included in the first exports from America, shipped from Jamestown in 1608, and in the earliest cargoes from Plymouth. The Massachusetts settlers in earliest years received from six to eight shillings a hundred-weight. By 1670 those settlements which now comprise the states of Maine and New Hampshire derived their chief wealth from the fats and wood ashes they exported.

The first patent issued by the United States Patent Office, on July 31, 1790, to Samuel Hopkins of Philadelphia, later of Pittsford, Vermont, was for an improvement in "the making of Pot Ash and Pearl Ash by a New Apparatus and Process." The Patent Office began its present numbering system in 1836. That year fire destroyed all Patent Office records; some were later replaced.

Wood ashes were received in trade by all trading posts, stores, and peddlers. The earliest rate of exchange seems to have been about three cents on a bushel.

When Joel Hull, who removed from Massachusetts to Dryden, New York, built a small addition to his house for a store in 1801, his stock in trade—which he bought in Aurora, about 30 miles distant—consisted of one chest of real Bohea Tea, wholesaling at $1 per pound, a keg of whiskey, two or three pieces of calico, some narrow sheeting, a quantity of Cavendish tobacco at three shillings per pound, and two or three rolls of pigtail tobacco, which sold at three cents per yard, cash. It was generally understood that one bushel of wood ashes would buy one yard of pigtail.

By 1816, according to the Day Book of the Roland Clapp store at Turin, New York, wood ashes were being credited at a shilling a bushel.

A record book has been preserved, bear-

PLATE 11. A New Hampshire ashery from which ashes were carried to Keene for making into yellow soap. (Courtesy *The Earth Earthy*.)

PLATE 12. Pigtail Tobacco. Sturbridge Village General Store.

ing on the title page: "Herman Stickney's Ash Book, Turin, June 24, 1825." The purchases entered start from that date and continue until 1841. Prices he paid varied from 6¢ to 12¢ per bushel. The cheaper, noted as "field ashes," were from woods burned in the open and were not as clean as those burned inside. They may also have been leached by the rain.

Some men, like Herman Stickney, made potash their complete business. They made their own ashes and bought more, leached them with water, and boiled down the lye to potash crystals. Many merchants found it profitable to add an ashery to their other enterprises. Frequently they completed the potash process, using their own ashes along with those they took in trade.

The ashery was usually a small building laid up with stone, sometimes no larger than six by ten feet, with an opening near the top to stoke the wood, which was fired on a grade, and a hole underneath to rake out the ashes. Evergreen ashes made poor potash and were avoided whenever possible. Black ash, maple, basswood, beach, and hickory were good potash producers, and the water elm, where a single tree might yield as much as 200 pounds of the black potash crystals, was best of all.

A simple leaching vessel was a section of a hollow tree, a sycamore or gum by choice. This would be raised a few inches from the ground on stones or stumps, and an inside bottom fashioned of a thick network of branches and straw. The wood ashes were placed in the leach, water poured over them, and the resulting trickle of liquid lye which came through the sieve-like bottom was caught in a trough. Barrels were sometimes set up in the same fashion, resting on a "leach stone" or "lie stone," in which a furrow had been chiseled to channel the liquid into a suitable container.

The iron potash kettle in which this liquid was boiled was made to be hung over the fire by iron chains, and a three-inch ear, quite close to the top, slanted down on each side to hold the chains in position. It was from three to four feet across at the top, but narrowed quickly to a much smaller base in a sort of half-eggshell shape. The bottom was heavily cast to stand the weight of the lye as it evaporated to a heavy mass. Few settlers could hope to have expensive iron kettles for every purpose, and frequently their potash kettles served for watering stock, boiling clothes, maple syrup, or a venison stew.

In 1753, "Salisbury Iron Ore" was used in casting potash kettles for New Hampshire users; in 1790 one New Jersey iron furnace was concentrating almost entirely on potash kettles; and in 1798 such kettles were being cast for Vermonters at Sheldon.

Some ash works went a step further and refined the black crystals to a bluish white crystal known as "pearl ash," which commanded a higher price. This was done in a brick kiln at a temperature high enough to consume the carbon.

A ton of potash required from five to seven hundred bushels of ashes, according to their quality. Potash, through the years, brought varying prices from $3 per hundredweight, or $60 a ton, in pioneer times to more than twice that much in the early 1870s.

When the Erie Canal opened its 363 miles of waterway from Lake Erie at Buffalo to the Hudson River at Albany, in October 1825, the first east bound freight was equally divided between wheat, whiskey, and potash.

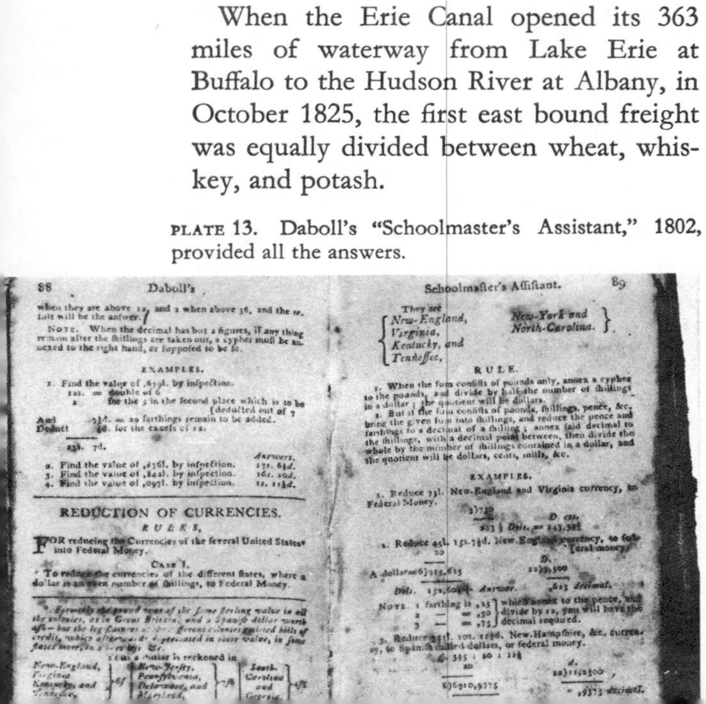

88 Daboll's

when they are above 12, and 2 when above 36, and the result will be the answer.

NOTE. When the decimal has but 2 figures, if any thing remain after the shillings are taken out, a cypher must be annexed to the right hand, or supposed to be so.

EXAMPLES.

1. Find the value of ,679l. by inspection.

12s. = double of 6
2 for the 5 in the second place which is to be deducted out of 7
And [illegible] = 10 farthings remain to be added.
Deduct [illegible] for the excess of 12.

13s. 7d.

	Answers.
2. Find the value of ,876l. by inspection.	17s. 6¼d.
3. Find the value of ,842l. by inspection.	16s. 10d.
4. Find the value of ,097l. by inspection.	1s. 11¼d.

REDUCTION OF CURRENCIES.

RULES,

FOR reducing the Currencies of the several United States* into Federal Money.

CASE I.

To reduce the currencies of the different states, where a dollar is an even number of shillings, to Federal Money.

* *Formerly the pound was of the same sterling value in all the colonies, as in Great Britain, and a Spanish dollar worth 4s6 — but the legislatures of the different colonies emitted bills of credit, which afterwards depreciated in their value, in some states more, in others less, &c.*

[illegible] a dollar is reckoned in

New-England, Virginia, Kentucky and Tennessee, 6s; *New-Jersey, Pennsylvania, Delaware, and Maryland,* 7s6; *South Carolina and Georgia,* 4s8.

Schoolmaster's Assistant. 89

They are *New-England, Virginia, Kentucky, and Tennessee,* | *New-York and North-Carolina.*

RULE.

1. When the sum consists of pounds only, annex a cypher to the pounds, and divide by half the number of shillings in a dollar; the quotient will be dollars.

2. But if the sum consists of pounds, shillings, pence, &c. bring the given sum into shillings, and reduce the pence and farthings to a decimal of a shilling; annex said decimal to the shillings, with a decimal point between, then divide the whole by the number of shillings contained in a dollar, and the quotient will be dollars, cents, mills, &c.

EXAMPLES.

1. Reduce 73l. New-England and Virginia currency, to Federal Money.

3)730
D. cts.
243⅓ Dols. = 243,33

2. Reduce 45l. 15s. 7½d. New-England currency, to federal money.

20
A dollar = 6)915,625 D.
12)7,500
Dols. 152,604+ Answer. ,625 decimal.

NOTE. 1 farthing is ,25 / 2 — = ,50 / 3 — = ,75 — which annex to the pence, and divide by 12, you will have the decimal required.

3. Reduce 345l. 10s. 11¼d. New-Hampshire, &c. currency, to Spanish milled dollars, or federal money.

£. 345 : 10 : 11¼
20
6)6910,9375
d. 12)11,2500
,9375 decimal.

PLATE 13. Daboll's "Schoolmaster's Assistant," 1802, provided all the answers.

Charge It, Please

THERE'S an old story of an early merchant who hung up two boots, one on each side of the chimney, and put all the money he took in into one, and all the receipts and vouchers for monies he paid out into the other, and balanced up once a year by emptying the boots and adding up. Quite possibly this is true, but by 1802, when Daboll's *"Schoolmaster's Assistant, Third Edition,"* was published account keeping was anything but simple.

For several years after the Revolution, when the English currency was dropped, there was a great deal of confusion about the dollar value. Daboll explained—

Formerly the pound was of the same sterling value in all the colonies as in Great Britain, and a Spanish dollar was worth 4s 6, but the legislature of the different colonies emitted bills of credit which afterwards depreciated in their value, in some states more, in others less.

This resulted in varying dollar values in different states. In New England, Virginia, Kentucky and Tennessee, a dollar was figured at 6 shillings, the shilling being worth 16 2/3¢; in New York and North Carolina, the dollar was worth eight shillings, with a shilling at $12^1/_2$¢; in New Jersey, Pennsylvania, Delaware, and Maryland, a dollar contained 7s 6d, and South Carolina and Georgia, 4s 8d.

If this was not enough to make a storekeeper's head swim, he had also to contend with a flood of bogus ha' pennies some clever English were making in Birmingham and exporting as "hardware."

Since the storekeeper traded two ways—with customers who exchanged their potash and beeswax for penknives and bustles, and the wholesaler who supplied the latter in exchange for the former, his profit depended on his astuteness in both trades, and it was important that he keep abreast of monetary differences.

By 1792 the United States mint was in

operation, and the circulation of Federal money began slowly to straighten out the situation. However, as late as 1818, the Roland Clapp store at Turin, New York, was still putting a premium of $2.12 on $85 of "Massachusetts currency."

The merchant was also handling goods from England, France, Spain, and other countries, and must know the packaging and weights and measures peculiar to each country.

Even measuring off yard goods necessitated a separate table in Daboll's *Assistant:* For this it was customary to mark off a section of the counter with nails or tacks, whereby a yard was divided into four squares, with each square similarly divided into sections of $2\frac{1}{4}$ inches. (The term "thumb" is an ancient measure of $2\frac{1}{4}$ inches or the length of the thumb to the second joint—hence "rule of thumb.")

"Getting down to brass tacks," Daboll gave the cloth measure thus—

4 nail (na.) make	1 quarter of a yard	qr.
4 quarters	1 yard	yd.
3 quarters	1 Ell Flemish	E.Fl.
5 quarters	1 Ell English	E.E.
6 quarters	1 Ell French	E.Fr.

There were tables for Wine Measure by which all brandies, spirits, mead, vinegar, oil, etc. were measured, he gives—

4 Gills make	1 pint	pt.
2 pints	1 quart	qt.
4 quarts	1 gallon	gal.
$31\frac{1}{2}$ gallons	1 barrel	bl.
42 gallons	1 tierce	tier
63 gallons	1 hogshead	hhd.
2 hogsheads	1 pipe	p.
2 pipes	1 tun	T.

He notes that 231 solid, or cubic, inches make a wine gallon, but a beer gallon contains 282 solid inches. A bushel contains 2150 4/10 solid inches.

In long measure, he gave "3 barley-corns (b.c.) make 1 inch; 1728 solid inches in 1 solid foot; 40 feet of round timber or 50 feet of hewn timber to 1 ton or load; and 128 solid feet, or 8 feet long by 4 wide and 4 high, to a cord of wood."

Once the would-be storekeeper had mastered the intricacies of necessary weights and measures, Daboll advanced him to Tare and Trett, the practical rules for deducting certain allowances which merchants made in buying and selling goods by weight—

Gross Weight, *which is the whole weight of any sort of goods, together with the box, cask, or bag, &c, which contains them.*

Tare, *which is an allowance, made to the buyer, for the weight of the box, cask, or bag, &c, which contains the goods bought, and is either at so much per box, &c, or at so much per cwt, or at so much in the whole gross weight.*

Trett, *which is an allowance of 4 lb. in every 104 lbs. for waste, dust, &c.*

Suttle, *is what remains after one or two allowances have been deducted.*

To give himself the most complete freedom in a barter, the merchant marked his goods in code. Favorite code phrases were: BLACK HORSE, MISFORTUNE, FISH TACKLE, CASH PROFIT, SO FRIENDLY, WHITE SUGAR, GAINFUL JOB, NOW BE SHARP, or other ten-letter combinations in which no letter was repeated. The new and trusted clerk could study such equations as NOW BE SHARP (123 45 67890) and know that $3.35 would be written WWE, and $4.57, BEH. The two together on an article, WWE/BEH would indicate quickly the cost and asking price. Sometimes to avoid the repetition of a letter or figure, which tended to make the code too easily broken down by curious competitors, the letter "O" would be used as a repeater, so that $3.35 instead of appearing as WWE, would be WOE. Particularly cautious merchants devised more complicated codings.

When *The American Grocer* was first published in 1869, it began almost immediately to stress the importance of bookkeeping records. An 1874 editorial suggested a double entry bookkeeping system be kept, and that "it would be a good thing for wholesale merchants to note on their bills, not only as some did that they were insured, but also that they *kept a correct set of books.* It would serve as a constant reminder to their customers of the importance of the subject and save, perhaps, many a dollar to both parties."

Such an editorial would indicate a general laxity in the keeping of store accounts, yet there survives documentary proof that the double entry bookkeeping was practiced by many successful stores long before the editorial was written. The E.B. Holden store in Turin, New York, for one, was using day books and ledgers as early as 1837. However, there was no standard procedure for bookkeeping, and each merchant followed the system that suited him best, or perhaps worked one out that only he himself could understand and figure.

An example of individual bookkeeping is found in the records of a large machine shop in New England in the early 1860s. Two castings had been made for a customer, each 3 feet square and 8 inches thick; one solid, the other having a circular hole in it about 20 inches in diameter. The bookkeeper entered both as solid. Then discovering his mistake, he computed the weight of a piece of cast iron 20 inches in diameter and 8 inches thick, and credited the customer "By one hole, weighing 432 pounds."

Up to about 1845, the merchant made his own quill pens, and usually his own ink. A trade card put out by Pearson and Little of Exchange Street, Boston, in the mid 1700s, advertising their writing, wrapping and letter paper, quills, lead pencils, inkstands, penknives, paints, slates, India rubber, wafer, Rice, Gold, Morocco and Fancy paper, carried a handy shilling table in one margin, and the directions for cutting a pen on the other.

Some of the old inks have withstood the years better than others; perhaps some storekeepers were more skillful blenders. Mrs. L.G. Abell in her 1848 edition of *The Skillful Housewife's Book,* gave a recipe for ink powder—

Reduce to powder 10 oz. gall nuts, 3 ounces of green copperas, 2 oz. each of powdered almond and gum arabic; put a little of this mixture into white wine and it will be fit for immediate use.

At the beginning of the 19th century, pens of very fine steel, cut and slit to resemble quill pens, appeared in England, but Americans clung to their quills until the mid 1840s. Though various attempts were made to popularize steel pens manufactured here, none succeeded until Richard Estabrook brought out his steel pen in 1858. (Estabrook pens today produce 216,000,000 annually.)

As for lead pencils, William Monroe of Concord, Massachusetts, was making some by hand in 1812, using his own formula for grinding the lead. In 1837, Louis J. Cohen began the first manufacture of lead pencils by machinery, but competition from Germany was too much for him, and he discontinued shortly, leaving the market to German control.

Though the merchant may have designed his own system of record keeping, he was obliged to keep his accounts in some semblance of accuracy. It was quite the usual thing to carry charges that were settled only once a year, with a large proportion of business done in anticipation of a coming crop. Since he was well acquainted with his creditors, he was often in a position to protect his investments. Roland Demerritt, who with his brother clerked in his father's general store in Stephens Corner, New Hampshire, in the 1880s and 90s, tells of a chicken raising creditor who was nearly $600 in debt for feed when the hens began to ail. The Demerritt boys did a neighborly act—and saved their $600 at the same time—by furnishing free medical advice and sitting up

nights with sick chickens until the flock was in condition again.

Storekeepers also were called on to act as middlemen in another sort of trade. When D. T. Mitchell of South Butler, in 1888 wanted to pay Mr. J. Rising $1.04 for services rendered, he gave Mr. Rising a due bill or order on the Graves Store for that amount. Mr. R. got the groceries, and the $1.04 was put on the Mitchell account to be settled later. When such a due bill was brought to a store and payment was made, it was voided by tearing off the signature. Occasionally some one was careless, and enough of the signature remains on examples preserved to indicate the process.

The T. Kingsford Cornstarch factory at Oswego, New York, in the 1880s issued considerable trade notes or script to their help, and these were generally accepted in Oswego stores as currency.

During the depression days of 1873, *The American Grocer* did a bit of thinking about the virtues of a good cash business and wrote several editorials extolling the idea. One concluded—

The value of a snug cash business has never had a better opportunity to commend itself to merchants than during the past two months. The men who have gone on serenely and quietly in business, unmoved by the storm around them, are those whose day books show few charges and whose tall balances may be presented on a few lines. They are the men who are able to walk into the biggest house in this city with a roll of bank bills in their pockets, ask for bottom prices, and if they don't get them, walk out again . . . who seeing a slip of sugar quotations can send a certified for 50 to 100 bbls . . . who are ready to take a customer's cotton or produce and pay him either in cash or trade and command a fair margin for their profits.

So it was that Hard Times dreamed up the Cash and Carry that Good Times would later make a reality.

◀ PLATE 14. Such Currier & Ives prints were popular store wall pieces after the depression of 1873. Lettering about "poor Trust" is composed of "dead-beats." (1881).

Women Lend a Hand

WOMEN, in the dark ages before 1900, may not have worked outside the home, but they frequently did their share in kitchen, buttery, and long winter evenings, to advance the family finances. Not that they received cash money for such labors. They took their pay in trade, and energetically supplied storekeepers throughout the land with things they could make in exchange for things they couldn't. In the end it was the same as cash in hand.

An early "cash" crop, which pioneer women worked with the men to prepare for market, was maple syrup. They called it "maple molasses." Homemade Indian brooms, fashioned by women as well as by men, brought 8 cents apiece in trade in 1837 —somewhat less than they had in 1818 when they were worth some 19 cents apiece.

Practically every household boasted a clock reel for measuring off thread as it was spun. (After forty revolutions the clock reel snaps, indicating a lay or knot, with twenty lays making a skein). The early Shakers made and peddled these conveniences in great quantities, selling them to stores or to individuals for as much as $1.50 to $2 apiece. With such reels, women wound off skeins of woolen thread at home—sometimes the storekeeper furnished the wool—and turned them in at the local store for trade. The merchant then passed on the yarn they had

PLATE 15. Clock Reel for measuring skeins of yarn, Shaker model.

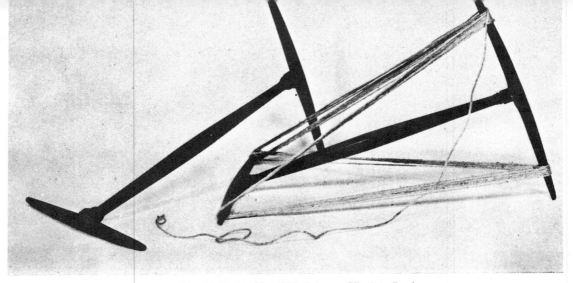

PLATE 16.   Niddy Noddy, 1733. Courtesy Virginia Parslow.

wound to knitting customers and bought back the finished garment.

The niddy-noddy, a hand reel, was also used to measure yarn. The story is told of one too enterprising New England lass who in early days was fined—and also jailed—for shortening her measure. She had cut an inch off the shaft of her niddy-noddy!

Mrs. Alice Steele of West Cummington, Massachusetts, wrote of her grandmother, Aurelia Todd Gudwith, who lived in Chesterfield and later in Worthington, as one who kept her larder stocked, bought all her clothes, and whatever gewgaws she fancied in the country store, without a penny spent. She dried apples, blackberries, blueberries. She made buttonholes in men's suspenders —they came from the factory in two strips and had to be sewed together across the back and the buttonholes set in. She knit stockings with the storekeeper furnishing the yarn, some black, but mostly white, at 75¢ a pair. If she put down more salt pork than the family could use, the excess went to the grocer. If there were extra potatoes, the grocer got them.

Many a woman churned butter and took it to the store in five and ten pound crocks. In fact there wasn't much a woman could fashion that the storekeeper couldn't use. All such items, brought in by busy women, were credited to the family account. The pay had to be taken out in trade. It is hoped that once in a while the ladies got first chance at the weekly buying.

CHAPTER TWO

EARLY STORES AND STOREKEEPERS

The First Real Stores

GOVERNMENT restrictions on independent trading were released gradually, a few picked men at a time being given protection in their merchandising endeavors. Thomas Stanton of Hartford was one who was so protected by the Connecticut General Court of April 5, 1638—

It is ordered that none shall trade in this River with the Indians for beaur [beaver] but those that are hereafter named (Vitz); for Harteford, Mr. Whitinge, Tho. Staunton; Wythersfield, Geo. Hubberd & Rich. Lawes. . . .

Like the others named, Thomas Stanton was an important man in the Colony. As a boy he had landed in Virginia and had worked his way up the coast to Massachusetts by trading with the various Indians along the way. He was appointed an interpreter by the Massachusetts Bay Colony, and his efforts in that concern are best remembered today because it was to him that Uncas, the last of the Mohicans, came when he wanted his will drawn.

Ten years after he had begun his trading in the Hartford area, there were enough white settlers in the section to warrant a trading house and he was granted permission to erect one near the mouth of the Pawcatuck. He chose a site on the west bank near Pawcatuck Rock. Vessels coming up the deep water channel could load and unload on the Rock itself, practically at his door. Thus he was relieved of the necessity of building an expensive wharf.

While isolated traders like Stanton could more or less set their own rules, early city merchants were hemmed in on all sides by government restrictions. The General Court believed in keeping prices down, and forbade competitive bidding at the docks lest it force prices up. The General Court also held down profits, sometimes limiting them to as low as five percent.

Merchant Capt. Keayne, in 1639, was convicted, fined by the Court, and censured by the church—some wanted him excommunicated—for taking more than sixpence profit to the shilling. As late as 1676, Massachusetts law was regulating the price of shoes to "five pence ha'penney a size for all pleyne and wooden heeled shoes, and seven pence ha'penney a size for well wrought French falls" (a 17th century shoe with wooden heels).

By 1650 when there were some two thousand inhabitants in Boston, and half as many in New York, retail stores began to open in the cities. Storekeepers tried to operate by remembered English methods. John Cogan, said to be Boston's first storekeeper, patterned his shop on that of his brother Humphrey's in Exeter, England.

Though they would have preferred to specialize in the English city store fashion, only tobacconists and apothecaries found

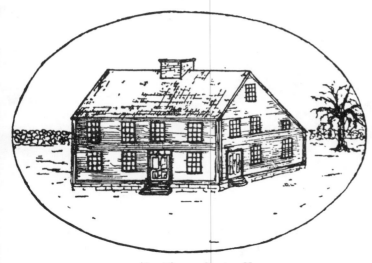

PLATE 17. Thomas Stanton House.

it practical at first. Most carried a mixed stock of whatever merchandise was available, and many followed the European vogue of setting up shop in a room in their dwelling house. Goods were arranged on shelves, over doorways, and suspended from ceilings. However scant his stock might be, every storekeeper hung out a bright sign, picturing his wares so that those who could not read might at least see what business he was in.

The shop-in-the-house was popular for many years. When Silas Peirce left his home in Egypt, Massachusetts, to seek his fortune in Boston—he was to found S. S. Peirce & Company in 1831—his brother who remained at home opened a country store in the wing of the family homestead.

PLATE 18. Penny Store in the House of Seven Gables, Salem, Mass., made famous by Hawthorne's novel in 1851. Early portion of the house was built in 1670, later enlarged. (N.Y. Public Library Print collection.)

John Hull, Boston Merchant

THE DAYBOOKS of John Hull, whose mercantile establishment, or warehouse, was on Dock Square, Boston, tell a great deal about wholesale merchandising in the latter 17th century. John Hull died in 1682, and his son-in-law, Samuel Sewall, succeeded in the business. The existing daybooks cover both regimes.

Typical of early merchants, Hull was active in civic affairs. He was a master goldsmith and mintmaster—with his partner Robert Sanderson he coined the Pine Tree shillings, the first money minted in America. He served as Magistrate, Deacon in the church, and Captain in the Ancient and Honorable Artillery Company. He engaged in navigation to far ports, and financed fishermen in closer waters. Like everyone in the shipping business, he suffered losses by captures, wrecks, and casualties, but on the whole, he prospered.

Among his customers were many pioneer traders, striking out for the "western country," to whom he furnished supplies, usually on credit. The "West," though still in Massachusetts, was a week away from Boston for a man on horseback. The trail through dense forest was for miles distinguished only by marks on trees.

Hull's records for 1688 show that on August 18 he furnished supplies to Samuel Bartlett, and on October 18 to Preserved Clapp, both of Northampton, with notations "To pay in the Spring." Later entries show these obligations were met when Samuel Bartlett shipped 22 bushels of pease and two bushels of wheat, and Preserved Clapp, 10 bushels of pease. Edward Taylor of Westfield, another "western" settlement, was given credit for supplies received by "six barrels of tar and three barrels of ditto, wanting a great deal of being full." The Rev. Jno. Williams of Deerfield, is noted as owing "9s 6d for four bushels of salt; 2s 6d for a barrel to Putt it in, and 6s for portage on board."

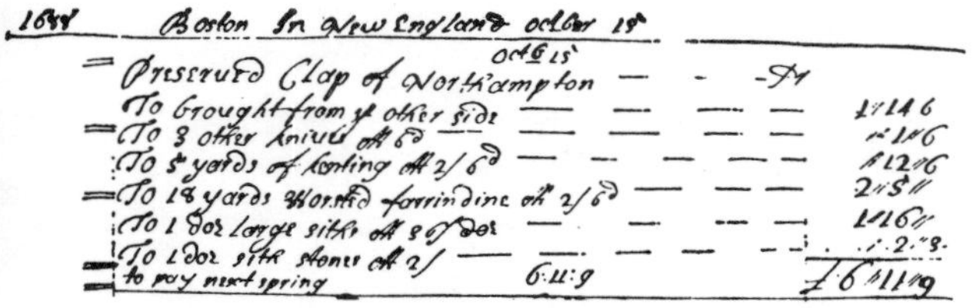
1688 Boston In New England october 15
Preserved Clap of Northampton octo 15 Dr
To brought from ye other side 1:14:6
To 3 other knives at 6d 0:1:6
To 5 yards of corling at 2/6d 0:12:6
To 18 yards worsted farrindine at 2/6d 2:5:0
To 1 doz large sithes at 8s doz 1:16:0
To 1 doz sithe stones at 2/ 0:2:8
to pay next spring 6:11:9

PLATE 19. Entry in John Hull's records for October 15, 1688, show Preserved Clap of Northampton the purchaser of 3 knives, 5 yds. of cording, 18 yds. worsted farrindine, 1 doz. large scythes, and 1 doz. scythes stones, "to pay next spring."

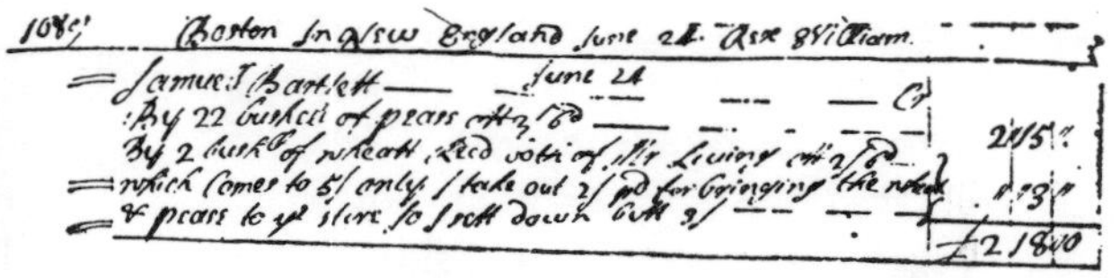
1689 Boston In New England June 21 Anno 8 William
Samuel Bartlett June 21 Cr
By 22 bushels of peas at 2/6d
By 2 bushels of wheat Recd which Mr Living at 2/6d 2:15:0
which comes to 5/ only / take out 2/ pd for Grinding the wheat 0:3:0
& peas to ye store to sett down but 2/
£2:18:0

PLATE 20. On June 21, 1689, John Hull recorded James Bartlett's payment by 22 bushels of peas and 2 bushels of wheat "brought in by Mr. Living." Pease were credited at 2.15s, and wheat, valued at 5s, at 3s, making subtraction of 2s cost of grinding.

A page from the Daybook, under Samuel Sewall's operation, shows the type of merchandise, including luxury items, imported for customers in the back country. This invoice of goods was shipped on board the *Barque Lloyd*, Mr. Joseph Chickley, Commander, to Isaac Pepper in Hartford, sometime in the late 1680s. The prices are carried out in pounds, shillings and pence—

	L	s	d
To 8 doz glass bottles at 3s pr. doz.	1	4	
To 8 stone juggs at 4d pr. . .		2	
To 64 [?] cotton wool at 8d pr.	2	3	4
To 1 doz printed books at 3s .	1	16	
To 1 doz Chathachisms at 6s .		6	
To 20 yrds wt flannell at 22d yrd	1	16	
To 20 yrds yellow ditto at 21d pr yrd	1	15	
To 2 doz horn combs at 3s pr doz.		6	
To 1 ps of calico at 25s 11 yrds	1	5	
To 1 doz worsted stockings at 44s	2	4	
To 27½ collered [?] ferrindine at 2s 6d	3	8	
To 26 yrds 4 hair camlett at 4s pr yrd	5	5	
To 3 sheep sheers at 2s pr . . .		6	
To 2 ps black ferritt ribbin at 11s pr.	1	2	
To 1 ps green ditto at 10s . .		10	
To 1 ps redd tafata at 10s . . .		10	
To 1 ps cotton ferritt at 4s 6d .		4	6
To 1 doz tapes at 6s 6d		6	6
To 1 doz hollon [Holland] tapes 14s		14	
To 28 yrds printed linnen at 10d yrd	1	3	4
To 18 yrds ½ kersy at 3	3		
To 1 ps ditto at 55	2	15	
To 2 ps wood silk at 24 ps . .	2	8	
To 35 M pd naills at 4s 3d. . .	7	7	9
To 2 ps Kenting at 7s ps . . .		14	
To 45¼ worsted crape at 17d .	3	3	10
To 12½ farrindine, more at 2s 6d	1	14	3
To 1 trunk 8s		8	
	47	18	4

The Country Corbins

THE MAN who kept store in the outlying country was less influenced by English tradition than the city tradesman. Specialization would have been impossible for him and the thought of it never entered his mind. His merchandising problems were unique, and in his adjustment to them, he set the pattern for the general country store in America.

In his own way, and on a lesser scale, he followed the precedent of John Hull—he traded for commodities, operated on credit, and was an important person in the community. Often he was the only one for miles around who could read and write. He served as lawyer, magistrate, and mentor.

Two lively back-country merchandisers in the late 1600s were James and Jabez Corbin, sons of Clement Corbin of Muddy River, Massachusetts, who crossed the river to establish a store at Woodstock, Connecticut. Their shop at Plains Hill supplied arriving settlers with necessities, and took in return furs and turpentine from the woodsmen, surplus produce from the planters.

To transport their wares to and from Boston, a distance of some seventy well-forested miles, the Corbin's built a great cart, and "James Corbin's cart, drawn by four oxen and four horses," became Woodstock's chief means of communication with the outer world. The huge cart was continuously breaking down on the rough roads, most often between Wooster and Menden, and the Woodstock folk were always uneasy when the cart was "on the road."

Once, in 1700, when Indians were harrassing the settlement, and the Corbin cart was overdue from Boston, sixty armed men went out to meet it and escort it back to Woodstock. (It had been laid over along the way for repairs, not plundered by the Indians as they feared.)

Jabez Corbin, the younger brother, was listed in town records as "merchant and weaver." He was also a Lieutenant in the militia or Training Band. In 1694, a square piece of land in front of Corbin's store, some four or five acres, was set aside as a training ground. It still forms part of Woodstock's pleasant common. Quite naturally the Corbin store became the meeting place and headquarters of the militia. During the troublesome times of 1700, James Corbin was formally requested not to furnish ammunition to any Indian, unless "sanctioned by Captain Sabin or the Reverend Mr. Dwight."

In the late seventeenth century, settlers began to take up land and migrate westward along the Connecticut River. For many of them the trading post was their only contact with the world they left behind. Such posts began to expand and to stock articles the settlers needed. Like the Corbins in Connecticut, or Preserved Clapp and Samuel Bartlett in Northampton, they risked hazardous trips back to Boston for merchandise.

There were boat peddlers, too, who called at settlements along the streams, and peddled short distances inland from their boats. Eventually peddlers' carts came along to service stores like the Corbin's as well as individual families.

New Jersey in Wartime

THE JACOB Vosseller & Company's store at Pluckemin, New Jersey, was in the thick of military activities in the bleak winter of 1776–77 when the British played hounds to Washington's fox over the frozen New Jersey countryside. Soldiers under both flags were everywhere on the move, skirmishing forward, scurrying back, turning the countryside upside down, sleeping in farmhouses when they were lucky, on the ground when they were not, always hungry, always cold. A stranger might be friend or foe, or a disgusted deserter off on his own.

Through it all Jacob Vosseller kept store, selling his chocolate, his rum, his snuff, and his Almanacs, entering his accounts neatly in his Daybooks, a penny here, a six-pence there, to be added up when some sort of peace made payment possible.

His accounts that winter carried many

PLATE 21.   Post office section of the old Ullman Store, Montclair, N. J. now owned by Mr. and Mrs. R. E. Tomlinson, and restored as a country store museum.

charges for powder and flint, and for odd jobs indicative of his talents and the needs of his neighbors. His entries included "for mending hoes," "made shoes and mended same," "cured leather," "made grat-coats." He charged for the letters he wrote for those who could not write themselves, for the errands he ran, and the trips he made for them. Most storekeepers performed these favors freely, but this was wartime—a man might be excused for charging. He served as lawyer, drawing up notes and mortgages for sixpence each, bonds for a shilling.

To Peter Moelich of Basking Ridge, on whose farm General Charles Lee's army was quartered, he sold the makings of a cheerful evening—rum, some allspice, a jew's-harp. There was less merriment on the night of December 13, when Lee, Washington's enigmatic second-in-command, was seized in the night in a nearby tavern by Banastre Tarleton and his Light Horse Dragoons, and hustled away to New York in his nightshirt. No one knew what the morrow would bring in New Jersey!

Money was a worry, too. The store had to gamble on what Continental specie might be worth next week, next month, next year. Yet Vosseller gave Peter Wortman a three pound, one shilling and threepence credit for a seven dollar bill, and Richard Compton Jr. twenty-one pounds, thirteen shillings, fourpence for "50 Contenantle dollars." On January 1, 1777, with fighting gory in the fields around him, he took his patriotic stand, and noted in his Account Book at the beginning of the New Year: "All that is sold hereafter to be proclamation money charged, except mentioned in the book."

On January 3, the day of the Battle of Princeton, his books show only one entry, and no more until the 6th, when Washington's successful army moved on to winter quarters in Morristown.

Oh, wartime was unsettling for everyone concerned. Perhaps Jacob Vosseller had good reason to pen for handy reference on the fly leaf of his account book—

Cure for Fits
Take the root of a young mullen, the root of a large thistle, it has a narrow rib,
The root of five finger,
The root of a yerb call'd fit yerb
Boyl them together.
Quite likely he charged for this prescription, too!

The Roland Clapp Store in Turin—1816

IMMEDIATELY after the Revolution, pioneers began a serious push westward from New England toward the fertile Finger Lake region in New York State. General John Sullivan had dispersed the Indian threat from the section, and many of the new settlers were men who had been with him on his famous march, drawn back by the remembrance of the Indian's rich fields and plentiful harvests.

Settlements like Turin, New York, began to take shape, and general stores appeared at closer intervals to serve the growing communities. Turin had a population of 440, according to the 1800 census, consisting of 77 families. All but 15 men and 11 women were under forty-five years of age.

Fortunately the record books of the Roland Clapp store in Turin, from its opening date in 1816, through various ownerships, to 1913, lacking only the years 1818 to 1833, have been available for study. These records comprise some two hundred and fifty daybooks, ledgers, cash books, order books and the like.

From them the acute observer can read the story of all general country stores of the period, and more besides. There's the background picture of the farm where self-sufficient pioneers raised all the foodstuffs the family used with the exceptions of such

luxuries as coffee, tea, spices, salartus, molasses, salt, and sugar, and of those only salt
was indispensable. There's a hint of romance when Aaron Fenton purchased in
one afternoon a set of teaspoons, 63¢; a
handkerchief, 38¢, and a pair of white silk
gloves, $1. There's a teen age problem when
Winthrop Sheppered, Jr. was put down
in the charge book for "Buttons 25¢;"
and "Cash 25¢, to go to a dance." A run on
half-quires of paper at 16¢, or on pen or
pocket knives, 25 to 50¢, or hair combs, 25¢,
indicate that word had got around of a new
shipment just received.

The first few pages of Clapp's earliest daybook, were devoted to notes: "J. D. Doty
(clerk) began to board to Reuben Wool-
worths 6 Nov. 1816"; "R. Clapp began
the 21st Dec. 1816, both at 11s per week."
"J. D. Doty absent at home while my father
was at Albany in April, 17 days, 1816."
"James D. Doty left off boarding at R.
Woolworth's on Monday 20 May 1816,"
and "Roland Clapp left off boarding to R.
Woolworth's on Monday 15 July, 1816."
Vacations were noted: "Absent at the Salt
Springs 7 days myself," and below "Doty
absent to the Salt Springs 4 days." (The
Salt Springs was Syracuse).

Though there were a few advance sales,
duly noted, the daybook really began with
the official opening of the store on January
1, 1816. On that day $105.95½ was charged
on the books; no record was made of the
amount of cash taken in. There were 28
charge customers, with 51 entries, and 127
items charged. Many of the curious made
more than one visit—Consider Williston

PLATE 22.   Typical Country Store.

PLATE 23.   Backwoodsmen. From an etching by Basil
Hall, 1829.

was in four times, and David Kendall, six;
almost everyone came in twice.

The first customer was Justus Woolworth who bright and early bought 2 quarts
of brandy at $3 a gallon, and eight sleigh
bells at $2.

Of the charge items, ten were for tea at
$1.50 a pound; seven for sugar, totalling
$4.76; one for nutmeg at 12¢; one for pep-
per 16¢. Stephen Hart got one pound of
sugar 31¢, 1 pint of brandy, 38¢, 1 block tin
teapot at $1.79, and one-quarter pound of
tea 37¢. John Ives bought a chamber pot at
37¢; Henry Graves, 10 sleigh bells at $2.50.
Several sets of "teas" (teaspoons) were sold
at 63¢; teapots at 38¢; three tumblers for
38¢; 4 bowls at 50¢. Someone bought a
pound of tobacco at 37½¢, and someone else
a lesser amount at 12½¢. David Phillips was
set back 28¢ for a pint of rum. Most of the
entries were for drygoods, clothing, and
shoes.

The second day, January 2, business
dropped off. There were only 37 entries,
with 18 charges, one of which was to John
Whittlesey who borrowed $5. Total busi-
ness, $24.26.

The third day business dropped still
more; only $9.16 was charged, including
a 40¢ slate and pencil to Roland Nimox, and
another pint of brandy at 38¢ to Stephen
Hart. That day the bills began to come in.
Fortunately these could be paid without
money. Loami Taylor and Consider Williston, who had each brought a load from Albany, were credited $30 on the books.
Thomas Kilam also found a way to beat the
money problem—he bought a $2.50 axe
and paid for it with deerskins.

The first credit for wood ashes appear on
January 5, when Judah Barnes charged a

PLATE 24. *An Embryo Town,* from an etching by Basil Hall, 1829.

pound of tea at $1.50 and 4 papers of tobacco at 12¢, and his account was noted "to be paid in ashes at Graves." Apparently "Graves" was an ashery, and some three-cornered trading was already in progress. Entries later in the year show Henry Graves credited $13 for 52 muskrat skins and 37¢ for a mink; John Whittlesey, $50 for 20,000 shingles; John Case, $5.76 for field ashes at 9¢ a bushel; Alfred Books, $11.25 for beaver. Rush Davis was marked down for credit "144 ash rails or near that number. Davis says 150. No price on them."

The following New Year's, John Kilam and David Phillips switched from brandy and rum to cheaper whiskeys, which sold for 13¢ a half pint, or 31¢ a quart. (This was still profitable to the storekeeper, for whiskey could be bought wholesale for 25¢ a gallon.)

Of interest to those who want to know exactly what a country store carried in 1837 is the 24-page inventory, forty items to a page, totalling $1773.75, which was taken on May 6, 1837 when Roland Clapp turned the store over to E.B. Holden and Company. Dry goods took up most of the inventory, two full pages being devoted to calicos alone, ranging from 9¢ to 26¢ a yard.

The following items, selected from this inventory, are listed at wholesale prices. The shilling mark (/) and pence mark (d) were used occasionally for individual items. The New York shilling was then valued at 12½ cents.

5 splint brooms .42; 2 mop sticks .20; 6 axe handles 1/ea; 1 pr. large steelyards 2.25; 4 brass candlesticks, 6/2d, 1.25; 1 stone china pitcher .38; 5 pink and black pitchers 2/, 1.25; 2 glass lamps 1/6d, 1.44; in the neighborhood of 60 gross screws; 1000 clout nails .56; 6 sheets of corn plaster @ .02; 3 prs. of spectacles 2/3d, 1.84; 4

razor strops 1/4d, .67; 2 razors @ .10; 258 papers of garden seeds .06¹/₄ a paper; 17 papers of onion seeds 1/; toothbrushes @ .07; 40 lbs. salt @ .08; 1 doz. bed cords 3.38; 1 molasses gate [faucet] $1; 1¹/₂ set of tin measures 1.75; 2-gal. jug .34; 1-gal jug .22; 3 3/4 lb. coffee @ .10; 4¹/₂ lb. pepper 1.41; 5₁/₂ lb. spice .50; 7¹/₂ lb. starch .55; 1 cask tobacco, 190 lb. @ 18 ¹/₂, 35.15; 1 box of pipes 1.19; 3¹/₄ lb. of twine .47; 3¹/₂ lb. rope .15; 12¹/₂ lb. of B snuff @ 2/, 3.12; 2¹/₄ lb. of ginger @ .08; 2 chests of green tea @ .50, 102 lbs. 61.20; 1¹/₄ lbs. raisins @ .10; 2 lbs. rosin .04; 70 lbs. salartus @ 9¢, 7.11; 7 lbs. of alum @ 7, 1.49; 1 bbl. logwood 3.44; 8¹/₂ gal. molasses @ 35¢, 2.97¹/₄; 10 gal. oil @ 8¢, 1.00.

Lightening mathematicians, making quick estimates between tea paid for at 60¢ a pound and charged in the daybook at $1.50, may conclude there was an unusually high mark-up on "luxury" items. Transportation was the storekeeper's hidden expense. Frequently it cost him as much, or more, than the goods themselves. Wholesale prices on imported goods—sugar, coffee, spices—were in a constant state of flux, subject to inflation whenever unsettled world conditions made shipping difficult. The War of 1812, for instance, played havoc with imports, sending loose sugar to 31¢ a pound and loaf sugar to 50¢ a pound. Coffee, which the Roland Clapp store was selling at 44¢ a pound in 1816, while the effects of the 1812 conflict were still being felt, dropped in 1830, when things had quieted, to 19¢ a pound.

An Early Chain

THE STORY of John Meeker's chain store operation, one of the earliest in the country, has to be pieced together from newspaper clippings, brief accounts in county histories, and extracts from letters, for no records have been preserved.

PLATE 25.   Jedediah Barber's Great Western Store, in Homer, N.Y. built in 1811, destroyed by fire in 1856 at an estimated loss of $50,000.   Homer was reputedly the "Homerville," and Jedediah Barber, the "David Harum," of the book by that name.

Meeker, from Hinsdale, Massachusetts, was an entrepreneur with merchandising vision who took advantage of the early 19th century trek to upper New York state. He chose locations, set up stores, and with great good judgment selected young men as his partners to operate them. At one time he was reported to be operating fifteen stores.

He shared with his junior partners the profits of their particular location while he attended to the trading of all produce taken in barter, and the supplying of manufactured goods for the retail trade. Four-or six-horse covered wagons hauled the potash and wheat and oats from his country locations to the Hudson River at Albany, and returned with hardware, drygoods, groceries, and drugs. From many of his stores, the trip to Albany required at least two weeks.

The Smith boys, Azariah, Calvin, and Joseph, were sons of one of Meeker's Middlefields, Massachusetts, creditors, and he set them up as managers of trading centers in Onondaga and Cayuga Counties, New York. The boys wrote home frequently, and their letters, now in the possession of one of their descendants, throw light on Meeker's operation. Early in 1808 Azariah, then at Manlius, wrote of Meeker—

He has now in Albany about 1000 bushels of Wheat and four tons of Potash and due to him in various places about $14,000. The store at Onondaga remits money the fastest and from my best observation in proportion to that of this Store in Manlius as 8 to 7, to that in Marcellus as 8 to 6. Since you were here in September last, he has established two Stores; one in Aurelius at the outlet of the Owasco Lake, and one in Homer south of Tully and about thirty Miles from this. . . .

Late in June 1809, Azariah again mentioned Meeker in his letter home—

Mr. Meeker has lately returned from New York where he purchased about $40,000 worth of Goods, which to distribute occasioned me considerable labor, having to send a bill of them

to each of his stores, six in number, besides this at Manlius, he having lately established a seventh store at Nine Mile Creek in Marcellus. Each store stocked with about $8,000 worth of property, which with two stores at Homer & Tully, four Asheries, Gristmills, sawmills, and his distillery, dairy, and farm with thirty laborers must furnish business enough to confound a common man, and more than he or any other can attend with profit. Whether he sinks or swims, time must determine. He has agreed to give me $14 a month for my extra trouble. For two weeks past I have had to labor intensely, as well in body as mind from sunrise to midnight not even having opportunity of leisure more than one half of the Sabbath.

Time determined that John Meeker should sink. While he had made it possible for his partners to save money, he himself had over extended his credit, either by over-buying or in unwise trading. In 1882 he was an insolvent debtor, and his last years were spent on his farm on Meeker Hill in Madison County.

Many of the boys he had chosen so carefully, and trained so capably—young Jedediah Barber, and the Smith boys among them—went on to have their own successful stores.

The letters that Azariah Smith and his brother Joseph wrote home over a twenty-year period portray the "frontier sequence" in the merchant's rise. Almost all successful storekeepers followed the same path. Azariah was first a clerk, working for another; then a junior partner, furnishing energy and brains to the senior partner's contacts and capital. Next he engaged in

PLATE 26. Flyer for Meeker's store at Delphi, N.Y. indicates types of conveyances in use: horse, stagecoach, train, balloon, and top-hatted winged travellers of the future. Interest in ballooning was increased by Thaddeus Sobieski Coulincourt Lowe's record hop from Cincinnati to South Carolina coast in 9 hours, in 1861, and by Lincoln's use of an Army Balloon Corps.

business for himself, and at last branched out as a factory owner, member of the legislature, and substantial citizen of the community.

His brother Joseph went one stage further—recording economic disaster when his town of Manlius was bypassed by the route chosen for the Erie Canal.

Jedediah Barber, another of Meeker's young men, had come to Onondaga Hill in New York State from his Hebron, Connecticut, home, with no definite plans in mind. He worked as a travernkeeper's helper in the summer at $8 a month, and as a teacher in the log schoolhouse in the winter at $10 a month. When Meeker started one of his chain of stores in Onondaga Hill in 1806, he gave Jedediah a few pennies more per day than he was getting to try his hand at storekeeping. Meeker was building up the Red Store at Tully to be the leader in the area, and he soon moved Jed over there. Though he made Jed a junior partner at $1,000 a year, Jed apparently thought it was not enough. He quit and went to work with his brother-in-law, William Hibbard, a blacksmith in Homer. But storekeeping was in his blood, and he soon left the smithy to set up his "Great Western Store" in Homer.

One of his sources of capital without currency is illustrated by the advertisement which appeared in the *Cortland Republican*

newspaper of October 21, 1815—

5000
*Bushels; Flax-seed
Wanted
The subscribers would inform the
public that they carry on the business
of*

*Manufacturing
Lindseed oil
in the village of Homer where they
will pay the highest prices for
Flax-Seed in exchange for Oil,
or in Goods at Jedediah Barber's
Store, or in Cotton Yarns and Goods
at the H.C.M. Company Store
R & H Bishop*

Here again is triangular trading. Jed made a profit on the merchandise he exchanged in his store for the flaxseed desired by the R & H Bishop Company, and used the credits from Bishop to exchange for merchandise to replace that which was swapped for flaxseed.

The Great Western Store grew and prospered. When Barber celebrated his 42nd anniversary in 1854, he advertised $50,000 worth of goods, including three barrels of buffalo robes, 100,000 superior butter firkins and tubs, and as always "Barber's four-shilling tea."

In 1856, the store burned to the ground, with a loss estimated at more than $50,000. Undaunted, Jed was back in business in a few months, letting his son George run the store under his own name—the George J. Barber Company—while he devoted most of his time to the bank he had just started. With George he carried on a running price war with the Great American Tea Company, later the Great Atlantic and Pacific Tea Company. A sample advertisement in this exchange appeared in 1867 when Barber offered his "superior Quality Japan Tea and China Young Hysen Tea" at $1.00, warranted "as good as any that can be purchased of the American Tea Company at $1.25 or Money refunded. All other qualities and prices in same proportion."

Jed was not one to sit in a rocking chair in his declining years, and when one of his competitors, Uncle Billy Sherman, suggested they both close their businesses and retire, Jed replied: "You can rust out, but I'll wear out." And until his death, in the late 1860s, the old gray haired man, with his long skirted coat and high beaver hat, carrying an ivory headed cane symbolic of his age and position, was familiar to the streets of Homer.

The *Syracuse Journal* wrote of him in his old age—

Plain, honest and truthful, possessing a genial temperament exceeding the affable, though sometimes blunt in his expressions, he has succeeded in securing the good will and esteem of all . . .

He did not live to see the Great Atlantic and Pacific Tea Company organize in 1870, nor to comment on their expressed purpose of "importing and distributing pure and reliable teas and coffees, subjecting the purchaser to but one profit from the foreign factor."

Added Service

ABSENTEE storeowners were not uncommon. Ebenezer Coles Merriman of Elbridge, Onondaga County, New York, built a store in Wayne County at South Butler, and never went near it. Orin King operated it for him, and the location came to be known as King's Crossroads. Since Butlerites had been going to Auburn for the necessities, a distance of some twenty to thirty miles over roads which only an ox team or a saddle horse could travel, the new store was hailed with delight.

When Mr. Merriman died in 1839, Richard Pomeroy, also of Onondaga County, bought it from the Merriman estate, and set his son and son-in-law to run it for him. In 1846, his brother-in-law, Henry King Graves, of Butler, purchased

PLATE 27. 1905 photograph of the Wilson Bros. store in South Butler, N.Y. Store's history traced back through Graves & Wilson, George Graves, Henry K. Graves, Charles H. Graves & H.A. Graves, Henry King Graves, Richard Pomeroy, to Ebenezeer Merriman, absentee owner, who hired Orin King to run it.

the property for $2400, the same price Mr. Pomeroy had paid for it seven years before.

Stores were carrying much more merchandise by 1846, and Mr. Graves, who ran the store himself, proved an up-to-the minute merchandiser. His Ledger No. 1, for the period July 25, 1846 to April 18, 1849, presented the names of 515 customers. Between those dates, Mr. Graves offered 746 different items of goods.

Of foods that were not home grown, he carried candy and chocolate, lemons, figs, oranges and raisins, ginger, cloves, cassia, cinammon, spice, red pepper, black pepper, nutmegs, codfish and mackerel, tea and coffee, salaratus, sugar, sugar loaf, salt, soda and Palmer's Extracts. He also stocked soap and shaving soap.

On his medicine and herb shelves were antimony, madder, Gridley's and Jeffery's ointments, opium, opodeldoc, linament, paragoric, peppermint, rhubarb syrup, sal ammoniac, saltpeter, sarsaparilla, soda, sugar acid, sulphur, wild cherry wine, port, brandy, worm medicine, vitriol, vermifuge, "old man" (imported from Jamaica for use by saddlers and coachmakers), gum arabic, assafetida, camphor, balsam, and castor oil.

Inventory books showed stock on hand April 1, 1863 as $4040.36, and on January 1, 1868 as $6036.29, indicating the growing demand for goods in the post-Civil War period.

George K. Graves, who succeeded his father, was equally progressive. Not only did he manage to get appointed as Post-master from 1867 to 1871, with the post office located in his store, but he also began to sell subscriptions from a list of over 150 publications. This not only added to his revenue, but brought more people to the store when they came to pick up their magazines and daily papers.

Among the more outstanding publications for which he found ready subscribers were *Atlantic Monthly, Albany Journal, Chicago Times, Country Gentleman, The Northern Christian Advocate, Harper's Weekly, Harper's Bazar, New York Tribune* (daily), *New York Times* (daily), *Onondaga Standard, Onondaga Gazette, Syracuse Journal* (daily), and *True Flag,* Boston.

Though the post office surely brought store customers, the post office work was not all roses. Then, as now, there were "Complaints." On a nail near the Graves' post office window, hung a dog-earred memorandum book, filled with notations such as—

Nov. 8, 1881—J. E. Rodgers orders his mail not to be delivered to F. F. Farlaw MD.

Nov. 11, 1881—Charles Scott orders his mail not to be delivered to anyone but himself or wife.

Jan. 10, 1882—Will Barcliff orders his mail not to be delivered to Eddy Caywood.

Feb. 4, 1882—F. L. Belknapp orders his mail not to be delivered to Peter Bagerly or any of his family.

April 28, 1882—Myron Rising orders his mail not to be delivered to Sidney Rising.

Sept. 11, 1883—Mrs. J. Cartner orders their mail not to be delivered to anyone except their own folks and Will Wood and wife.

Since Mrs. Cartner had been a Wood, it must have cheered Postmaster Graves to know that at least one person in town trusted her own sister-in-law to carry the mail.

PLATE 28.   Advertising card, Graves & Wilson, 1877.

Way Out West in Iowa

WESTERN storekeeping in Kansas, Iowa, and Missouri Territories was not for the faint hearted. Many, like a Mr. Sherman of Vermont, who had hopefully loaded his store, complete with assorted braids, buttons, edgings and trimmings, in a covered wagon, crossed miles of difficult country, and ferried over the Mississippi, took one look at the wide and empty country, and turned the horses back toward the green hills of home.

For the pioneer storekeeper who persisted, the West offered tremendous opportunity. Real estate promoters, starting a town, offered free lots to those agreeing to erect store buildings. When two or three merchants, a lawyer, and a doctor, who usually operated a drug store, too, succumbed to this enticement, the town was ready to be built.

The western storekeeper's profits were high. Saddles costing $5 in seacoast cities brought $12 to $15 in St. Louis, even more in smaller towns. Farmers, fearing to keep money at home, deposited it with merchants, to withdraw at will or to apply on goods. The merchant became a banker.

Wholesale houses in New Orleans, New York, Philadelphia, and Baltimore, eager for the growing trade, extended the western merchant credit for six months, payable in a year, with interest of six to twelve percent after the first six months. Sometimes they waited willingly for two years before collection.

As in the east, farmers paid for their

goods in furs, meats, wheat, flax, hemp, whiskey, ginseng, honey, and beeswax— beeswax in the 1830s was quoted from 18¢ to 22¢ a pound. Commission houses bid for the merchant's produce business, and sometimes advanced money on produce customers were yet to bring in.

Once a year the western merchant went east, usually in company with others bent on buying their year's supply. They'd arrive in St. Louis on horseback, take the steamboat down the Mississippi to the juncture with the Ohio, then up the Ohio to the east. On board they played cards, and talked storekeeping and politics. In the city, their coarse boots, huge blanket coats, foxy caps and long beards spelled "Western trade," and city merchants sent their best salesmen to court their business. For two or three weeks they "saw the city," living in hotels, attended by merchants, inspecting stock and selecting "best goods at cheapest prices." In the evenings they visited museums to see rare animals or mechanical marvels; spent $1 for a box at the opera, or 25¢ for a seat in the gallery; or arranged gay evenings at somewhat livelier spots. At home again, they were filled with enough new ideas for business and conversation of "back East" to last till the next trip.

A typical story of western success is that of Stephen Beckwith Ayres, who after some twenty years in other people's stores, set out from his native New York State for Fort Dodge, Iowa, to go into business for himself.

When he first opened his store in 1857, Fort Dodge was a frontier town with less than a thousand inhabitants. By the time

PLATE 30. A Prairie store scene, "A Market Report 'Corn is Up,'" by Robert Henry Roth, 1903.

the population had reached that round figure, Stephen had four competitors.

Perhaps Stephen was not typical, for his was one of the very few general stores that did not carry whiskey. Most Iowa stores had a handy "customer's barrel" with a tin cup hung beside it, and proffered a swig to farmers travelling in from a distance and bade them godspeed, when trading was done, with another "for the road."

Though his conservatism may have lost him some trade, it possibly advanced him in other more respected ways. He became agent for the Aetna Fire Insurance Company of Hartford, Connecticut, a land agent, interested in bringing immigrants to the country, and banker of some repute. His advertisements appeared regularly in the newspapers, indicative of his wide interests.

WANTED:
*$20,000 worth of prime furs
for which the highest market price will be paid.*
STEPHEN B. AYRES—*Jan. 17, 1865*

Agent for Tapscott Bros. & Co's Foreign Exchange and Emigration Co. Will sell exchange on England, Ireland, and Scotland, at current rates and Passenger Tickets from Liverpool to New York by their favorite line of Packets. For particulars, see large bills. STEPHEN B. AYRES —*Dec. 1864*

EXCHANGE OFFICE:
The subscriber is prepared to buy Exchange on all the leading commercial cities of the United States and Europe. Also American and Foreign Gold Coin, and Uncurrent Bank Notes of all kinds that have a determinate value, and will sell sight Drafts on New York City in sums to suit. STEPHEN B. AYRES—*April 21, 1863*

While Stephen Ayres' interests were wide, he never fogot the primary purpose of the

PLATE 29. Stephen B. Ayers started his general store in Fort Dodge in 1856 in the little brick building with gable end and awning to the street, added the larger building in 1861-2.

store—to buy and sell goods. His merchandise was much the same as that carried by eastern stores of the time, but frontier needs were not forgotten. His full column advertisements always ended, with the notice in the largest of print:—"AND I shall keep a full supply of TRAPS AND BUY FURS. At all times paying the full market Prices."

Just Step Inside

WHOEVER thinks the country store must have been a hodgepodge, thinks exactly right. From the earliest mud-chinked log cabin establishment to the late model brick emporium, "the Store" was a housekeeper's horror.

There were soaps and spices, salt and salaratus, dishes, books and drygoods on the shelves. Hardware and leather goods shared floor space with barrels of flour, sugar, and molasses. A cat in the cracker barrel was commonplace. Axes, log chains, kettles, pots, pans, kegs of nails were piled in corners or hung from the rafters on cords. Shoes were piled loose in a big "shoe box;" saddles and harnesses added to the variety.

PLATE 31. Country store signs, fixtures, and merchandise, arranged on shelves at the L.A. Johnson Supermarket display, in 1950.

The drug corner lined up patent medicines, physics and sedatives—laudanum, paragoric, rhubarb, assafetida, turpentine, sweet oil, opium, and epsom salts. Coffee, cheese, and tobacco crowded the counter along with piles of Russian sheeting, shirting, bed ticking, and Cassimeres, superfine and common. Women who bought yard goods material had to hang it out to air before they started "making it up."

Whiskey was usually out of sight, but not of smell, in the back room or basement. Pins, pens, paper, buttons and collars, black silk gloves and palm leaf fans were always "around somewhere."

When, about the turn of the 19th century, frame buildings made log cabins obsolete, up-to-date store quarters were built with cellars cool enough to store cheeses, butter, and eggs, and roomy enough for hogsheads of molasses, casks of whale oil and camphine. But new products were coming out all the time and shelves and counters were as crowded as ever. After 1860, barrels of the popular kerosene added a new and distinctive odor.

Heating arrangements took up space—fireplaces in the earliest stores; later, Franklin heaters and cast iron 10-plate stoves. The pot-bellied stove, first used by railroads, came to store use only when coal became a cheaper fuel than wood.

Every store, of course, had scales—both steelyards and balance scales. The steelyards were probably imported but balance scales were made by local blacksmiths until patent scales came into use.

There had been platform scales in England prior to 1796, for in that year, a Mr. Solmon was granted a patent for improvement on them. But it was 1831 before the first platform scales were patented in this country. Erastus and Thaddeus Fairbanks of St. Johnsbury, Vermont, were the inventors. In another ten years, in 1841, Dale's Improved Patent Scales were on the market. These used only two weights of small size, and could weigh from a quarter of an ounce to 28 pounds. Nothing resembling a truly modern scale appeared until 1900 when Allen De Vilbiss Jr. of Toledo, Ohio, was granted a patent for computing scales.

The big colorful coffee mills were standard store equipment after the 1860s when coffee first became popular. The Enterprise Manufacturing Company of Philadelphia was turning out their well known model in 1868, and are still making coffee mills. They were advertising colorfully in *The American Grocer,* in the 1880s with comparison pictures, cartooning the obsolete methods used by O. Phogy & Co., and the strictly up-to-date coffee-grinding methods in the Enterprise New Store. Lone Bros. of Millbrook, New York, "Established in 1845," were advertising at the same time and in the same publication their Swift Mill, another popular make.

Somewhere around the store there was sure to be a dried fruit augur, used for losening the dried fruits that were shipped in barrels. A sugar grinder was needed, too, so that the chunks of hardened sugar, loosened by the same dried fruit augur, could be put between rollers and broken fine enough to sell.

Purchases were wrapped in "pokes" or "papers." The capable clerk could manufacture one in midair. Judson Green, storekeeper at Spring Lake, New York, some sixty years ago was one of the most adept

PLATE 32. "American" Meat Chopper, butcher's size, on 15" block, promised grocers from 1 to 3 cts. more per pound for sausage than any other "grinder" in use. It cut from 50-60 lbs. an hour; weighed 120 lbs; cost $25.

PLATE 33. National Cash Register, shown in American Grocer and Dry Goods Chronicle, 1884, was manufactured at Dayton, Ohio, in various models, sold at $40. to $150.

at this legerdemain. After he had the desired amount of bulk commodity in the hopper of the scale—rolled oats, sugar, beans, maybe nails—he would reach under the counter and bring up a sheet of wrapping paper. With his right hand he'd toss it in the air, holding one corner in his hand. A quick flip and a twist of the wrist, and he held a cornucopia. Folding the small end upward, he'd pick the hopper off the scales and pour whatever was in it into the cornucopia, jounce it once or twice to settle it, fold the top over, reach above him for the string dangling from the stringholder and tie up his package—all in the twinkling of an eye.

Before the Civil War, cotton bags were used for shipping flour and grain and other produce. Came a scarcity of cotton, and New York traders, who were shipping such foodstuffs down the Erie Canal to New York City, began casting around for some sort of paper container to take the place of the almost non-existent cotton bags.

Some ten years earlier, in 1852, Francis Walle of Bethlehem, Pennsylvania, had patented a machine which would cut paper, fold and paste it with flour paste into a bag. Other patents had followed but there was little interest until a real need for paper bags arose. Then inventors got busy. The best known of early paper bag machines was built by a Mr. Pettee. He began licensing his apparatus to printers in 1865 and collected a royalty on its use. But not until 1869, when the best features of all types of paper bag machinery were purchased and put together in one machine by the Union Company of Pennsylvania, did the paper bag industry really get under way.

In May 1870 *The American Grocer* put its accolade on the paper bag, and wrote, in regard to Howlett Brothers, Patent Machine Paper-bag and Flour Sack Manufacturers and Printers of 204 Fulton Street, New York—

PAPER BAGS FOR GROCERS

We invite attention to the advertisements of Paper Bags in our present issue. The use of such bags has become absolutely necessary, and the firms whose cards appear are prepared to supply every size and quality. Write for prices and styles.

As for the store counter itself, the top board usually extended well out in front; the siding sloped back toward the bottom. Reputedly so built for the comfort and convenience of ladies in hoop skirts, this offset continued in use long after hoop skirts were out of fashion. Even in 1879 when Kunkel's

PLATE 35. Papier mâché figure, 3 ft. tall, advertising Quaker Oats, frequently appeared on shelf or counter. (Courtesy Wm. Underwood Company Museum, Watertown, Mass.)

combined counter and refrigerator was advertised, its "no offset style" was almost as much of a selling point as its refrigerating process.

As more goods came on the market competition among wholesalers grew keener. Suppliers began to give storekeepers all kinds of fancy fixtures printed with their advertising. An iron flag holder to hang from the ceiling advertised Day's Soap. A wooden bag rack for the counter, holding a dozen different sizes of paper bags, called attention to Griffin and Hoxie, Wholesalers at Utica, New York. Mustard maker G. C. Mulford gave away an eight day clock made by the Ansonia Brass Company of Connecticut. None Such Mincemeat gave out another Ansonia clock—in the shape of a pie. They also distributed pie-shaped thermometers. The Ambrosia Five Cent Cigar handed out a wooden thermometer, and Boschees German Syrup, one which cheerily listed the different ills it would cure.

"Andrew Coat, Agent," provided elaborate spool cases for thread; so did the Clark Company, advertising O.N.T. (Our New Thread). P. Lorillard and other tobacco companies gave showcases, tobacco cutters, and other such accessories.

The storekeeper accepted all tokens gratefully, and hung them on his crowded walls or set them on his cluttered counter. While the general effect was of one of added

PLATE 34. Loafers enjoyed such lithographed advertising signs as this, announcing "The Fragrant Vanity Fair is now, and ever shall be The Best Cigarette in the World." (1883).

confusion, at least the storekeeper could easily read the time, the temperature, and for once, knew where to find the thread!

The Clerk and The Lounger

IN 1938, the following rules for employees, reputedly posted in a Detroit store in 1854, were widely reprinted. The Kallfelz Bakery in Syracuse, New York, was one who used them in an advertising bulletin—

THE FOLLOWING RULES WILL BE PUT
IN FORCE AT ONCE
Store must be promptly opened at 6 A.M. and remain open until 9 P.M. the year round.

Store must not be opened on the Sabbath Day unless absolutely necessary and then only a very few minutes.

Any employee who is in the habit of smoking Spanish cigarettes, getting shaved at a barber shop, going to dances and such places of amusement, will most surely give his employer reason to be suspicious of his integrity and all around honesty.

Each employee must not pay less than $5.00 per year to the church and must attend Sunday School every Sunday.

Men employees are given one evening a week for courting purposes, and two if they go to prayer meeting regularly.

Leisure time must be spent in reading good literature.

Though these rules seem exaggerated, they differ little from the basic requirements set forth by Adams and Park of Chester, Vermont, some forty years later. Among the letter copies preserved in their Letter Book for 1891 are some replies by Mr. B.A. Park to the Rev. E.J. Ward of Hyde Park, Vermont, who was lining up a position for his son. Wrote Mr. Park—

We always commence our year's help in April . . . He to sleep in store, board nearby where he may elect, so as not to be gone too long to his meals, and do his own washings.

If he should come, should want his best efforts & attention to our business and on it. That is to say, not off on some party or something of the kind. Wednesdays we close at 6 o.c. which gives us all one evening out. We open store and sweep out at 6 A.M. & close by 9 P.M. He to take charge of grocery side & keep the stock in shape & full. Also to work wherever needed. Let us hear from you and Oblige.

The Rev. Ward had further questions, and a few weeks later, Mr. Park wrote—

We pay our help every Sat. night for what time they have worked. Most stores only pay them what they (clerks) are obliged to have, & bal. at end of year, but we settle as we go & if gone a day or part of day, it is all fresh Saturday night & can be settled at the time.

We talk plainly what we want & expect and do not picture any easy nice time so they can be disappointed in that line, but the opposite, for if they can be scart out, the sooner the better if before they commence. They should not start in it unless they are decided & bound to follow it. They do not want to waist their time in what they are not to follow, or we spend ours if not to Stay.

Adams and Park's clearly pointed out what they expected, but Adams & Park's records do not indicate whether or not the preacher's son was "scart out" before he commenced.

Boys who didn't have a farm to work on —the preachers', lawyers' and doctors' sons, often started out as store clerks, and the training they received stood them in good stead in other professions. Particularly did the country store turn out politicians. When Grover Cleveland's father preached at Fayetteville, New York, young Grover clerked in the village store at $50 for his first year, and was offered $100 for his second. Horatio Seymour, twice Governor of New York (in 1852 and 1862) started out as a clerk in his father's store in Pompey, New York. Records indicate that James Duane Doty, Governor of the Territory of Wisconsin, and in 1863 of the Territory of Utah, under appointment by President Lincoln, an ex-storekeeper himself, was the J.D.

Doty, Clerk, of the Roland Clapp 1816 Store Books. Samuel Pomeroy laid the groundwork for the Free Soil Party in Wayne County, New York, in 1848, while working in his father-in-law's store in South Butler. He ended up a Senator from Kansas.

Many clerks stayed with the business and became storekeepers themselves. The University of Missouri studies by Louis Atherton found that 46 percent of country merchants investigated had begun their careers as clerks in the stores of other people. Few inherited their capital. Most of them saved it. In frontier communities young men had few opportunities to spend money, and if they frugally forswore those, they might end up the year with almost every cent of their year's earnings intact. When employers did not object, a clerk could invest his savings in a little trading on his own. One young western clerk, permitted to buy furs, netted an additional $350 a year—more than seven times his yearly salary.

"Willing to Work" was the prime requisite of a clerk's job—and sometimes he could trade this willingness for capital. Mr. J. M. D. Burroughs, an early merchant in Davenport, Iowa, told of such an instance. When he himself had just started out in business, a hotel clerk introduced him to Mr. R.M. Prettyman, "a capable and worthy young man who wanted to clerk in a store." Burroughs felt he couldn't afford a clerk just then, but Prettyman said he'd be glad to work for nothing for a while. At the end of the month, he'd proved himself so valuable that Burroughs put him on salary. In less than two years he was a partner.

A clerk's life might be eternally rushed and confining, but it was never dull. Almost everything that went on in town fanned out from the country store. Sometimes the clerks made their own private jokes that were good for a chuckle years later. When Nathan Grant, who ran the country store in South Butler, and Charlie Betts, who was editor of the county paper, were boys, they clerked for a while for John E. Hough.

Nathan still grins as he tells of a cold February morning when he and Charlie had been fooling around and failed to start the wood fire that John E. expected to find going when he arrived at the store. When they saw him coming down the street, they hastily snatched some candles from the shelf, lit them, and tossed them inside the wood stove. Old John E. came in, saw the flickering flames through the crack of the stove, backed up to it, and rubbed his hands, muttering, "Guy, Guy, Guy, boys, a fire feels good this morning!"

There was always coming and going in the store, and plenty of "settin'" too. On rainy days farmers who couldn't work outside came to the store to lounge a while with the regular "setters." There were always chairs around the fire, crackers in the barrel, and someone to talk to. A German peddler in the West warned his friends: "Don't come out here to make a living peddling—everyone wants to go to the store for free gossip."

Sometimes the loafers got too much for the storekeepers. One merchant expressed himself in an advertisement in the *Missouri Republican* on 12 September 1825—

Mr. Printer—I am a storekeeper, and am excessively annoyed by a set of troublesome animals called Loungers, who are in the daily habit of calling at my store, and there sitting hour after hour, poking their noses into my business, looking into my books whenever they happen to lie exposed

PLATE 36. Wire springs on front legs of arm chairs made lounging even more pleasant and restful.

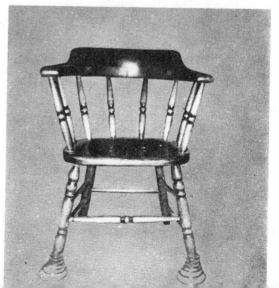

to their view, making impertinent inquiries about business which does not concern them, and ever and anon giving a polite hint that a little grog would be acceptable.

Do, Mr. Printer, give this an insertion: some of them may see it and take hint. If it should not, however, answer the purpose, I shall certainly be under the necessity of disposing of my goods the best way I may, shutting up shop, mounting a Vide Poche Cart and crying "March donc," take myself off to some more favored country where I shall not be bored to death by loungers.

Yrs . . .   T. Will Yardstick

Clerks kept their sharp eyes on the loungers, quietly moving a raisin barrel out of reach when a hand dipped too frequently, pushing a cuspidor suggestively closer, toning down horseplay, the teasing of cats and dogs that roamed the store, and the baiting of village unfortunates.

But the loungers had nothing to do all day but try for a laugh, and some of their dry witticisms were repeated all over town. Even teetotallers had to smile when a town drunk, watching a pious deacon leave the store with a sack of meal on his shoulder, paraphrased the good man's words: "There he goes, pore ole man, spending all that good money for meal. I'll bet he ain't got a drop of whiskey in the house."

As stores grew more crowded with merchandise, loungers and loafers got pushed into corners, or sometimes into a little fenced-off space near the stove. When steam heat came into use, and stoves were no longer necessary fixtures, the loafers' chairs and benches moved to the porch, or the sidewalk in front of the store. The supermarket even did away with those.

Recently advanced grocery marts have again begun to spare space for rest areas, sectioning off easy chairs for footsore shoppers and kiddy corners for moppet-size loungers.

PLATES 37 & 38. Salemen's cards present a thoughtful view of the variety of items carried in country stores in the 80's and 90s. Many firms used both sides of cards for their messages.

Drumming Up Trade

A SALES book kept by Boston wholesaler S.S. Peirce in the year 1829 records frequent trips taken by his partner William Stearns to Lowell, Salem, and New Bedford in Massachusetts, and to Portsmouth, New Hampshire. For a respectable merchant to go out and solicit trade was at that time an almost unheard of affront to good taste and fair play, yet it is evident that was just what the enterprising Peirce-Stearns combination was doing. Today's S.S. Peirce Company, (established 1831 and incorporated in 1894) proudly credits Mr. Stearns as being the first travelling salesman in the country.

Though other firms soon succumbed to "drumming," the custom was for a long time looked upon unfavorably. New York merchant Asa Green, in 1834, aired his views in *The Perils of Pearl Street*—

Drumming in mercantile phrase . . . is chiefly used in reference to country merchants. Instead of waiting patiently for these persons to come and purchase, a merchant or his clerk goes to them and solicits their custom. In this manner the sale of goods is often expedited; and though the practice of drumming is held by some to be neither very modest nor very dignified, still it must be owned to add pretty largely in certain cases to the amount of goods sold. Indeed, without drumming, it is

greatly suspect that sundry houses, which make a remarkable show and noise, would do very little business, and for various reasons . . . first, that they have seldom any great variety of goods, and secondly, that those which they have are rarely first quality.

But if the character of these houses is not of the first degree of respectability, neither is the custom which they obtain by drumming, in general, of the best kind. It consists chiefly of the younger class of country merchants who have not had time to acquire property, who have no money to pay for goods and who, in due time, all things considered, may be expected to fail . . . Those who are well established in business are not likely, for very obvious reasons, to become the prey of trimmers. They can go to the most respectable houses and purchase . . . because they are old customers and their credit is undoubted.

The Pearl Street of which Mr. Green wrote was then the wholesale center of New York City. Another "peril" which concerned him was the growing number of drummers from unimportant houses who "made deals with hotel clerks" so that they might be the first to know when prospective buyers turned up in town. They would then descend upon the unwary country buyer and seek by fair means and foul to wean him from his familiar sources of supply. The buyers themselves found these unsolicited drummers a nuisance, especially in New York and Philadelphia where the practice was widespread. Almost every contemporary mention of them in notes or published writings, by country buyers as well as "respectable" city merchants, was derogatory.

Slowly the picture changed, and more and more wholesalers, including the most dignified, began sending drummers on the road. The early bagmen were frequently picturesque individuals with a penchant for flashy dress. Their gay waistcoats, vivid neckties, heavy gold watch chains and diamond rings, occasionally real, set the fashion for dudes across the country. But for all their outward elegance, their lot was

not the easiest in the world, and their success demanded far more than a fancy appearance.

Charles S. Plummer, who wrote his own selling experiences in *A Drummer's Diary* in 1889, after he had retired, set forth the exacting requirements of a good drummer:

The commercial Traveler . . . is himself an organizer, a governor, and a civilizer. He is, or should be, a natural orator, a master of the art of pleasing, a genial companion, a politician, something of a statesman, an elecutionist and good storyteller, a walking encyclopedia of prices and an authority on tariff, capable of umpiring anything from a yacht race to a game of baseball, an expert in art, music, cookery, etiquette—and a good salesman.

Mr. Plummer's first employment as a drummer was with a wholesale-retail stationery store in New York City; his first assignment, to visit all principal cities up the Hudson River, then along the New York Central as far as Buffalo and Lockport. He carried two trunks; in one were his samples, in the other, boxes of pens, pencils, and such small

PLATE 39.   E.P. Briggs who began his career as a drummer in 1861, wrote an account of his adventures in *Fifty Years on The Road.*

articles as he could deliver direct to the purchaser. His instructions were to keep a correct account of sales and monies taken in, and to use the cash received to help pay his travelling expenses.

Edward P. Briggs, who began his drumming career in 1861, and wrote about it later in *Fifty Years on the Road,* travelled for a cutlery house. His first job took him regularly to Washington, then a ten-hour train trip from New York. There were no Pullmans, but the trains did provide, for one dollar, a sort of sleeping bunk, and he usually made the trip at night. Later he travelled down the Mississippi River from St. Paul to Memphis by steamer, and after the war, on to New Orleans. On side trips, a stagecoach was frequently the order of transportation. On one 75-mile trip through Iowa in an old fashioned swinging coach drawn by four horses he recalled that six changes of horses were required.

It was not unusual for a drummer to be on the road for a year before getting back to home base. In each town he would stop at the principal inn, arrange his samples, and in the forenoon go forth to visit the shopkeepers. He would then get off his reports, his orders, and funds collected to his employers. In the evening, customers frequently dropped in at the hotel to go over his line more carefully, or just to visit. As there might be as many as five or six drummers stopping at the same hotel, the customer could count on a gay, as well as busy, evening.

Though transportation was expensive, hotel charges were cheap. The best country hotels ranged, with meals, from $1 to $1.50 a day, and similar accommodations in the larger cities were about $2. There is no doubt the drummer was the mainstay of the hotel business in those middle century years. By 1860 there were about 60,000 commercial travelers abroad in the land, and by 1883, the *Hotel Gazette* estimated the number exceeded 200,000. One experienced drummer, a worthy "Knight of the Road,"

PLATE 40.   Attention getting papier mâché figure for counter display, shows drummer; about 3 ft. tall; key wind mechanism makes head nod, cigar move. Late 1880s.

was reported, in 1899, to have decorated a whole wall of his bachelor apartment with "a trophy composed entirely of hotel keys."

Mr. Briggs listed as the smallest hotel bill he ever paid one presented by Illinois hostelry in the early 1860s. A good dinner, the transportation of his 200-pound trunk back and forth from the depot to the hotel, and the use of the parlor as a sample room, cost him fifty cents. He sighed, in 1911, for "the good old days"!

In spite of the number of drummers on the road, some die-hard opposition to "drumming" persisted. In 1874, the *Boston Commercial Bulletin* carried an exchange of letters and editorials on "Does Drumming Pay?" Several of the largest houses expressed the opinion that by making prices low and sending out occasional samples, the buyer could again be drawn to coming himself to market and canvassing the trade. They considered the greatest pitfalls of the drumming system the failure of the salesman to investigate customer credit, and his zeal for orders which lead him to overload a willing customer with unsaleable merchandise. Both practices resulted in the customer's asking unhappily for an extension of credit—and the merchant's even more unhappy compliance with the request.

The drummer himself felt quite differently, for as Charles Plummer wrote in 1889—

Without him factories and workshops would never have been built. He is responsible for the great emigration to this country; for without a demand for labor occasioned by the sales of all manufactured goods displayed and sold by the drummer, our country would not have increased as it has during the past fifty years.

Actually the drummer's life was much less adventurous than smoking room stories would indicate. For the most part, these travellers were ambitious young men, seeing the country and learning the business, with hopes for a stay-put position in the main office once their apprenticeship was served. Other successful salesmen became so wedded to life on the road they didn't mind getting up, more often than not, at four in the morning to catch the next train or steamer or stagecoach for another town, another hotel room, year after year. The Gideon Bibles, found on the nightstands of all commercial hotels today, have been placed there by the Gideon Society, an organization formed by a group of earnest commercial travellers in 1899 at Janesville, Wisconsin. Samuel E. Hill, a travelling man from Beloit, was their first president.

The growth of the chain store system thinned the ranks of commercial travellers. Today's salesmen are sound businessmen, trained in merchandising and, like drummers of yesterday, bring the storekeeper new items, new ideas, and keep merchandise moving from factories and warehouses to the counters where people can see and buy.

The American Grocer

THE first edition of "The American Grocer" appeared on September 15, 1869. It was published in Philadelphia by Professor John Darby, head of a firm of Consulting Chemists, and was patterned on the London-published *The Grocer,* first issued in 1862.

The purpose of this new publication—was stated editorially:

Every department of commercial interest is represented by a special journal except that of the grocery trade. . . . The American Grocer comes to fill the hiatus, and takes its stand with the "Dry Goods Reporter," "Engineering and Mining Journal," "Druggist's Circular," "American Artisan" and "Scientific American" to do for the grocer what the above journals are doing for their various specialities. No one can see why this vacancy should not be filled, and all are surprised that it has not been filled before. We intend to fill it.

In his second issue Mr. Darby began to hint at extending the scope of the subject matter to include items other than food products—

The range of subject to be looked after is very great. . . . Whatever is used as human food

POEM OF
"DER DRUMMER."
BY CHAS. FRANCIS ADAMS.

Who stops at der best hotel,
Und takes his Oysters on der shell,
Und mit der ladies cuts a swell?
    Der Drummer.

Who vas it comes into my store,
Throws down his pundles by de floor,
Und never stops to shut de door?
    Der Drummer.

Who dakes me by der hand, und say:
"Hans Phiffer, how you vas to-day?"
Und goes for Bisness rite away?
    Der Drummer.

Who spreads his goods out in a trice,
Und says: "Just look vonce; see how nice;
You bet, I've got der bottom price?"
    Der Drummer.

Who punch my ribs, call me a sport,
My oldest daughter dries to court;
Sells goods cheap, because he's short?
    Der Drummer.

Who varrants all de Goods to soot
De customers upon his route,
Und ven dey comes dey ish no goot?
    Der Drummer.

Who calls by my house ven I'se been oud,
Und drinks my beer, und eads my krout,
Und kisses Käderlena in der Mout?
    Der Drummer.

Who, ven he comes agin dis vay,
Vill hear vat Phiffer has to say,
And mid a black eye go avay?
    Der Drummer.

Mr. M. B. CURTIS AS SAM'L OF POSEN. "DER DRUMMER IS THE MOST INNOCENT MAN ON THE ROAD."

PLATE 41. The verse "Der Drummer" which appeared on the program of the play Sam'l of Posen, was written by Charles Francis Adams, railroad expert, civic leader, historian, son of Charles Francis Adams, and grandson of John Quincy Adams.

or drink, or in a daily operation of the family, comes legitimately within our province. If we enter a wholesale grocery, we find sugars, syrups, teas, coffees, liquors, meats, fish, soaps, candles, spices, etc.

In the retail grocery we should not only find the above, but in addition, butter, cheese, vegetables, and a thousand and one things used by every household. To all these things our eyes are opened; and it will be our business to lay before the readers of The Grocer *items of interest in regard to any or all of them. Every intelligent grocer would certainly like to know the character of the articles in which he deals—their origin, qualities, liability to adulteration and the means of their detection, and we intend to make* The American Grocer *the medium through which such intelligence may be conveyed.*

The good professor had already started his attack on adulterations in his first issue when he devoted a thousand word editorial to the subject of kerosene, writing frankly against unscrupulous manufacturers, jobbers, and retailers, and the necessity of the honest storekeeper to keep his customers informed of mischievous practices of adulteration—

The remedy lies with the people. Buy nothing that will not bear the test and the vitiated materials will soon disappear. Benzole is only about half the price of good kerosene; and there is a strong inducement on the part of the retail dealers to adulterate what might have been good kerosene with this dangerous element. Let every community see to it that they are not imposed upon.

The *American Grocer* proved immensely popular, and in the early seventies it began to adapt itself to the needs and wishes of its many country subscribers, who stocked many items other than groceries on their shelves. While it continued to print the same amount of market news and advertising on food products, the number of its pages was increased to accommodate full pages on market prices of non-food products such as dry goods, hardware, and other commodities in which the general storekeeper was interested. About this time, it went from a bi-weekly to a weekly, bringing to the subscriber the latest market prices of the commodities the country storekeeper took in trade—butter, eggs, cheese, grains, ashes, and beeswax. Its advertising pages listed up-to-the-minute wholesale prices on the merchandise the storekeeper would exchange for produce.

Thus it was that when the country storekeeper swapped his bustles for beeswax, he had only to consult the latest issue of *The American Grocer* to know that he was making a fair trade.

CHAPTER THREE

THE MERCHANT'S THORN

The Boat Peddler

THE peddler, unlike the early store-keeper who established himself in one spot and drew his trade from the community around him, sought the settler on his home ground. Wherever a man swung an axe in a clearing, however isolated it might be, there came the peddler, on foot, on horseback, or by boat, to exchange his wares for those products of farm and forest he could conveniently carry with him.

The frontier peddlers were men of courage and resourcefulness. To make the hazardous treks, alone and unprotected into the wilderness, required, in addition, an adventurous, perhaps even a wild and reckless, temperament. Many disappeared. Only the most rugged—and luckiest—endured. Not only were they beset by the dangers of the wild, but by the hazards of civilization as well.

In the Lenox Collection of the New York Public Library is an eighteen-page pamphlet, the only copy known to exist, printed and sold by William Bradford in Philadelphia in 1692, entitled—

Rex et Regina V Lutherland
Blood Will Out or An Example of Justice
in the Tryal, Condemnation, Confession
and Execution of Thomas Lutherland who
Barbarously murthered the Body of
John Clark of Philadelphia

and was Executed at Salem in
West Jersey the 23rd of February, 1691.

John Clark was a boat peddler on the lower Delaware, and a temptingly prosperous one. The pamphlet starts off—

In the beginning of November last, John Clark late of the city of Philadelphia was trading at Salem with several sorts of goods, according to his usual manner; and upon the 12 day of the said month, his boat was found on shore at Sandy Point, near the Mouth of Salem Creek; John Clark was not in the Boat; the Boat and goods that were in her, were secured—there was several persons present that were with John Clark the day before in his Boat and they affirmed, that they did see several parcels of Goods then in the Boat, which goods were considerable and now missing.

The Prisoner's Confession, printed in full, began boldly—

I have been a great Sinner, and have continued in my sins until this fortieth year of my age, and have committed more sins than man could almost commit, for Drunkedness, Whoring, Swearing, Tempting Young Women to Debauchery and then leave them; then for theft, and now for murder.
I pray good people take care of your goods, and leave them not in out houses carelessly, which are great Temptations to sinners. The Devil takes such opportunity to persuade sinners to Steal & Rob; I declare I never took any goods out of a House that was lockt.

The detailed inventory of the recovered

goods belonging to Clark, signed by John Thompson and Samuel Hedge, is still on file in the Surrogate's Office in Salem, New Jersey. It bears witness to the surprising variety of goods available to Jersey folk in 1692, as well as to the merchandising processes of the peddler.

Priced in pounds, shillings, and pence, it includes: "shirts, neckcloaths, coates, breeches, childrens and adults wastecoates, gloves, hatts, blankets, children's and men's shoes, women's braided shoes, sashoons, silks, 1 yd 3/4 broadcloth, course kersey, flanel, ffillitin, drugget, silk saye, searge, silk-white-narrow-blue—culld tape, gimp, loop and thread lace, tobacco, pipes, thimbles, 30 doz thread buttons, 2 dozn of smale combs, 20 large hand combs, 1 dz childs books, garden seeds, 4 doz of brass bells, 11 pairs of cissors, 1000 pines [pins], thredd and glass buttons, knives, 20 doz gun flints, ramm rodd, 7 lb. ½ of ginger, 7 lbs of bees waxe, 7 prs. of tobacco tongues, rasps, hammers, chissels, cooper heding knive, shovells, hoes, gimletts, still-yards, candlesticks, saddle girts, headstalls, hobbles, briddlerains, trenchers, pewter spoons, and porringer, glass pendants, and a paire of Pendants sett in gold."

There were listed, in addition to "childs books," titles to answer every seeming need: "arethmitick," "Lilles Gramr," and twenty-three others including "The Way to Make All People Rich," "The Discourse of Dreams and Visions," "The Marrow of Prayer," "The People's Ancient and Just Liberties," and "Observieations of Health & Longe Life."

The inventory noted such items taken in trade for merchandise as "39 lbs old iron, 2 small Doe skins, 15 bushells of barley, 10 bushells of wheat, 9 lbs of bees waxe, 1 halfe Bushell & 1 bushl of mault."

The records show that Clark extended considerable credit. What was owed him in conveyances, bills, and obligations amounted to some £64.6d, double the amount of his merchandise inventories.

Clark's extensive inventory and his prosperous records make it apparent why merchants in Pennsylvania and New York, as well as those in New England, complained loudly against peddlers. Their wails resulted in various laws whereby peddlers were taxed severely, or prohibited altogether. Philadelphia required all peddlers and "chapmen" to be licensed.

But the settlers on the frontiers, the farmers, the small communities wanted and welcomed the peddler. Even if he cheated them, which he sometimes did, it was worth it for the excitement of having something new to talk about. By 1700 the peddler was firmly entrenched. Merchants have yet to see the last of him.

The Yankee Tin Peddler

PRIOR to the War of 1812, there was little settlement in mid-America. Permanent trading posts were set up only in those few sections where a smattering of white settlers had gathered. As for the thinly populated areas along the Missouri and the upper Mississippi, the Yankee trader found his way to them, peddling his merchandise or auctioning it off in larger settlements.

PLATE 42. A fanciful illustration of an early "peddler" in disguise, appeared in *Leslie's Magazine*, May 1861, later in *Harper's Weekly* for June 20, 1863.

Even as late as 1833, travelers on the Ohio River reported flat boats drawn up at many of the villages, offering corn, pork, bacon, flour, whiskey, and cattle, along with notions from such river towns as Cincinnati. The heterogenous stock on one flatboat was recorded specifically as of brooms, cabinet-furniture, cider, plows, and cordage. If trade was not good in one town, the merchant-trader simply moved along to the next. When the stock was all gone, he'd sell the flatboat too, and take the steamer home.

During the Revolution many stories were circulated concerning spies who assumed the role of peddlers. Gamaliel Painter of Middlebury, Vermont, completed a successful mission at Crown Point, disguised as a feebleminded peddler of notions. Young Oliver Wolcott of Connecticut, similarly disguised, sat in the kitchen of the great DeLancey Mansion on New Year's Eve and picked up stray information from the servants who were passing refreshment among the merry-makers at that British headquarters. This spying was dangerous business, and most peddlers were too busy minding their own to engage in it.

During the 1700s a good many young men began to peddle locally items that they or their family produced. Connecticut newspapers by 1793 were publishing lists of articles that could be bought from such neighborhood sources: excellent good leather, brown, white and striped tow-cloth of home manufacture, blue, white and striped mittens, stockings, shoe thread, cheeses, butter, goose feathers, rags, rabbit skins, and furs.

Encouraged with local success, peddlers added other lines to their packs, went farther afield, and stayed out longer. There got to be so many pack peddlers on the road that early tavern keepers were known to post notices that no more than five should sleep in one bed, and that all boots must be removed before retiring. More peddlers probably put up in haystacks or country barns than they did at such persnickity inns.

In New York state, even the Indians took up peddling. Dr. Arthur Parker, Indian archeologist, and former head of the Rochester Museum, tells of Indians, living near the settlements, who learned to make wooden plates or trenchers and sent out their own peddlers on horses panoplied with wooden dishes hung on strings.

In 1741, two young Irish immigrants, William and Edward Pattison, who had learned the tinsmith's trade in England, settled in Berlin in the Connecticut Valley. It was a time when new industries were badly needed in New England. The little tin shop they set up in their home, to pound out plates and pans and teapots from sheet tin imported from England, was the first of its kind in the New World.

When the brothers had made up a sufficient supply of shining plates, teapots, kitchen utensils and such, they packed a sack, and set out on foot to nearby settlements to sell their wares from house to house. Their tinware was so tempting that they soon advanced to horseback, attaching ingenious baskets to the saddles to hold

PLATE 43. Though peddlers usually spent their winters in home quarters, or travelling through the south, *Leslie's Magazine*, Dec. 26, 1874, pictures one hardy Vermonter undeterred by snow or sleet.

their wares, and travelled further distances. Before long they were taking on young apprentices to learn the tinsmith's art, and selecting the likeliest to go out with one or the other of the Pattison brothers to learn the equally important business of trading tinware for caraway and mustard seeds, feathers, and old metal.

Feathers were much in demand, and peddlers brought home, from the New York region at least, Passenger pigeon feathers as well as goose feathers. In an inventory that accompanies the will of Peter Doty, who died in 1811 in Shaticoke, New York, a pigeon net and rope were valued at $1.25, and a pigeon featherbed tick at $5.

The Pattison brothers did so well that others, observing their success, started tinshops of their own and sent out salesman. By 1750 the Yankee tin peddler was on the road—and the road led to every kitchen door in the country from Charleston, South Carolina, and Savannah, Georgia, to Detroit and the Lake Erie region, down the Mississippi through St. Louis and Memphis to New Orleans.

In 1778 merchant-peddler Thomas Danforth, credited with the first chain operation in America, settled in Connecticut at Rocky Hill, now Stephney. According to his accounts, now in the possession of Mrs. E. W. Williams, he dealt in almost every conceivable article of hardware. He manufactured goods in Brittania, tin, pewter, copper, brass, lead, and Japan ware. He had a brother in Hartford, and another in Middletown, who were both engaged in the same line of manufacturing and trading. The establishment at Rocky Hill, a sort of "half way" house, became the center of operations.

Danforth sent out peddlers with his goods, and did a thriving business in Weathersfield, Berlin, New Britain, Farmington, and other Connecticut towns. He took his son-in-law, Richard Williams, into the business in 1794. His own sons he set up in shops in strategic spots all along the coast, as far south as Savannah, Georgia. They engaged in retailing Danforth's goods, and also supplied and outfitted peddlers with the same.

One popular repeat item in the Danforth peddler stock, unused today, was a fine imported sand, which village housewives sprinkled over the bare floors of family or sitting rooms, often working out designs with the sand to simulate the carpets they didn't have. This sand absorbed the dirt and grit, and in a few days was swept out and a new "carpet" laid.

To many the stamp T.D. on goods made by Danforth was a guarantee of good reliable manufacture. Some say he was responsible for the clay "T. D. pipe," but this has never been satisfactorily established.

Peddling attracted the ambitious, the adventurous, the "born salesman" and, no

PLATE 44.   Yankee Tin Peddler from a drawing by C.G. Bush in *Harper's Weekly*, June 20, 1868.

doubt, those juvenile delinquents of the day who had not already shipped off to sea or gone adventuring toward the west. It was a colorful occupation and colorful men engaged in it. That there were many one-trip get-rich-quick peddlers who indulged in sharp practices there is no denying

Timothy Dwight, President of Yale University, Chaplain in the Revolutionary War, and writer on New England customs, took a dim view of the peddler and wrote in 1821: "No course of life as the peddlers tends more rapidly to eradicate every moral feeling."

Yet even then the foundations of some of the most eminently respectable—and most lucrative— businesses in America were being laid by enterprising young peddlers. It might also be noted that Dwight frowned on football, too. He forbade the game to be played at Yale, and violators were punished with a fine, "not to exceed one-half dollar."

Any Old Rags Today?

TIME brought roads, more people to sell to, and more goods to sell; and the peddler's commodious cart, hung with dozens of articles, and as many more concealed in its ingenious compartments, clanked and rumbled throughout the land. Laden with tinware, glassware, brooms, washboards, clothespins, matches, pots and kettles, flatirons and trifles, including a host of household remedies, the peddler's cart set out in the spring, right after mud season, and travelled through the summer and fall till the first snow flurry, replenishing its stock at wholesale centers along the route. In the cold months horses rested, and carts were refurbished for next year's trip. An occasional intrepid "carting gentleman" worked through a northern winter.

The invasion of peddlers from New

PLATE 45. Miller's peddling cart on the road, near Oneida Lake, N.Y., 1880. Carts of the '80s and '90s were ingeniously built with dozens of compartments to hold goods taken in trade as well as fresh stock for sale.

England in other sections caused great distress to storekeepers and local peddlers. Rumors were rife of Yankee hams made of basswood, cheeses of white oak, nutmegs of wood.

The term "Yankee" which H. L. Menken held was the anglicized form of the Dutch "Jan Kaas," meaning a freebooter, and applied by Dutch settlers to all New Englanders, became more or less of a general term. It did not indicate a citizen of any one state, nor necessarily a New Englander, rather, any stranger to the locality.

The wooden nutmeg story is thought to have originated with Sam Slick, a character introduced by Canadian humorist Thomas Chandler Haliburton in his book *The Clock Maker* published in 1837. Sam, the Yankee clockmaker once met up with a friend in Washington, D. C.—

Said the friend: "Which way are you from Mr. Slick, this hitch?"
Said Sam: "I've been away up South speculating in nutmegs."
Said the friend: "That eternal scoundrel, that Captain Allspice of Nohant. He used to trade to Charleston and he carried a cargo once there of fifty barrels of nutmegs; well, he put a bushel of good ones into each end of the barrel and the rest he fulled up with wooden ones, so like the

real thing no one could tell the difference. . ."

To settle the nutmeg myth, Rawson W. Hadden, curator of the Mattatuck Historical Society of Waterbury, Connecticut, recently took a nutmeg to an expert wood carver and asked how long it would take him to produce an acceptable imitation. (A true nutmeg is a kernel of the fruit of an evergreen tree cultivated in the Spice Islands in the Dutch East Indies, and has a wrinkled surface like nothing else in nature). The wood carver estimated a full day to produce a single imitation. Mr. Hadden then determined that with ninety to ninety-five kernels in a pound, selling in 1857 from 55¢ to 72¢ a pound, no true Yankee peddler would ever have engaged in so unprofitable a venture.

However, wooden nutmegs *were* made and peddled at the World's Fair in 1892 as a fun souvenir. They sold so fast the concessionaires had to buy real ones to peddle for phonies.

A hundred years ago, in 1856, the Syracuse, New York, Business Directory listed seventy peddlers by name; the only business group that exceeded them in number were grocers, the only profession, law.

Cash seldom figured in peddling transactions. The most common medium of trade was old rags. White, kept separate, were worth more than mixed rags. There were no complicated market rules. If a bag of rags did not weigh enough to pay for the article selected from his stock, the peddler noted the indebtedness in his little book, to be paid on the next trip around. If it came to a few cents more, he noted the credit, or shuffled out some extra item like clothespins to make up the balance.

Vermonter Lon Newton was conceded the king of the road, king of the tin peddlers, champion tale teller, and man of business, and Julian Ralph once wrote of his two-day trip through Rutland County beside him in the peddler's cart—

"*Anything for the tin peddler this morning?*" was Lon's usual approach, which enlarged to

PLATE 46. *Yankee Peddler*, painted by John Whetton Ehminger, dated 1853.

"*Haven't you got any rags, iron, lead, copper, pewter, brass, zinc, any kind of old metal, hides, pelts, skins, furs, or beeswax? H'ain't there anything ye can trade with the tin peddler this morning?*"

One of his stories, which illustrates pretty well any tin peddler's turn of mind, Mr. Ralph set down in Lon's own words:

The secret of peddlin's that you must do a trade, even if it hurts your principles, where there is a possible chance. I remember how I once managed with an old fellow who wouldn't have nothin' to do with me. He was so confident and sure he warn't going to trade that I made up my mind he'd got to.

"I've got wooden nutmegs, pocket sawmills," says I, "and horn gunflints, basswood hams, tin bungholes, calico hog troths, white oak cheeses, and various other articles too numerous to mention, including cast iron rat holes—and if any of them ain't big enough to answer, I'll knock the bottom out of a frying pan, and that will let any rat through that you got, I guess. "Whoops," says I, "I'm from way in the mountains of Hepsidam where the lion roareth and the wang doodle mourneth for her first born." The old man just look on and shuk his head. "I'll take pewter, copper, zinc, iron, rags, anything" says I, "excepting money and old maids." But the old man on'y shook his head. I simply had ter start a trade. I saw a pair of old boots, and I said them was just what I wanted.

"What?" he says, "d'ye buy old boots?" And I said them was my partickler specialty. "How much d'yer give?" he asked, and I says "Half a cent a pound s'long as half cents is coin," says I. He didn't take no heed to my meaning but began to rummage around and git out three or four pair. They weren't no good to Newton, but I was starting a trade.

"Now h'ain't yer got some rags?" I says. "Them was what I asked for first, and the old miner said he didn't have none; and now stirred up by the chanst of gitting somethin for his old boots, he brought out seventeen pounds of rags, and we done a brisk bit of trading for tinware. I left the old boots sitting beside the gate when I drove away. Them will come in handy to start another trade on, next time I come."

No story of peddlers would be complete without mention of Henry W. Carter, "the merchandising prince," who saw the possibility of selling wholesale to the numerous stores throughout New England. The "Carter Teams" coming through town, drawn by beautiful well matched horses, with silver mounted harness, and handsome wagons with gay scenic paintings, were as exciting as a circus. At one time, Mr. Carter had five teams on the road, four with four horses each, and one with six horses. Though other travelling wholesalers followed him on the road, none could match his teams for glamour. Their single teams and lighter stock presented little competition. Carter was "big business."

Pack peddlers of the early 20th century are well remembered by those who lived in country towns in the early 1900s. David Thumpsky was one who travelled the upstate New York area, carrying two tin trunks, the one in front loaded with jewelry, that on his back holding tablecloths and other textiles, both suspended and supported by wide leather straps over each shoulder. Welcomed at every farm house as an old and exciting friend, he'd spread his wares, and if night was coming on, he'd be asked to stay over. In the morning, to pay for his board and room, he'd leave doilies or laces for the ladies, maybe a jacknife or a mouth organ for the boys, or a string of coral beads for Little Miss. (Later David Thumpsky, beloved of so many farm families, left off peddling to join the police force in Syracuse. He was killed in the line of duty.)

Peddling was no doubt the best possible education in down-to-earth merchandising, and many major fortunes were started via the peddler's route. B.T. Babbitt, the soap man, was a peddler; Corlis P. Huntington, the railroad magnate, sent out as a boy to collect bills for a clock peddler of Connecticut, later became a peddler himself. James Fisk, turbulent Wall Streeter, sold dry goods and geegaws from town to town in the Connecticut Valley. His father was a peddler, too, but Jim's gaudy wagons, drawn by long teams of horses, hung with glistening harness, outsold his father's more modest conveyance.

Sears & Roebuck's Julius Rosenwalt, along with Isaac Gimbel, pack-peddled in Indiana; Nathan Strauss, a native Bavarian, through the southern states. David May, another whose stores are now nationally known, started out selling from a pack.

Of the many who couldn't take the rugged life, the best known is perhaps Louisa M. Alcott's schoolteacher father, Bronson Alcott, who gave up after one season of peddling tinware and Yankee notions in the South.

Gone is the color and romance of the country peddler with his cheery "Scuttles and cans, buttons and bows, I'll cure your ills, and cheer your woes" resounding nasally in the open air. Gone, too, are the dirt roads his cart rumbled over.

But today's farm housewife still opens her door to the Watkins man, the Grand Union man, the men from Jewel Tea, Cook Coffee, Fuller Brush, to ladies with Beauty Counselor or Avon products. She buys her bakery products from bread trucks, and occasionally, when the hens are laying extra good, engages in a little peddling of her own.

CHAPTER FOUR

ON THE SHELF

Indian Gifts

THE INDIAN was generous to the white man. In sharing his secrets of survival, he not only kept the settlers alive —though he changed their dietary habits in doing so—but he set the course of the new America toward its powerful agricultural development.

The Spaniards who discovered the cultures of Mexico, Central America, and Peru found that Indian agriculture far surpassed that of any European country. According to Edwin F. Walker of the Southwest Museum in Los Angeles, the Indian had not only developed more than twenty important products from wild growth—Europeans in some 450 years on this continent have developed none, with the possible exception of *guayule*—but had so cultivated and utilized them that once acquired by the world, they now aggregate more than half its agricultural wealth.

To the North American colonists the introduction to new foods began with maize. The Indians taught them how to plant it in rows, to hoe it, to hill it, to fertilize each hill with fish, and when it was ripe, to grind it and cook it.

The hardy "first ones over," dreaming of their favorite English breakfasts—"a draught of beer and a toast," or a "wooden noggin of good porridge and bread" —

approached Indian corn with trepidation. Many feared it was as unhealthful to eat as water was to drink. The Pilgrims' first three years were lean and hungry. Then Governor Bradford commanded each family to raise a plot of corn, and no more nonsense about not eating it!

Soon cornmeal mush was the accepted breakfast dish and evening meal. They called it "hasty pudding," after an oatmeal porridge they had known back home, and forgot their early fears.

Corn proved convenient, for if there were no mills for grinding,—some towns provided bolting mills—it could be pounded in a mortar, or soaked and run through a quern. If no proper mortar was at hand, one could be improvised, Indian fashion, from a hollowed cut stump, with a heavy rounded stick tied to a strong sapling to act as a pestle. The coarse crushed corn pounded out in this way was known as samp.

There were countless ways to prepare corn. Mixed with dried fruits, put in a bag and boiled for hours in the same pot with the meat and vegetables, it made a tasty pudding. "Rye and Indian" cakes of cornmeal and buckwheat could be baked on a stone, or a hoe, or on an oak board before the fire. Hominy, pone, suppawn, samp, and succotash—all Indian dishes, with Indian names, made from Indian corn—were relished at the settler's table.

In the south, Colonists found sweet

PLATE 47. Wild water rice, growing in swamp districts of the big lakes, furnished the chief vegetable food to many tribes. Women bent bunches of rice over the gunwale and beat loose the ripe grain with wooden mallets. (After an engraving by Schoolcraft.)

potatoes growing abundantly, and these tubers became a staple food. They were roasted, boiled, made into puddings, or beaten into pancakes to be taken with tea for breakfast. Corn pone was enjoyed, too, and patrician planters who substituted it for their important "wheaten bread on the table" had, as early as 1720, established the continuing Southern custom of hot bread at every meal.

For greens, plantation-grant lords, wise to ways of Kings and Courts, turned to the ancient English practice of making salads of violets and roses. The Indians showed them that American flowers of the sassafras family were tasty, too, and blossoms of the red bud best of all. Boiled poke leaves took the place of spinach, and "poke sallet" is still on southern menus. In the north, Indians introduced settlers to such greens as nettles, cow cabbage, and cowslips.

Not only did the Indian share his vitalizing foods, strictly home grown, but he passed on his democratic traditions. Universal suffrage, for women as well as men, the pattern of states within a state, the idea that chiefs are servants of the people, and the insistence that the community respect the diversity of men and the variance of their dreams—all were part of the American

way of life before Columbus landed.

The Indians left us beautiful place names for our towns and mountains and rivers, and they gave us, too, a common word heard every day around the house. "Okay," when backwoodsmen Andrew Jackson first introduced it to the English language did not signify a misspelled "All Correct," as his detractors would have us believe. Rather, it has been interpreted from the Choctaw to mean, "We have reached a point where practical agreement is possible, however far from perfection it may lie."

To the sports world Indian invention gave tepees, moccasins, canoes, hammocks, pack baskets, toboggans, snowshoes, rubber balls, and all the popular munchables and chewables that go along with American sports—chocolate, peanuts, popcorn, chewing gum, tobacco. Much that is distinctive about America is Indian, through and through.

The trading posts and country stores acted as intermediaries between Indian and European cultures. Trading in local produce, they encouraged the use of home grown food, and placed on their shelves each new development from the cornfield —the starches and cornstarches, the cereals, and vegetable oils, the candy and peanuts and gum. Depending on time, place, and need, they carried in stock all the sporting and hunting equipment the Indian had introduced. It was at the country store, too, that early settlers gathered to discuss the problems of the day, and brought into focus the fundamentals—long in practice among American Indians—that they most desired for their own democracy.

Crackers and Cheese

THE CRACKER was the American answer to the sailor's need for a bread that would keep well on long voyages. Made without yeast, of flour, water, and a little salt, mixed and kneaded by hand, rolled out and shaped

PLATE 48. A hardtack, full size.

individually, and baked in a hot charcoal oven, this flat hard cracker had been a home industry product long before Theodore Pearson set up a commercial cracker bakery North of Boston in Newbury Port, Massachusetts, in 1792. Pearson's venture into Pilot crackers, or Ship Bread, was the first cracker bakery in the country of which there is any trustworthy record.

In 1801 Josiah Bent, in Milton, to the south of Boston, began making "Bent's Hard Water Crackers." With his family to help, he stirred and kneaded and baked his crackers three days a week, and delivered them, by wagon, on alternate days to the stores in nearby towns.

In Arlington, to Boston's west, Artemas Kennedy started the Kennedy Biscuit Company in 1805, which was to continue in operation until it was absorbed by the National Biscuit Company a hundred years later.

All through the clipper ship era, cracker, or seabiscuit, makers flourished. When gold was discovered in California in 1849, crackers proved as satisfactory a staple for adventurers on land as for sailors on the sea. When the Civil War broke out and hardtack, quite similar to Pearson's Pilot bread and Bent's Hard Water Crackers, became a

PLATE 49. Much of the hardtack used by the Northern Army in the Civil War was made in conveniently located Baltimore, shipped to the front in wooden boxes.

standard Army ration, the old time pile ovens were taxed beyond capacity.

There was, of course, a great deal of grumbling about Army hardtack, and many noisome stories of weevils and maggots afloat in dunker's coffee were no doubt based on fact. But soldiers were sentimental about hardtack, too, and in the Palmyra, New York, Historical Museum, can still be seen, framed under glass, along with the remnants of their flag, four pieces of hardtack left over from the last wartime breakfast of the 77th New York Volunteers.

In England, fancy cakes of the kind Americans call "cookies," were on the market by the 1850s, and two British firms, Huntley & Palmer, and Peak Freen & Company began sending them to this country. In 1865, Belcher and Larrabee of Albany, New York, unable to procure proper machinery in the United States, sent to England for cutters and machinery, and were soon turning out cookies which put an end to serious foreign competition.

The term "biscuit" comes to us from the Latin, through the French, and means "twice-baked;" according to Gibbon, it originated with the military bread of the Romans which was twice prepared in the oven. The cracker, which was of American origin, was not introduced into Europe until the 1880s, where it was promptly rechristened a "biscuit."

As for crackers' companion, cheese, that dairy product was another early staple.

Though the Pilgrims had brought over with them on the Mayflower a goodly supply of ale—like all Europeans of the time, they considered it dangerous to drink water —they neglected to provide for milk. There were no cows on the *Mayflower*. Necessity proved that water did them no harm at all,

but when in 1624, Edward Winslow's three heifers and a bull arrived from Devon, milk was welcomed as a pleasant change. By 1630, it was an important part in the daily diet, and was selling in Salem at what was even then a ridiculously low price of a penny a quart.

By the 18th century, butter was a commonplace instead of a luxury, and cheesemaking had become an accepted farm chore. Farmer's wives were making cheeses for their men folk to peddle or to take to the store to trade. Neighbors with only one or two cows would pool their milk and make up cheeses to be wholesaled.

When Jefferson was elected president there was considerable excitement in the little town of Cheshire, Massachusetts, which had been roused to fever pitch by its great pulpit politician, Elder John Leland. In fact, Elder Leland was said to be so far-reachingly eloquent in Jefferson's behalf that all New England voted the straight Democratic ticket for years. To celebrate the victory, Leland suggested that his flock present to the new president the biggest cheese the world had ever known. He proposed that every man or woman who owned a cow should donate a certain day's milk yield for cheesemaking. No Federal cows were allowed to contribute.

A huge cider mill was fitted up where the cheese could be made, and on the appointed day, the countryside turned out with pails and tubs of curds, and the cheese was solemnly put to press with psalms-

PLATE 50.   As it was in the 1900s—Laurence Johnson cuts a wedge of cheese in Johnson Market Country Store Restoration.

singing and prayer. When it was well cured, it weighed 1600 pounds. Much too important to be trusted to wheels, it had to wait until the midwinter snows for delivery when it could be placed on a sled and drawn to Washington. Elder Leland drove it all the way—a journey of some three weeks— proudly displaying it to curious crowds as he went along.

In Washington, Elder Leland—and cheese—were received in state. Mr. Jefferson made a speech, and in the presence of heads of departments, foreign ministers, and other notables, cut the cheese and served it with bread. Considerately, he cut a great wedge which was sent back to its Cheshire makers with Elder Leland, to occasion a solemn and prayerful cheesefest.

There are many variations of this Jefferson ceremonial cheese story. One heard most often credits the cheese, weighing a mere 1000 pounds, to the cooperative efforts of the Republican Ladies of Massachusetts. The version given here is based on a reprint in *The American Grocer* for December 15, 1869, of Elihu Burritt's account first published in *The Gentleman's Magazine* and also reprinted in *Littel's Living Age*.

Another huge cheese made for a President was a New York cheddar, weighing some 1400 pounds, which was presented to President Andrew Jackson by some New York admirers near the end of his administration. This cheese was served to guests at a White House reception on Washington's Birthday. Many of them carried home large wedges for family consumption.

Cheesemaking remained a home industry until 1851, when Jesse Williams and his son George set up a joint enterprise—and a factory—near Rome, New York.

During the Revolution, David Williams of Connecticut had been stationed at Fort Stanwich, New York (now Rome), and had liked the country so well that he moved his family to a farm near Rome in 1792. His youngest son, Jesse, was born there in 1798.

The climate and grasses of that area were

ideal for producing cheddar cheese, and Jesse, who became a cheesemaker by trade, developed some special methods which produced consistently high quality cheeses. He did a thriving business and had many regular customers. In 1850 his son George, who had been working along with him, married and set up his own dairy business with a herd of several score of cows. Jesse began to turn some of his customers over to his son, insisting they pay George the same high prices for superior cheese that they were paying him. Buyers demurred, doubting that two lots of cheese made at different places would be alike in quality.

To avoid dispute—and to maintain their quality prices—Jesse and George pooled their milk, erected a factory, and made all their cheese in one lot.

The cracker barrel stood for years, hospitably open, convenient for sampling in every general store. The first inkling that the day of bulk crackers might pass came in 1898 when the National Biscuit Company began putting out their Uneeda soda crackers in family-size, patented, moisture proof packages.

As for cheeses, Kraft put an end to the familiar golden wheel when he developed processed cheese in 1903. Coming from Canada to Chicago with $65 in his pocket and a revolutionary idea, he began his experiments in a fifty-cent double boiler over his kitchen stove. In 1917 Kraft cheese was put into tins for "the boys overseas." In 1921 their first 5-pound loaf cheese wrapped in foil appeared.

A Dish of Tea

ACCORDING to Chinese legend, the first tea was brewed, quite accidentally, in 2737 B.C. by the Emperor Chinnung, revered as the source of agricultural and medical knowledge. The Emperor, it seems, was superintending the boiling of drinking water over an outside fire when dried leaves from a tea tree blew into the pot. The aroma was tantalizing; the Emperor dared a sip; and so—tea!

In India, the discovery of tea is credited to Darma, a devout Buddhist priest who, some nineteen hundred years ago, vowed to spend seven years in sleepless meditation. At the end of five years, growing drowsy, he snatched and chewed a handful of leaves from a convenient bush. Straightway he found himself awake, refreshed, and able to complete his vow. The leaves, of course were from a tea bush.

European literature seems to contain no mention of tea until 1517, and it was a hundred years or more later before Dutch adventurers brought tea to Europe. At first, it was used solely for medicinal purposes, but when the Chinese began sending teapots along with tea shipments to Holland, social tea drinking advanced.

In England, tea was still a novelty when Samuel Pepys noted in his diary for September 25, 1660: " I did send for a cup of tea, a China drink, of which I had never drunk before."

By 1703, the East India Company was placing such orders as "75,000 lbs. Singlo (green), 10,000 lbs. imperial, and 20,000 lbs. bohea," which sold at an average retail price of 16s per pound.

The first tea brought to this country, it is believed, came to the Dutch settlements in New Amsterdam about 1650 from Holland, where social tea drinking was already entrenched. Though it then cost from $30 to $50 a pound, fashionable hostesses in New Amsterdam society brewed several kinds, in different pots, offering each guest his preference.

By 1670, occasional chests of tea were coming into the Massachusetts settlements. Apparently no directions came with this "elegant" new beverage for it is recorded that early Salem residents, uninstructed, boiled the tea for hours, drank the bitter brew, and ate the leaves with salt and butter.

Even as late as 1745, tea was strange and untried outside the cities. In a letter preserved by her descendants, Ruth Starbuck Wentworth wrote in that year from Nantucket Island of the first tea ever seen there. It had been brought "in a large box from China" by her seafaring Cousin Nathaniel:—

Aunt Content has been much pestered in her mind because she knew not how to cook and serve the tea, and after our neighbors had assembled, she confided to them her perplexity. They all gathered about the tea chest, smelling and tasting the fragrant herb. Mrs. Lieutenant Marcey said she had heard it ought to be well cooked to be palatable, and Aunt Edward Starbuck said a lady in Boston, who drank tea, told her it needed a good quantity for a steeping which was the reason it was so expensive. So Aunt Content hung the bright five-gallon kettle on the crane, and putting a two quart bowlful of tea in it with plenty of water, swung it over the fire. Aunt Esther and Lydia Ann Marcey stayed in the kitchen to keep it boiling.

Before the brew was ready for serving, another two-quart bowl of tea had been added "for safety's sake," and the concoction boiled for an hour or more. The seafaring guests politely suggested that the mixture be saved to dye woolens, and proceeded to show young Ruth how proper tea should be made.

With the growing use of tea came a change in table appointments. The 18th century silversmith added tea services of silver to the tankards, beakers, and double-handled cups he had been making. He also turned out quantities of silver teaspoons. Dainty china cups and saucers, holding about a gill, appeared, and eventually porcelain dishes replaced all the customary everyday pewter.

On March 5, 1770, Lord North, seeking to placate the Colonies who were resisting "Taxation without representation," introduced a bill in Parliament to abolish all taxation in the American Colonies—except that on tea. To make this remaining tax more palatable, he proposed an ingenious scheme, whereby tea should be imported and sold

PLATE 51. The complete story of the Boston Tea Party appeared on the lid of this gay tin tea box, packaged by John A. Andres & Company of Boston, ca. 1876.

in the Colony at nine pence a pound cheaper than in England. However, Americans balked at the bargain on principle. Patriotic Whigs formed associations and signed oaths, agreeing not to use tea until the tax was removed, and went back to brewing tea as their ancestors had done—from home grown leaves of currant, strawberry, sage, and ribwort. A "Liberty Tea" was concocted from four-leaf loosestrife; Hyperion Tea, from the leaves of the raspberry plant. Even "cambric tea," of hot water, milk, and sugar, was patriotically sipped.

A hundred years later, history was being read on the lid of a gaily lithographed package of "Our Triumph Brand" Formosa Oolong, distributed by John A. Andres & Co., tea importers and coffee roasters of Boston:

THE BOSTON TEA PARTY
LIVERPOOL WHARF THEN GRIFFITH'S *was the destination of the Tea Party of December 16, 1773. It was a cold, wintry afternoon when the three vessels with their high poops and ornamental sterns were lying quietly moored to the wharf.*

They had been for some time under guard of a committee of twenty-five from the Grenadier Company of the Boston Regiment. The hatches were closed and this Vigilance Committee took care no attempt was made to land the cargo. The names of the three ships were, the "Dartmouth," the "Eleanor," and the brig "Beaver."

The number of persons disguised as Indians was not more than seventeen but the accession from the Old South, and of apprentice lads and idlers, swelled the number to more than a hundred. As many as sixty went on board the ships. Each ship had a detachment allotted to it under a recognized leader. Everything was orderly, systematic, and doubtless previously concerted.

The leaders demanded of those in charge the keys to the hatches, which were produced. As the chests were passed on deck, they were smashed, and then plunged into the dock. The contents of three hundred and forty-two chests mingled with the waters of the bay, and the work was done.

The tea, which records indicate, was shipped by Davison & Newman, was consigned to Richard Clarke & Sons, Benjamin Fanewil, Joshua Winslow, and Thomas and Elisha Hutchison (sons of the Governor). Captain Hall of the *Dartmouth* recorded in his log:

Between 6 and 7 o'c. this evening came down to the wharf a body of about 1,000 people ; among them were a number dressed and whooping like Indians . . . [they] cut the chests to pieces, and hove the tea overboard, where it was damaged and lost.

On March 7, 1774, sixteen chests of tea on the brigantine *Fortune*, consigned to Boston merchant Henry Lloyd, occasioned a similar and unrecorded Boston Tea Party. An account of it appears in a petition presented to the King of England by Davison & Newman and the firm which had insured the shipment in the amout of £480. They asked that "reasonable satisfaction" be made "all persons who suffered by the Riots and Insurrections at Boston." Davison, Newman & Co., still in business, has recently brought out a tea called "Boston Harbour," which they advertise "as rich in flavor as it is in tradition."

The first American trading ship to reach China was reportedly the *Empress of China,* which left New York in February 1784 and arrived in Canton in August. It returned to New York in May 1786 with a cargo of teas, and a great many china dishes of the type now called China Trade Porcelain

There was considerable rivalry between the shippers of green teas from China and those of black teas from Ceylon and India. From the first the green teas were popular in America, while England favored the black. An editorial of the 1870's conceded:
described their advantages—

The best tea is produced in the province oj Yamashiro. At Ogura, in that province, there are trees from four hundred to five hundred years old, producing tea worth five dollars per pound. . .

There is a difference. . .between black and green teas in the matter of firing. Black teas are fired in baskets; but the bluish green color of the leaf which is preferred in America is best produced by firing in iron pans. In the preparation of China green tea there is a mixture used of gypsum and Prussian-Blue or Indigo giving a glazed slate color. In Nagasaki an imitation of China green tea is prepared and exported under the names of Gunpowder, Hyson, Young Hyson, and Wankay. These are colored in this manner but nearly all the tea that goes from Yokohama or Hiogo is uncolored—that is, the only coloring it receives is from the reaction of the heat and metal pans.

Adulterations in tea were common, not only in the country of sale by wholesalers or storekeepers, but in China, the source of much tea. The London *Tricks of the Trade* in the early 1850's wrote of English problems in tea adulteration and the same problems echoed in America—

The superintendent (in China) takes a portion of Prussian blue, throws it into a porcelain bowl, not unlike a mortar, and crushes it into a very fine powder, at the same time a quantity of gypsum is burned in the charcoal fire over which the tea is roasting. . . .The two substances thus prepared are then mixed together, at the proportion of four of gypsum to three of Prussian blue, and forms a light blue powder. Then this coloring is added to the teas as they are turned in the roasting. The hands of the workmen become quite blue. The Chinese acknowledge that tea is much better without such ingredients and that they never drink dyed tea themselves.

Again—

The Chinese not only mix Prussian blue with their teas, but they also enclose in the curled-up

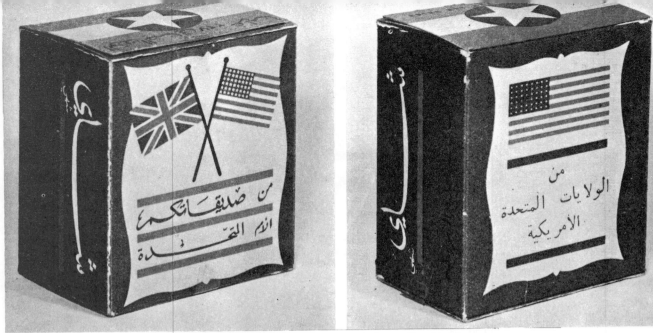

PLATES 52 & 53. Packages of green tea going to Spanish Morocco as a gift from the free nations during World War II bore the crossed flags of the U.S. and Great Britain; packages for French territory where sentiment was strongly anti-British bore only the American flag.

leaves an immense quantity of iron filings to render them heavy, so that it not unfrequently happens when a chest has been tossed about, and the leaves have broken, a layer of filings nearly equal to one third of the whole will be found in the bottom of the package. If a magnet is thrust into a tea heap or chest, it not unfrequently is found, on withdrawing it, to be covered with small particles of iron.

The problem of adulteration in America reached even more alarming proportions. An editorial entitled "Bogus Tea" which appeared in *The American Grocer* of December 1, 1869, was reprinted in the Troy, New York, Press, and presumably in other newspapers:

Seems the leaves of the California Chapparal are gathered in great quantities upon that coast, and packed in bales and shipped to China, whence, after being dried and prepared by some process unknown, it is returned to San Francisco properly put up into packages, and branded and sold as a superior quality of tea. No doubt this tea, which is said to resemble closely the best black, reaches this market—in fact, is sold in all parts of the country. Latterly there has been in different quarters several mysterious cases of sickness after drinking so-called tea; and in Chicago two fatal cases. Other shrubs besides the Chapparal (which is not poisonous but very debilitating and nauseating) are no doubt employed in this nefarious trade, and it is not likely the swindlers are particular about avoiding those of destructive character.

The New Englanders' preference for green tea followed them westward through central New York to Michigan, Ohio, Indiana, Illinois, Wisconsin, and the North West. Shortly after the beginning of the Second World War, the U.S. Government, along with the Commonwealth of Great Britain, "froze" all the green tea and original chests, and took it off the market, reserving it for the thirty million Moslems in North Africa and the Near East whose friendship was desired. As the Moslem religion forbids the use of food or drink that is fermented, and the unfermented green tea is a standard item in Moslem households, it was deemed wise to have a supply on hand to proffer in combatting Nazi influence.

At home American green tea drinkers turned to substitutes. Tea suppliers tried to promote Yerba Matte, the popular tea drink of South America, eulogized by Theodore Roosevelt in his *Through Brazilian*

Wilderness as "a valuable beverage." Though similar in flavor to very strong green tea, it never became popular. Instead Americans turned to the black teas. Today over a hundred million pounds of tea are imported in the United States annually. More than 93 percent of this is black.

Though iced tea was the desperate invention of a young Englishman, Richard Blechynden, it was first made and popularized in the United States. Other countries still prefer their tea hot. Young Blechynden, from Calcutta, representing Indian and Ceylon teas at the St. Louis World Fair in 1890, had prepared a very colorful booth with several young Singhalese, wearing bright turbans and jackets, to serve tea to visitors. Unfortunately the weather turned extremely warm, and the crowd bypassed steaming hot tea in favor of iced drinks. In disgust, Blechynden filled some tall glasses with ice and poured hot tea into them, and dared anyone to try the new drink. The crowd was in a gay and gambling mood, and by the time the Fair had ended, iced tea was the drink of the day.

The tea bag is also an American contribution. It was the practice of wholesalers to send their customers samples of their teas in small tins. But in 1890, according to the Tea Council of America, Thomas Sullivan, a small wholesaler in New York City, feeling the need of economy, had several hundred little silk bags made up by hand, slipped his samples in them and shipped them off. Orders began to pour in, much to Sullivan's surprise, for tea "packaged in those little bags." His customers with no coaching had discovered the advantages of the tea bag.

Lest anyone should worry about adulterated tea today, it might be noted with satisfaction that today's tea is bought at auction, either in India, Ceylon, Pakistan, or Indonesia where it is grown, or in auction rooms in London or Amsterdam, shipped in aluminum foil-lined tea chests to principal United States ports of entry, and placed in bonded warehouses until it is approved for entry by the U.S. Board of Tea Experts. This board of seven men— six from the tea trade, one from the government—operates under the Pure Food Administration, and sets the standards for tea sold in this country.

Sugar Is Sweet

THE history of sugar reads like an ancient travel brochure with space allotted to every known country within the thirty five parallels north and south of the equator where sugar cane could flourish, combined with a backward view of sugar's powerful influences in shaping the world of today. A universal sweet tooth and its demand for satisfaction played a forceful part in building rich seaports, in discovering a continent, developing an economy, and fomenting the rebellion that gave us the United States.

Sugar, like tea, originated in the Far East, most probably India. It was sponsored in England and on the Continent by returning Crusaders and was first used for medicinal purposes. Only with the development of social tea drinking did it become a staple commodity.

The earliest written mention of sugar cane appears in the record of Alexander the

PLATE 54. Tea caddies and canisters in fancy pasteboard "handsomely decorated in gilt and fancy ink in rich colors" sold wholesale in lots of 100 boxes at $7 for 1 lb. size up to $40 per hundred for 20 lb. size. Storekeeper packaged the tea himself in such containers and used them as counter display. (1870).

Great's expedition down the Indies River in 325 B.C. where "honey bearing reeds" were noted. Tai-taung, Emperor of China in the early 5th century B.C. sent envoys to India to learn how to extract syrup from sugar cane. (The resulting syrup, boiled to a thick, dark, crystalline mixture was somewhat similar in color to today's darkest brown sugar.) Diascrides, a Greek physician, writing at the time of the Roman Nero's fiddling, enthralled credulous readers with accounts of "a sort of hard honey . . . called Saccharum, found upon canes in India . . . grainy like salt and brittle between the teeth, but of sweet taste withal."

Arab traders in the Middle Ages took sugar cane to Sicily and the south of Spain. Dom Enrique, Infante of Portugal, surnamed The Navigator, transported it to Maderia in 1420. From there, in 1502, it went to the Canaries, then to Brazil, Haiti, and to Mexico, Cuba, Guadalupe, and Martinique.

The Italian Republics of Venice and Genoa grew rich and powerful with trade between the Far East and the northern countries. In London, in 1319, a shipment of 10,000 pounds of sugar from Thomasso Loredano, merchant of Venice, was recorded, to be exchanged for wool. The accounts of the Chamberlain of Scotland that same year show payment of 1s 9½d per pound for sugar—a dear price, even for medicine.

When the Turks captured Constantinople in 1453 and levied a high tribute on passing caravans, Mediterranean merchants watched their sugar and spice trade slip away. They would have been much happier if Columbus *had* discovered the new route to India he set out to find instead of an unknown America. However, Columbus did his best for them, and on his second voyage carried along cuttings of sugar cane, which he reported as "planted in fertile fields and in luxuriant growth."

A hundred and fifty years later, far too

PLATE 55.   From Washington Irving's *A History of New York:* "To sweeten the beverage . . . an improvement was introduced . . . suspend a large lump directly over the tea table, by a string from the ceiling, so that it could be swung from mouth to mouth, an ingenious expedient which is still kept up by some families . . ."

late to benefit the Italian Republics, the West Indies was engaged in a brisk trade of its own in the product of the cane—rum, molasses, and sugar.

The Pilgrims in Massachusetts first traded for such necessities with the Dutch in New Amsterdam. But soon the New Englanders were trading direct with "the Indies"—to such proportions that molasess became the "life blood of Colonial commerce." In 1728, the Colonies imported some 2, 124,500 gallons of rum alone. When the English Parliament passed the Sugar Act in 1733, levying a high duty on importations from the West Indies, irate Colonists promptly turned to smuggling rum, sugar, and molasses, and began to think seriously of breaking with the Mother Country.

Napoleon met the challenge, when France was blockaded by his enemies and imports from the West Indies cut off, by putting out a call for men of science to find a substitute for cane sugar. Franz Carl Achard, once a pupil of Andreas Sigismund Marggraff in Berlin who had announced in 1747 that the sugar beet would become the basis of a great industry but had done nothing to prove it, made up a quantity of beet sugar, and donated his process to the Institute of France. Beet sugar still reigns supreme in France. In the United States it is used mostly in the Central States. The coastal states find it more practical, mainly for freight rate reasons to use offshore cane sugar.

Sugar in early days in America was a luxury. The usual sweetening was found in home-produced honey and maple products, and molasses. As late as 1860, twenty-five million quarts of maple syrup were produced and sold annually, twice the amount used today. Molasses was for the most part imported, though farmers in warm sections, some as far north as Maryland, produced their own, raising a little patch of cane to be ground and processed locally. Sugar cane had been introduced in Louisiana in 1751 by Catholic missionaries from San Domingo.

Up to the middle of the 19th century, sugar was molded in cones, weighing up to 55 pounds. The smaller cones, under 12 pounds, were fashioned with a rounded nose, and were commonly called loaves. This once-familiar shape lent the name Sugar Loaf to many mountains in this country.

The refining method was to melt the raw sugar, then add milk of lime, egg albumen,

or oxblood to the pot. This caused many of the impurities to coagulate and rise to the surface where they could be skimmed off. The resulting light colored syrup was boiled to a heavy consistency, then poured into cone-shaped molds to cool and crystallize. The syrup which trickled through the apperture of the mold was collected and sold under the name of Treacle. Sometimes Fuller's Earth was run through the cooling cone to collect the dregs of molasses. The next step was to knock the loaf gently from the mold, trim it so no colored part remained. Then neatly wrapped, first in white, then in purple paper, it was dried at a temperature of 130 to 140 degrees in a drying oven from three to five days. Loaf sugar is made in Europe and Africa today in much the same fashion. It is used to greatest extent by native North Africans.

Colonists and early settlers soaked the purple paper wrapper for extra fancy dye; genteel young ladies learned the art of breaking pieces from the loaf with a sugar hammer and cutting them into lumps sugar shears for table use. Lump sugar, according to recipe books of the middle 1800s, weighed in at a quart to a pound, the best brown at 1 lb. 2 oz.

Granulated sugar did not become popular until after the Civil War. Even then it was coarse and brown, and so hardened in the barrel or hogshead in which it was shipped that a special augur was needed to loosen it, and a sugar grinder was part of the grocer's necessary equipment.

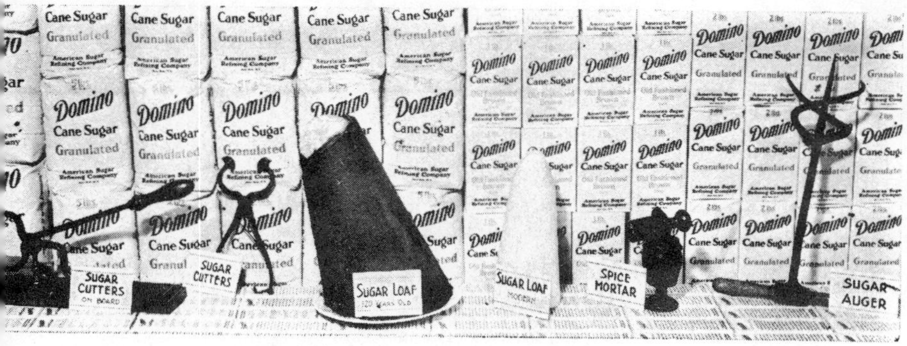

PLATE 56. Display of old time sugar utensils at the Johnson Supermarket Country Store: left to right, sugar cutters; old sugar loaf, from the home of Gideon Granger, postmaster general under Jefferson; modern sugar loaf; spice mortar; sugar auger.

Chocolate and Vanilla

TWO very happy products that the New World gave the Old are chocolate and vanilla. The Spaniards found them both in Mexico in 1520. *Chocolath,* from *choco* (Cacao) and *lath* (water) had long been enjoyed by the Aztecs. Historian William Hickling Prescott recorded in his *Conquest of Mexico,* in 1843, that the emperor Montezuma of Mexico was "exceedingly fond of it . . . no less than 50 jars or pitchers being prepared for his own daily consumption; 2000 more were allowed for that of his household." Cocoa beans, in various size bags, were also recognized as currency in the Aztec country.

Hernandez Cortez included some cocoa shells in the treasure he took back to Spain, and the use of chocolate as a beverage spread from Spain to other European countries. By the end of the 17th century in England, fashionable London folk had a choice of chocolate or coffee with their light breakfast at nine or ten in the morning—breakfast in itself was a novelty then. Chocolate was served in London Coffee Houses when they first opened about 1653. Tea was being introduced about the same time, and of the two, chocolate was the more popular. A century later everyday people were taking

PLATE 57. Cocoa shells, boiled for an hour or so in water and milk made a healthful breakfast drink, popular with the Shakers and children everywhere. Eagle Sweet Chocolate, also powdered, were Baker products.

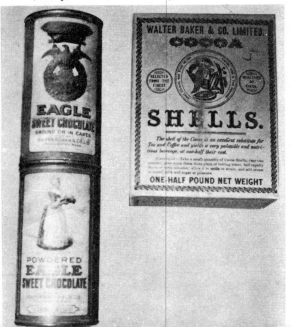

breakfast, too, and substituting chocolate for the ale that had been their customary morning drink.

For chocolate in America, Dr. James Baker is to be thanked. His chocolate was on the market before the Battle of Bunker Hill or the winter at Valley Forge; it was sold in stores when the British burned Washington in 1814; it was the only trademarked package food sold by Abraham Lincoln in the Berry & Lincoln store at New Salem, Illinois, in 1833; it was with us in the dark days of the Civil War, and is with us today.

In the fall of 1764, Dr. Baker of Dorchester, Massachusetts, befriended John Hannon, a penniless young Irish immigrant. Hannon, a chocolate maker by trade, lamented the fact that no one had the initiative to set up a chocolate mill in the New World where he could work. Dr. Baker obliged by leasing James Boies' new mill on the Neponset River, and supplying the capital to get started. Their first expenditures were for a run of millstones and a set of kettles. The mill started production early in 1765, and the business prospered from the first.

Though the Revolutionary War period brought its labor and price problems—by 1775 one-third of Dorchester's men over 16 years of age were in the Colonial Army, sugar was seven shillings a pound, and a sack of flour cost between six and seven dollars—the chocolate enterprise weathered the times. It suffered a blow, however, when John Hannon started off for the West Indies in 1779 to purchase cocoa beans, and was never heard from. Presumably he was lost at sea for he never reached his destination.

Dr. Baker then took over the business. The year following Hannon's disappearance he acquired the full ownership of the plant, and began making a blend of quality chocolate which he called "Baker's." In 1791, he took his son Edmund into partnership, and they worked together until 1804 when he retired. Edmund's son Walter joined the company in 1818, and when Edmund retired six years later, Walter gave the company the name by which it is known today. The business remained in the Baker family over a hundred years.

Walter Baker, like his father and grandfather before him, believed in advertising, and used newspaper linage to advantage. The trademark, "La Belle Chocolatiere," still used today, was adopted in his time. The original of this portrait, done in pastels, hangs in the Dresden Gallery.

Story has it that a young Austrian nobleman, Prince Ditrichstein, ventured into one of Vienna's quaint chocolate shops to try the new beverage. He was delighted with the drink, and more than pleased with his waitress, attractive Anna Baltauf, daughter of the impoverished Knight Melchoir. When they were married—for the story had the proper Cinderella ending—his wedding gift to her was this portrait, painted in the chocolate server's dress she had worn on the day they met. However true this charming tale may be, the French artist Jeanne Etienne Liotard, who painted it, was in Vienna around 1742 to do the portraits of the Imperial family. (He had just come back from a trip with Lord Duncannon to Constantinople and had, in colorful fashion, adopted the Oriental costume—they called him in Vienna "the Turkish painter.")

It may be that the fortunate Baker surname had something to do with the success of the company's advertising; it would have been hard to chose one, if the opportunity had been given, more appropriate to the product. However Walter Baker's German Sweet Chocolate found on practically every grocery shelf in the United States today includes the use of another surname whose connotation is misleading. The man who worked with Walter Baker in the development of this sweet chocolate and who was rewarded with a spot in the tradename, was his coachman, a man named German. He was an Englishman.

Though vanilla was introduced in Europe at the same time and from the same source as chocolate, its return to the Western Hemisphere was at a considerably later date. Sixteenth century Europe had been excited by the new flavor, which they called "Vaynilla;" but it took European botanists three centuries to succeed in growing it outside its native Mexico. Charles Morran of Liege, Belgium, finally went to Mexico to study the plant firsthand. There he figured out a means of artificial pollinization, and now the vanilla plant is grown in all semi-tropical countries.

Toward the middle of the 1800s, a lady who had spent some time in France, went to a chemist in Boston to see if he couldn't work out a vanilla flavoring for her sauces and desserts, such as she had been getting

PLATE 58. Joseph Burnett's Remedy for Asthma had won him a reputation as a chemist long before he brought out the first Vanilla Extract.

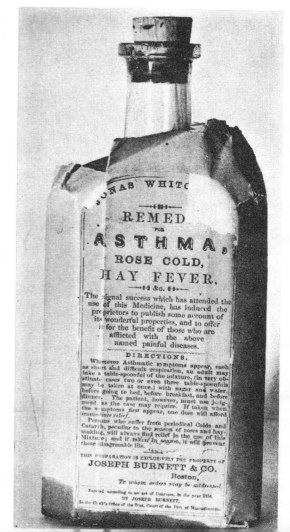

in Paris. However, she didn't much like the method the French chefs used—they cut up one or two vanilla beans, put them in a little bag, and dunked it, like a tea ball, into the sauce to be flavored, the flavor growing weaker with each using. She considered this method clumsy, unsanitary and inconvenient, and couldn't Mr. Burnett improve on it?

Joseph Burnett, whose inventive genious had already turned out a popular Asthma Cure and other money-making household remedies, could and did. He bought a pound of best vanilla beans and experimented. In 1847 he made the first vanilla extract ever sold in this country. The lady who instigated the idea said it was far superior to the French product.

Both vanilla and chocolate suffered at the hands of adulterators until the Pure Food Laws put an end to such shenanigans. *Tricks of the Trade* in London, 1856, reported that great accumulations of cocoa bean husks, a waste product in the manufacture of cocoa, were being ground up and mixed with the pure product, or being sold profitably in Ireland for use by the poorer classes. In fact, England was so successful in getting rid of this waste product that Italy and Spain were selling husks to London dealers under the name of "miserable."

Chocolate was also adulterated with flour, potato starch, and sugar, as well as coconut oil, lard, or even tallow. It was quite profitable to extract the rich cocoa fat or butter from the bean, sell it to the druggist for medicinal purposes, and replace it with animal grease or tallow. The Pure Food and Drug Act, let us thank a kindly Congress, was passed in 1906.

Cleanliness Is Next

SOAP making in Colonial America was largely a household art. Housewives saved their fats and ashes and made up their own soft soap, and even evolved a species of hard soap, usually molded in the form of a ball.

When Miss Agnes Adele Kinsbury, in 1955, gave an interview to a Syracuse, New York, newspaper on the occasion of her 98th birthday, she described the soap making process as she remembered it from her girlhood. The method was substantially the same as used by Pilgrim women in 1620—

Once or twice a year we made soap, yellow soft soap. There was a thing called a leach in the back yard. It had an opening a couple of feet square at the top and then it slanted in all the way down to the bottom to just a little hole for water to run out. We'd save up the wood ashes in this leach, and when we wanted to make lye, we'd pour on pails of water and let it run down through the ashes. Sometimes it took all day for one pailful of water to run through and come out at the bottom as lye. We kept on putting water through until we got all the lye we wanted.

Through the year, we kept all the grease from cooking, hog killing, beef killing and the like. When we came to make soap, we put the lye into the big iron kettle that we used to scald hogs in and built a fire under it. Then we added some grease and let it boil up with the lye. It would thicken, just like gravy. When it got cool, we'd take it down cellar and pour it into a barrel. Sometimes the soap would be almost hard as it cooled, and sometimes it would stay runny. We used it whatever way it was.

People in the cities were letting others make their soap for them long before "boughten" soap became commonplace in country stores. By 1800, John Slidell & Company at 50 Broadway, New York, was a well established soapmaker. In 1809, David Williams set up his soap business on Greenwich Street, near Barclay, in New York, and there were many other companies in that city and elsewhere. Most of them combined candle making with their soap manufacture.

PLATE 59. Homemade soap, taken in exchange for other goods, appeared frequently in country stores.

I used your soap two years ago and have not used any other since

Kirk's Flake
WHITE
Soap
James S. Kirk & Company
CHICAGO. U.S.A.
FOR UNIVERSAL USE

PLATE 60. This drawing by Henry Furness originally appeared as a Pear's Soap advertisement in *Punch*. It was adapted in this country for Kirk's Soap, before Kirk's was purchased by Proctor and Gamble.

Keeping the Country Clean

"ANY fool can make soap, but it takes a clever man to sell it," is an old saying in the trade. The story of commercial soapmaking in America is largely a record of these "clever" men.

WILLIAM COLGATE & COMPANY

William Colgate was fifteen years old in 1798. The farm in Harford County, Maryland, where he'd lived all his life, had just been lost through faulty title. He had to go to work—and at once. He hired out to a Baltimore soapmaker, and for two years he learned the trade. We are told he was industrious, faithful, and highly efficient.

When he felt he had enough experience, he took the stagecoach to New York—the Big City was even then exerting its pull—and found work with John Slidell & Company, the largest tallow chandlers in the city. When he was twenty-three, he struck out for himself, renting a two-story brick building at #6 Dutch Street, and installing the necessary manufacturing equipment.

The first day he opened his shop at seven in the morning and waited till nearly closing time for his first customer. Then an elderly gentleman came in, sniffed around, and bought a two pound bar—the first soap of his own that Mr. Colgate ever sold.

So successful was he in this and other manufacturing ventures that his sons, Samuel Colgate and James B. Colgate could contribute generously to Madison University in Hamilton, New York; the name was changed to Colgate University in 1890. To it, Samuel, a prominent philanthropist, left his collection of some 30,000 volumes of documentary records of the Baptist denomination.

William Colgate himself, and those who came after him in the business, manufactured so many items at various times that not all of them have been recorded. Nearly twenty years ago in an attic over the old Graves store, started at South Butler, New York, in the late 1840s, was found a little wooden box, stenciled on one end "William Colgate and Company, 6, 8, and 10 Dutch Street, New York." Pencilled on the top was "Fig Blue." "Fig" was the storekeeper's expression, then in common usage, meaning "small bits of." Inside were several little inch and a half round tablets of bluing, stamped with the picture of a very young Queen Victoria, encircled with the words "Royal Victoria Queen's Blue."

The Colgate Company confessed they knew nothing of the product. Quite possibly these little bluing tablets had been brought out soon after Victoria became Queen in 1837, and had been continued on the Colgate list until 1854–58 when the Colgate Company occupied the 6, 8, 10 Dutch Street address.

Early advertisements often turn up information lacking to company records. Of their Oleine soap, a green bar, Proctor & Gamble records show a trademark registration in 1874, a refinement in the product in 1878 when it became "Oleine Oxate," and end of production shortly after the turn of the century. However, an advertisement for Proctor & Gamble's Oleine Soap in *The American Grocer* of August 30, 1873 claims, in italics, "This soap has been sold for more than *eighteen years.*"

P&G

Out in Cincinnati, in the 1830s a young Irishman, James Gamble, was also making soap in a small way. William Proctor, a candle dipper from England, had just arrived in town and decided it was a likely place to set up a business. Candles were then being brought to Cincinnati from Philadelphia at great cost in transportation. Tallow was plentiful, and he got off to a good start. He asked Gamble if he wouldn't carry his candles along with his own soap, and from this first agreement, a partnership was evolved in 1837. Incidentally, they married sisters.

At first Proctor & Gamble were best known for their "Star" candles, which were shipped down the Ohio River to the various valley towns. As many of the stevedores could not read, large stars were painted on the ends of each box as a means of identifi-

PLATE 61. Proctor & Gamble's advertisement in *The American Grocer* for August 30, 1873, and July 12, 1873, indicates that Oleine Soap had been made for 18 years before registration of the trade name in 1874.

PROCTER & GAMBLE'S

CINCINNATI

OLEINE SOAP

Is the most popular Soap sold in

NEW YORK CITY, PHILADELPHIA, BALTIMORE.
Also, CITIES and TOWNS throughout the
EASTERN and NEW ENGLAND
STATES.

———:o:———

This Soap has been sold for more than *eighteen years.* It is economy to use it, as it is sold at the price of ordinary soaps and does more service.

Sell the PROCTER & GAMBLE BRAND, as all good articles are imitated.

More than TWELVE HUNDRED GROCERS sell our Soap, and its sale is increasing.

cation. An artistically inclined shipping clerk added a half-moon and a ring around both moon and star—the beginning of the trademark so well known today. Later twelve more stars were added as a symbol of the 13 states and the pioneering spirit which marked the company as well as the country. "Star" candles were still being advertised in *The American Grocer* in the early 1870s.

As burning fluids began to supplant candles for illumination, the soap business stepped to the fore. Their first soaps were not put out under brand names, but were delivered to the storekeeper in bulk to be cut off and sold by weight. They called their best grade simply "white soap" though they recognized the need for a more distinctive name.

It was Mr. Harley Proctor, or the second generation Proctors and Gambles, who hit upon Ivory. He was attending services at the Episcopal Church at Mount Auburn, Cincinnati, when the passage was read from the 45th Psalm: "All thy garments smell of myrrh, aloes, and cassia; out of the ivory palaces, whereby they have made thee glad." Mr. Proctor was indeed made glad, for "Ivory" was to become one of the country's best known, and most used, soaps.

The Proctor and Gamble Company was of the opinion that their first Ivory Soap ad appeared in December 1882, until a similar ad was recently uncovered in the August 25th issue of the *Grocer's Criterion* published in Chicago in 1879.

In explaining the appearance of the earlier advertisement the company believes Chicago was being used as a test market for the soap which was advertised three years later on a national scale. Harley Proctor used to travel frequently to Chicago—legend has it he kept an extra umbrella on each of the Chicago trains—and it was logical for him to select Chicago as a test market away from the Cincinnati area.

ONE THAT FAILED

Not all soap companies were successful.

PLATE 62. Cakes of Fuller's Earth, mined at Vienna, New York, were sold for a short while only, by unsuccessful promoters, The Fuller's Earth & Soap Manufacturing Company, Rome, N.Y.

Spotless Town

THE FIRST commercial scouring powder or abrasive manufactured in this country was Sapolio. In early days, housewives were content to use sand for their scouring; then for a long period the imported Bath Brick was the popular abrasive. This was of natural clay, formed by the slime deposits cast up by the bore of the Parrett River at Bridgewater in Somersetshire England, which was collected and shaped into bricks and dried. (Bath is the county seat in Somersetshire—though some say Bath Brick got its name from a laborer named Bathes who discovered its shining qualities). It had been known and used in England since the Napoleonic Wars when it was the English soldier's standard polish for guns and martial accoutrements. In American stores, by the mid-1800s, it retailed for about 10¢ a brick, and wholesaled from 55¢ to 75¢ a dozen. It was also available in powdered form.

Sapolio was brought out in 1869 by Enoch Morgan Sons. The company had a long soap making history. David Williams had established the company in 1809, and was succeeded in 1834 by his son-in-law, Enoch Morgan. When Enoch died in 1853, his eldest son, John Williams Morgan, then nineteen years old, took over. When he was twenty-one he purchased the business, and later took into partnership his brothers, William Henry and George Frederick Morgan. They operated under the name of Enoch Morgan Sons.

When Sapolio was first introduced, it was a brand new product. People had to be educated to its use, and many novel and elaborate advertising stunts were tried before it achieved its eventual success. For instance, in 1892 Captain Andrews, single handed in a fourteen-foot sloop called "Sapolio" successfully sailed from Atlantic City, New Jersey, to Spain, "to repay Columbus's visit." A few years later, the Spotless Town

A wooden box, found in the old Turin store about one-third filled with square brick soap, stencilled on the outside "The Windsor Fuller Earth and Soap Company, Rome, N. Y.," recalls one of them.

Fuller's Earth is a soaplike substance used in the cleaning of woolens. It is a mined product, and some of the deposits in Europe were very profitable. It was selling in this country in the mid-1800s at $35 to $60 a ton.

No doubt visions of great wealth inspired those who in 1866 in Rome, New York, formed a company, with a capital of $40,000 (8,000 shares at $50 each), to exploit the large bed of Fuller's Earth discovered some years prior in the town of Vienna, on land belonging to the Honorable Chauncey Drodock. The bed in Vienna was the second, and the larger, discovered in this country. The earth is slatey in color, entirely devoid of grit or common clay and of a greasy soapy nature, easily transformed by a chemical process into an excellent soap. However, the company was not in production long. The bed is still lying idle there in Vienna.

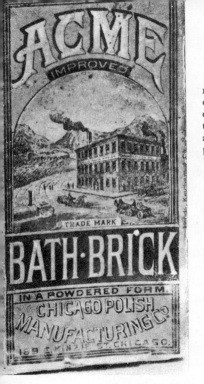

trademark appeared. Spotless Town limericks, used in their advertising, were widely quoted. One may still be read on a sign in Milton Swanson's Wayside Country Store in South Sudbury, Massachusetts—

In Spotless Town they got a bore
Who slyly spat upon the floor
They washed his mouth as white as snow
With water and SAPOLIO.
If you don't expect his fate
You must not Expectorate.

The trademark and the product became so well known that "Sapolio" like "frigidaire" and "victrola," could almost be considered a common noun. About the time of the First World War, Sapolio ceased its advertising. The company is still in business, but concentrating on export trade.

Stiff As A Board

THE ruff which characterized the costume of Elizabethan days was a prodigiously senseless fashion. It started mildly enough in the previous generation as a simple cambric collar with a gophered edge. But by Elizabeth's time, competing with the elaborate quiltings, slashings, puffings, embroideries and buttons of the day, it had taken on remarkable proportions. Ruff upon ruff, sustained by starch and wires, encircled the neck until the head appeared a separate member, supported on a tremendous linen charger.

Just as no man under a knight's degree was allowed to wear a neck chain of gold or a "garded or pinched shirte," and brooches from a goldsmith were forbidden those below the rank of gentlemen, so were ruffs denied the common people. It's quite possible the populace cared not at all, for these elaborate contraptions were not only uncomfortable, but costly, both to buy and to maintain. Starch in itself was a luxury.

The making of starch has a very ancient origin. Pliny, in the first century A.D., wrote of its being made from wheat on the island of Chios. But little more is heard of it until the ruff came into vogue. So scarce and dearly priced was it at that time that its use was confined by English law to the exclusive purposes of stiffening ruffs, and the making of hair powders by perfumers.

Though the Greeks had developed their starch from wheat, and had even worked out a food stuff from it, potatoes formed the chief source of supply in the sixteenth century. With the manufacture of cotton goods, and particularly after the development of calico printing which required sizing, there was an enlarged demand for starch. Early restrictions on its manufacture were removed and inventors were turning their attention to its cheaper and better production.

A hundred and fifty years ago there was not a starch factory in America. If starch was needed, the housewife simply grated the potato and washed the starch out of the pulp.

The first American wheat-starch factory on record seems to be that of Edward and John Gilbert in Utica, New York, in 1807.

However, it was the little wheat-starch factory started in 1827 in Jersey City, New Jersey, by William Colgate and Company, whose soap factory was also doing well, which brought its product forward to the present day.

In 1832 this company hired an ambitious young Englishman, Thomas Kingsford. Nine years later he was superintending the whole works, but he was not satisfied with the method of manufacture nor with the product made from wheat. He was convinced that native Indian corn would yield abundantly a cheaper and better starch, if only it could be separated from all foreign substances. His employers who were making money with wheat starch, saw no need for fooling around with so visionary an idea.

On his own, Kingsford began a series of experiments. For months his spare time was spent searching for a means by which he could separate the starch from the corn. He was close to discouragement the night he made a solution of wood-ash lye and poured it over the ground-up corn. Lye, he found, wasn't the answer, and he tossed the mess into a receptacle to be thrown away. He ground another lot of corn, treated it with a solution of lime. That followed the first lot into the discard. A few days later when Kingsford came back to his laboratory to try again, he found the man who tidied up for him had neglected to empty the debris. Kingsford was to

PTATE 64. Thomas Kingsford, a dedicated experimenter who developed starch from Indian corn, and laid the foundation for one of America's largest industries.

bless his handyman's laxness for, as he himself emptied the can, he found on the bottom a quantity of beautiful white starch, thoroughly separated. Perfecting his process was simple, and in 1842 he produced the first quantity of marketable starch made from corn.

William Colgate and Company was ready then to make the necessary investment to establish its manufacture if they could share in the profits. Corn was cheaper than wheat and the future looked rosy. However, it was necessary for Kingsford to design new machinery for his process. When manufacture began and the new starch reached the consumer, it met with prompt and universal favor, and soon crowded wheat starches from the market.

In 1846, Kingsford left Colgate, and with his son Thomson, founded the firm of T. Kingsford and Son. They built a small factory at Bergen, New Jersey, and began the manufacture of Kingsford Starch. His was the better mousetrap, and soon capitalists were coming forward with all kinds of propositions for investment in the business. One of these resulted, in 1848, in the incorporation of the Oswego Starch Factory, and the removal of the business to Oswego, New York, where suitable factory buildings were erected. Unfailing water power, a pure water supply for manufacturing purposes, and good shipping facilities were the chief advantages of this change in location. Oswego had a fine harbor on Lake Ontario, and freight on corn from the west was cheaper by water than by rail.

The business prospered, but Kingsford was still an experimenter. He began to think about a food substance which could be produced from corn, free from the objections inherent in cornmeal, nutritious, and at the same time suited to the delicate stomach—something to supplant the expensive arrow-root, sago, tapioca and similar farinaceous foods favored for infants and invalids. His experiments with different processes resulted in what was ultimately known as cornstarch.

The Kingsford Cornstarch factories eventually removed to the mid-west to be closer to the source of corn supply. Sometime after 1906, the company was acquired by the Corn Products Refining Company. Corn Products itself is unable to tell the precise date when the Kingsford interests were purchased. There were a number of mergers in the corn refining industry between 1848, when Kingsford built his Oswego plant, and 1906 when Corn Products was formed. It is altogether possible, they say, that the rights to the Kingsford name were purchased from one of those short-lived mergers, and not directly from the Kingsford Company.

Corn Products Company, listing Argo cornstarch, Argo laundry starch, Mazola and Karo among its present day products, still puts out a cornstarch under the Kingsford label, and oldsters who were "raised on it" can still find the familiar Kingsford package on the grocery shelf.

Few remember, if ever they knew, that Kingsford is the man to thank for the stiff starched pinafores of little girls, the "boiled" shirt of gala occasions, the glossy coated paper in magazines and books (it's done with cornstarch), for puddings, and pie fillings, and lumpless meat gravies. Statues have been raised to many a man who has contributed less!

Food From Thought

THE EARLY nineteenth century marked a period of psychic unrest in rural America. The first fierce and all-engrossing thrust in this new land had been made. The surging energy that had brought forth farmland from wilderness turned from the lonely monotony it had created to fall greedily on a world of ideas. A spate of religious fervor, economic experiment, political movement, and health fads swept the land.

Every movement directly affected the country store—gatherings brought added business; religious dictums made changes in food habits, put new products to the shelves; and talk of emancipating women roused greater interest in ladies' apparel.

Religious revivals were in the van. Summer camp meetings and winter revivals, where relays of preachers thundered through days and nights, with halts only for the preparation of meals over open fires, were times of congregation and relaxation. Farmers, readying for such gatherings, brought loads of produce, ashes, or charcoal to exchange at the store for new clothes for the family and added extras in the food line—tea, sugar, spices, coffee.

York State, with its fertile agricultural regions, was easily accessible from New England yet far enough away from Puritan dominated settlements to offer freedom for experiment. From the first it was a haven for religious sects and "isms." Anne Hutchinson, the first to bring her followers into New York State—all were massacred by Indians in 1643—is remembered

PLATE 65. Fashionable stiff-starched ladies "waists," petticoats, and light dresses of the 1900s set starch manufacturers vying for popularity with gaily labeled boxes.

PLATE 66. A Kellogg and Comstock print shows varied activities of outdoor camp meeting, including preparation for refreshment over the open fire.

today by the river which bears her name and the Hutchinson River Parkway which parallels it.

When the first tide of settlers reached the Genessee Country in the summer of 1790, they found on the western shores of Seneca Lake "fields of clover knee-deep, and golden grain ready for the cradle," planted by Jemina Wilkinson, prophet, priest, ruler, judge, physician, and self-termed "Universal Friend." With her flock, this Rhode Island born Quakeress had established her "New Jerusalem" three years earlier on 12,000 acres purchased from Phelps and Gorham at eighteen cents an acre. Her generous field of farm crops, herds of cattle, pigs, and sheep were an ever-available source of supply to incoming settlers.

The Shakers came in 1778 to establish, at Watervliet, a community that was to add invention and manufacturing to agricultural pursuits.

By 1820 other religious sects and all kinds of psychic manifestations began to appear. Diviners of hidden treasure, finders of water or stolen articles, dowsers with forked sticks were common. A wave of "digging for money" swept over western New York. Farmers assembled at night, in absolute silence, to dig for treasure in spots disclosed to them by diviners.

One young diviner who reached great renown was Joseph Smith, Jr., whose father and brothers pursued their livelihood near Palmyra selling cordwood, baskets, birch brooms, maple sugar and syrup. On public days, they pushed a "cake and beer" cart, laden with confectionery, gingerbreads, and root beer through the streets.

PLATE 67. A contemporary view of Main Street, Palmyra, New York, 1841, the town in which Joseph Smith, founder of the Mormon sect, began his public career. (Historical Collection of the State of N.Y.)

PLATE 68. Mormon Hill, 140 ft. high, about 3 miles south from Palmyra, where Joseph Smith claimed discovery of the plates containing the Book of Mormon. (1841) Historical Collection of the State of N.Y.

Young Joseph guided by vision to Cumorah Hill, found there, according to his own account, the golden plates of the Book of Mormon, and organized, in 1830, the Church of the Latter Day Saints. Vermont-born Brigham Young, a carpenter, then clerking in David Smith's store in Port Bryon, New York, was converted in 1832.

Persecuted by lawsuits, though none were successful, Smith moved on with his followers to Kirtland, Ohio, the first step in the long many-staged Mormon trek which ended at Salt Lake City in 1848.

The Mormons, industrious, capable, thrifty, and abstemious, abreast of the times in agriculture and commerce, prospered. They pioneered in dry-farming, and later brought irrigation to the desert. Their agricultural products have for the past century affected prices paid for farm products over the country.

Thousands of Millerites, followers of Massachusetts-born William Miller, who had settled in Low Hampton, New York, believed firmly in his prophesy that the end of the world would come to pass sometime between March 21, 1843 and March 21, 1844, and threw local economy into a tizzy by disposing of their farms and earthly belongings against that day. In 1845 when a start toward living had to be made, there were still some fifty thousand faithful Millerites to convene at Albany, where the name "Adventists" was adopted. The church has maintained its vitality, and still survives. Its present stronghold is at Alfred University, in Alfred, New York, an agricultural community strongly influenced by the sect which dominates it.

The Adventists, like many other religious sects, were strict vegetarians, and from them have come some of today's best known vegetable products. The remarkable Ellen Gould Harmon White who gathered the remnant of William Miller's Millenial group in New Hampshire to found the Seventh Day Adventists, was guided by vision to establish the Western Health Reform Institute at tiny Battle Creek, Michigan. Later, under the extremely competent Dr. John Harvey Kellogg, son of an Adventist pioneer, the institute was renamed Battle Creek Sanitorium. Dr. John's brother, Will K. Kellogg, developed the Kellogg Breakfast Health foods.

There were other less permanent evidences of the receptivity of the times to psychic forces. The Fox sisters, in 1848, startled their little village of Hydesville with mysterious rappings, and removed to Rochester where their spiritualistic manifestations continued to larger audiences and became known as the "Rochester Rappings."

Fowler, an American phrenologist, toured the country, and everyone who could afford it had his "bumps" read. He published a book advocating octagon houses—almost every community in New York has at least one of these unconventional structures.

PLATE 69. *Harper's New Monthly Magazine* in August 1831 took a poke at female aspirations : "The American female Emancipist marches on her holy war under the distinguishing garment of her husband . . ."

PLATE 70. Currier & Ives immortalized the Bloomer Girl in print. She was also "done in plaster" figurines. Both prints and figures are sought by today's collectors.

Sylvester Graham, a lecturer on temperance, proposed a cure for alcoholism by diet reform, theorizing that a vegetable diet was incompatible with a craving for stimulants. By 1830, several Graham boarding houses were in operation in various cities. He urged abstinence from meat, and the use of bread made of unbolted flour. His recommendations resulted in Graham bread, Graham flour, Graham crackers.

Soon after the first Women's Rights convention was held in Seneca Falls in 1848, Amelia Bloomer was preaching the absurdity of asking for social, civil, and political rights for women who continued to wear long skirts and corsets. The Bloomer Girl, in loose Turkish trousers, gaiters, and short jacket became a symbol of woman's freedom. Dr. Mary Walker, famous Civil War surgeon from Oswego, New York, was pictured in this costume.

This restlessness in religion, in civil and cultural ideals split many a family asunder. Children left their homes and followed new religions to new settlements, abandoned established customs and became "free thinking."

The economic effects of these changes were far felt, for they stressed and furthered agricultural progress across the country. Sylvester Graham and Will K. Kellogg contributed to today's food shelves definite products advanced from their deepest beliefs. Amelia Bloomer lent her name, at least, to another "best seller."

"Hands To Work and Hearts To God"

THE UNITED Society of Believers in Christ's Second Appearing, commonly called "Shakers" because of the leaping, shouting, and shaking that formed part of their worship ritual, had its beginning in a Quaker revival in England in the mid-1700s. Persecuted there, they were led by a vision vouchsafed to "Mother" Ann Lee, to America and in 1778 to the establishment of a colony at Watervliet, New York.

This was a communistic venture, and a celibate one. The sect would have early died a natural death but for the religious revivals in the region around New Lebanon, which swelled their number with converts.

The Shakers used no tobacco, alcoholic liquors only as medicine, and ate neither meat nor fish. The men did the farm and factory work, while the women cooked, kept the house, and made butter and cheese.

PLATE 71. Green corn slicer, invented and used by Shakers to cut off kernels for drying.

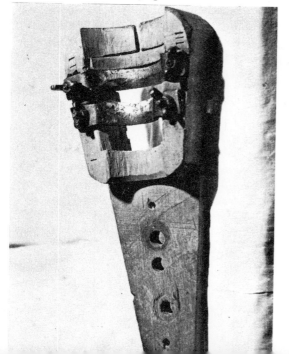

PLATE 72. Horsehair sieves in round ash frames were woven on a special loom by Shaker Sisters.

Through the years, Shaker colonies were established elsewhere in New York, in Massachusetts, New Hampshire, Connecticut, Maine, Kentucky, Tennessee, Ohio, Indiana, and Florida. An establishment in Georgia was unsuccessful.

Today only a handful of Shakers are left, a few each in the colonies at East Canterbury, New Hampshire, Hancock, Massachusetts, Sabbathday Lake, Maine and in Kentucky and Tennessee.

It was the practical vision of the Shakers, rather than their religious views which left an impress on the years. Their list of "firsts" speaks for their inventive genius both in manufacture and in the use of agricultural by-products, as they followed the precept of Mother Ann, "Hands to work and hearts to God."

The Shakers originated the seed industry in New York and seem to have been the first seed growers anywhere to put garden seeds in paper packets. They were the first to grow broom corn and make brooms, having begun the industry in 1798 at Watervliet; they clam invention of the flat house broom, and the tools to increase the rate of their manufacture. They cultivated various medicinal plants and gathered others from the woods, and put them up for the drug trade. They grew poppies and for a time made most of the opium used in America. They were among the first to evaporate fruits and vegetables for the market, especially corn, apples, and raspberries.

Although the Indians knew the art of drying corn for food, the Shakers are said to be the first to engage in the occupation on a considerable scale. At New Lebanon in 1828 they had built kilns for the purpose and were marketing dried sweet corn, as they did their seeds, in convenient containers. At first the process consisted merely of boiling the corn on the cob in great iron kettles, cutting off the kernels with hand knives, usually two or three-bladed affairs screwed to a vise or a table, and drying them in the sun on large boards. Later a drying house was erected.

The Shakers credit themselves with the invention of the metal pen, and claim to have been the first to cook medicine in vacuum pans, and the first to condense milk.

Their peddling wagons loaded with merchandise of their own manufacture went through the countryside selling their products wholesale to the country store and retail to the farmhouse. Besides brooms, brushes, and clothespins, they carried scythes, snaths, spinning wheels, and round wooden spittoons, or "spit-boxes," which were sold for 25¢ apiece. Sugar boxes brought 80¢ a nest, horn combs $1 a dozen, candlewicking 25¢ a pound. Floor mops made of tow, cotton, and wool sold at $2.25 a dozen wholesale. All kinds of whips were made and peddled along with leather mittens, diaper and other cloth, from 1809 on. In earlier times, around 1789, they had supplied felt colt's fur and wool hats, an important part of the country store's clothing stock, at nine shillings each, and "caster" hats (beavers) at one pound, 12 shillings.

They designed and built distinctive furniture, simple but efficient, reflecting

PLATE 73. Advertising cards of J.S. Banker, Genoa, N.Y. show views of "Sunday at Mount Lebanon, Strangers Coming to the Shaker's Meeting."

their religious intensity and aesthetic restraint. Their tables, chairs, benches and beds were widely distributed from Shaker communities, and as widely copied by other manufacturers of furniture.

They manufactured cotton and woolen fabrics, dying them brown with peach leaves or butternut bark, sand color with black walnut shucks. On special looms the sisters wove sieves into round ash frames from the hair of horse's manes and cow's tails. "Of all their inventions," commented James Brown, an authority on Shaker furniture and Shaker history, "the only one of which they were not proud was the horse collar!"

Shaker products were known and used in cities as well as country communities. Miss Leslie in *The House Book or a Manual of Domestic Economy,* published in Philadelphia in 1840, offered the housewifely suggestion—

In washing tea things (cups, small plates, teaspoons) it is a great saving of the hands to use a little cupswab or mop such as are made by the Society of the Shakers and are to be obtained wherever their wares are sold Taking one of these by the handle in your right hand and dipping the woolen or thrum end into the water, you can wash the thing very clean while holding it at the edge between the thumb and finger of your left hand.

The dish mop—another first?

PLATE 74.   Home of the Oneida Community, 1854.

The Oneida Experiment

IN 1829, Sewall Newhouse with his parents, William and Nancy, migrated from Brattleboro, Vermont, to Oneida county, New York, a wild and "western" country, scarcely more than a frontier settlement. Deer, bears, and wolves abounded in the great forest basin of Oneida Lake. Sewell became a hunter and trapper, so successful a woodsman that it was held unsafe for a muskrat, three miles away from him, to make an audible plunge. Because he wanted a better trap than those in use, he made one himself, learning from an itinerant mechanic how to temper the springs which he cut from worn out blades of old axes. His new trap worked well; it held what it caught.

He made up about fifty of them and sold them to neighboring Indians for 62¢ apiece. Then he made another supply and sold those. Off and on for twenty years, Newhouse worked at trapmaking, sometimes with a partner, sometimes alone. Perhaps he made from one to two thousand a year.

Then Newhouse joined a new religious cult, an American communistic society that had come to Oneida in 1847, and his traps became part of the community holdings. As such they ceased to be a purely local product and entered the national market.

This organization, a product of the religious revivals of the 1830s, was conceived by John Humphrey Noyes, a Dartmouth College graduate and a Congregational minister. One of its cardinal tenets was that selfishness was the chief sin of human kind and that communism was the best method of overcoming it. In the colony established as "Perfectionists" in Putney, Vermont, members pooled their property, renounced all religious observances, denied allegiance to the United States, and instituted a free-love marriage system, holding that monogamy was antagonistic to communism. The churches in Vermont could not quite condone polygamy, and the colony perforce migrated to Central New York in 1847. There they took the name "Oneida Community."

There were some three hundred members, mostly New England farmers and mechanics—industrious, able, and sincere. Converts like Newhouse added their skills to the group. The first ten years saw land cleared, crops planted and the groundwork laid for expansion. The Community, unlike most such groups, emphasized manufacturing rather than agriculture, and early put the Newhouse traps in production.

Like other experimenters in communism in this country, the Community found it could not live to itself. When conditions were looking very dark indeed, one of the members, a Mr. Olds, took a trunkful of the Newhouse traps to Chicago, showed them to the hardware firm of Hibbard and Spence, and met the response "We'll take all you've got." Under Mr. Noyes, the Community worked out a system of manufacture so that the price of the traps could be reduced. Soon Newhouse traps were known and sold wherever there was a frontier. Country stores and trading posts in Kansas, Colorado, Nevada, and Idaho called for traps and more traps. Wisconsin adapted the steel trap into her Coat of Arms.

To dispose of the goods they manufactured, Community members who had previously been peddlers, took to the road

PLATE 75.   Currier & Ives print, "In the Northern Wilds, Trapping Beaver," shows a Newhouse type trap in use.

again, travelling through New York, New Jersey and Pennsylvania. Finding that the articles which sold best were their packs of sewing and embroidery silks, the Community began to specialize, engaging in a wholesale jobbing of silk thread.

In 1877, the Oneida Community turned its attention to a branch of their order in Wallingford, Connecticut, which was turning out spoons of ungraded tin in patterns called "Lily" and "Oval." Silver-plated ware was becoming a popular and extremely salable product, and the Community converted their tin spoon shop to a manufactory of silver plate. From the start this proved a highly successful venture.

The Oneida experiment was abandoned in 1881, but the community was reorganized as a corporation, settling on the manufacture of a limited number of products, two of which are still very well known today—Community silverplate and New-house traps.

Coffee Break

ALTHOUGH the United States is today one of the heaviest coffee drinking nations in the world, coffee came late to the American table. It was known, and available, long before the Civil War, but its luxury prices denied it to the majority of people. As early as 1816, Reuben Woolworth of Turin, New York, who kept boarders, had to pay forty-four cents a pound—an exorbitant sum—at the Roland Clapp store, and according to Clapp's daybook only two or three pounds were sold each month. Thousands of young men in the 1860s had never tasted coffee until it turned up in their Army rations.

When John D. Billings, who served with the Army of the Potomac, came to publish his recollections of Army life, in 1888, he not only considered coffee of such consequence as to use it in his title, *Hardtack and Coffee,* but devoted several pages to its merits. "How often," he concluded, "after being completely jaded by a night march—and this is an experience common to thousands—have I had a wash, if there were water to be had, made and drunk my pint or so of coffee, and felt as fresh and invigorated as if just risen from a night's sound sleep! At such times it would seem to have had no substitute."

Billings, who was in the Quartermaster's Corps, and in a position to know, left an enlightening account of the division of coffee and sugar rations among the men. (Unless there was occasional canned milk in camp, they drank their coffee black.) Each soldier was issued a daily ration of pork, bacon or beef, hardtack and bread, or the flour or cornmeal to make his own —in those days soldiers cooked for themselves. Other foodstuffs, like beans or peas, potatoes when practical, pepper, molasses, coffee, tea, and sugar were assigned in given amounts, so much per hundred men, to the regimental quartermaster. The daily coffee ration (unless tea was substituted) was ten pounds of green coffee, or eight pounds, roasted and ground. When this had been apportioned among the ten companies, it was up to the sergeant in each company to make an exact division among his men.

First, two rubber blankets were ceremoniously laid out. On one, the coffee was divided into as many little piles as there were men to receive rations, care being taken that the piles looked of the same size. Sugar was spooned out on the other. In companies given to unruly grumblings about "my fair share," the sergeant would turn his back on the rations, and take out

PLATE 76.   Illustration from the book *Hardtack and Coffee,* 1888.

his roll of the company. On request, some-one would point to a pile and ask, "Who shall have this?" The sergeant, without turning, called a name from his list, and the one thus called promptly appropriated the pile specified.

No man was without a bag of some sort to put his coffee in. Starchy young soldiers, fresh from home, might bring out a fancy oil silk bag, lined with cloth, but the veteran was content with a plain cloth oblong bag, sometimes indescribably soiled, into which he scooped both coffee and sugar and stirred thoroughly. In this way, nothing was lost if the sugar got wet and melted in the rain.

Considering this complicated routine, it is to be wondered how the daily "1 lb. 4 oz. of pepper and 1 quart of molasses" were divided amongst one hundred men. Mr. Billings did not say.

In periods between battles, there was a great deal of fraternizing and considerable swapping between the boys in blue and the boys in gray. Between the lines drawn up before Petersburg, Virginia, in the winter of 1864-65, the "Dog Express" was kept busy. The protagonist in this friendly exchange was a strictly neutral canine, trained to answer whistles of either side. He ambled back and forth carrying coffee to the south, and bringing back tobacco and peanuts to the north. That higher-ups were aware of the Dog Express and sought to use it to advantage is evidenced by the following order which found its way to Confederate Lines in a can of swapping coffee—

HEADQUARTERS ARMY OF THE U.S.

IN THE FIELD, JAN. 4, 1865
                    SPECIAL ORDER No. 3:

Deserters coming in will be sent to their homes or to any part of the Northern States on taking the oath, or will be employed in commissary or quartermaster departments. Horses and Mules will be paid for.

U.S. GRANT, *General*

Having been so satisfactorily indoctrinated to coffee, the boys were not inclined to do without it when they got back home. In the wake of their demand, coffee companies got busy. There followed a tremendous rush of coffee importing and roasting apparatus invention, of far-fetched advertising, and "coffee wars." There was also considerable chicanery in adulteration.

The Oriental Tea Company in Boston, Massachusetts, hit the advertising jackpot when they brought out, in 1868, a "Male-Berry Java Coffee." This they claimed stood at the head of "all known varieties for powerful strength, richness of aroma, and healthy drinking properties." The Male Berry, it claimed, was "the round or fully developed bean, picked from the ordinary flat Coffee, by hand, in Java," and was, in their opinion and that of everyone who had tried it, "the very best coffee in the world."

Their advertising and promotions of the "Male Berry Java" must have given their competitors many uneasy nights, for the public rose to the name and the notion of "powerful strength."

Inspired by this advertising, *The American Grocer* on November 15, 1869, came out with a mildly admonitory editorial, replete with botanical reference. If the coffee berry had any sex at all, they concluded, it was certainly not male; the small round berries called "male" in the advertisment and claimed exclusively for Java, were found in many other types of coffee, particularly Mocha. They allowed that "Male Berry Coffee" was a very good coffee, but hinted broadly that others were just as good.

Unabashed, the Oriental Tea Company stuck to their story—the catchy "Male Berry" was their most expensive coffee. As late as 1873 they were warning their customers through their advertisements to beware of imitations.

Other companies worked hard to combat this "Male Berry" appeal. The first branded coffee noted in *The American Grocer* appeared in December, 1869. This was Osborn's Celebrated Prepared Java Coffee, which came "packed in a one pound foil paper; cases of thirty and fifty pounds; wholesale price, 18 cents per pound."

Their advertisement was headed "No Prize Packages, No Orders for Spoons or Dolls, but a Coffee Really Worth Its Price," and led off—

This coffee has been noted favorably to the trade since 1863. It is sold strictly on its merits, as the two to five cents per pound which other advertisers spend for fancy advertising, is devoted by us to improve the quality of the article.

Honest coffee roasters, wholesalers, and retailers were plagued by many unscrupulous competitors who were "fostering" adulterated coffee at lower prices.

Artemas Ward, editor of the *Philadelphia Grocer,* warned his readers—

The adulterations of ground coffee are very numerous, all sorts of wasted grains, nuts and shells having been used for this purpose, but chicory root has been the most extensive adulteration . . . It is even said that coffee beans have been made by grinding the chicory root to a powder, moulding it into proper shape, roasting it and coloring it in imitation of the coffee berry . . . By buying the whole, unground coffee, we may feel fairly sure of obtaining a pure article . . . but it is a mistake to suppose that whole roasted coffee is not easily adulterated. The roaster can, by manipulating the coffee in its roasting, glaze it with grease or gum, and add to its exterior appearance while materially injuring its real value.

English coffee men were running into the same problems. *Tricks of Trade,* in 1856, reported coffee adulterated with barley rye to the extent of 25 per cent; and chicory from 20 to 75 per cent. The same article referred to the machine invented, patented, and used for shaping substances such as chicory into coffee-berry shape, and took the Government to task not only for refusing "to prevent the public from having adulterated articles sold to them openly as genuine" but for granting "protection to the inventors of machines for producing the adulterating circumstances."

"Coffee Extract," a popular patent compound, containing little, if any, pure coffee, allowed the user to do his own adulterating. It was used extensively in cheap boarding houses by mixing it with real coffee, then selling at 35 to 40 cents a pound.

The glazing and polishing process brought on several advertising wars. One of the fiercest occurred between two leading Pittsburgh roasters, Messrs. Arbuckle & Co. and Messrs. Dilworth Bros. The former had a patented process for coating or glazing the coffee after it was roasted. The latter had a patented steam polisher for manipulating their berry. Dilworth Bros. claimed Arbuckle & Co. started the trouble by circulating a small handbill with a woodcut representing the interior of a coffee roasting establishment, purportedly Dil-

PLATES 77 & 78. Home coffee roasters could avert some of the commercial adulterations, which according to a list presented to Congress by James R. Mann, on June 21, 1906, might include roasted peas, beans, wheat, rye, oats, chicory, brown bread, charcoal, red slate, bark, and date stones.

worth's, with all sorts of unmentionables in boxes and barrels about to be used in the mixture; in the crowd of excited people at the door, one man was saying "No wonder I have been sick," and a woman was exclaiming, "I see what killed my children."

The ensuing newspaper advertising by both parties was exceedingly lively and followed the tone set by the handbill. It made fascinating reading. The segment of the public which classed "coffee drinking" with sin, enjoyed it avidly.

The consumer, all this time, had been quietly getting educated to coffee and had grown more discriminating. The coffee trade began to turn from bickering and extravagant advertising to concentrate on improving the product in quality and in blending.

About the time the coffee roasters were roasting each other in Pittsburgh, young Joel Cheek, down in Kentucky, turned twenty-one. With his "freedom dollar" in hand—presented by his father in the old time manner as a symbol of his freedom to venture forth—he rafted down the Cumberland River to Nashville, Tennessee. There he got a job as a travelling salesman with a wholesale grocery firm. Though he handled a variety of grocery products, he fell in love with coffee. He thought a lot about developing his own blend, which would be an improvement on all the blends he sold, but he was never long enough in one spot to experiment. Eventually he was promoted to a partnership in the business, and settled down in Nashville.

At first he limited his coffee experiments to his spare time. Gradually they demanded more and more of his working day. Finally

he reached a point where he had to choose between his job and his "coffee;" he quit work. That was in 1882.

It took him a year or two more to get his blend to his satisfaction, but when he was suited, he asked the Maxwell House in Nashville, one of the South's finest hotels at the time, to try it out. The guests, who included the elite of the country, liked it. "This Maxwell House Coffee, Sir," they said, "is superb."

Years later when Theodore Roosevelt was an honored guest at The Hermitage, Andrew Jackson's old home in Nashville, he was asked by his hostess if he would have another cup of Maxwell House Coffee. "Will I have another!" he boomed. "Delighted! It's good to the last drop."

And so were born, by chance, the name and the slogan so well known today.

In another section of the country, at about the same time, another famous name in coffee was getting its start. In the early 1850s, young James Sanborn was peddling garden seeds from a horse cart through the State of Maine. Acquiring a little capital, he started a coffee and spice business at Lewiston, Maine Soon he opened a branch office in Boston. There he came acquainted with Caleb Chase, the son of a Cape Cod sea captain, who in 1864 had started a coffee business in Boston. The two young men joined forces. Their firm was the first to pack and ship roasted coffee in sealed cans, and from 1878, when their sealed brand coffee, in one and two pound cans, first appeared in country store shelves, Chase and Sanborn have been familiar household words.

For those who may wonder about the origin of coffee itself, its use is recorded in Abyssinia in the 15th century, with the statement that it had been known for time immemorial. The name probably derives from the Arabic *K'hawah,* though some scholars take issue and trace it to Kaffa, a province in Abyssinia, where the coffee tree grows wild. Legend has it that a flock of sheep,

PLATE 79.   Wall-type coffee grinder.

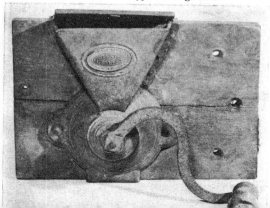

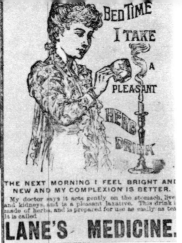

PLATE 80. Lane's Medicine and Kemp's Balsam were two of Orator Frank Woodward's successful patent remedies.

nibbling at the wild berries, became elated, and couldn't sleep at night. When the natives discovered what the sheep were up to, they mixed a little brew for themselves—coffee drinkers have been "counting sheep" ever since!

There's a Reason

THE popular "new" coffee had its detractors, of course. Seventeenth century England believed wholeheartedly that coffee drinking caused leprosy. In the 1870s and 80s, indeed even into the 20th century, American preachers, reformers, extremists, and faddists were predicting results almost as dire, and the men who ground up coffee substitutes were delightedly spreading these opinions—and advancing their own—by word of mouth, handbills, pretty little trade cards, and extravagant newspaper advertising.

Orator Frank Woodward of Leroy, New York, was one who capitalized on "the evils of coffee" and made a fortune with his Grain-o, which he put out in a package labelled "A Table Beverage Which The Children May Drink Without Injury As Well As The Adult."

Orator Frank Woodward began his career—at the usual age of thirteen—mixing up plaster-of-Paris "nest eggs" in a kettle bought on tick from James P. Gillette's hardware store in Leroy. These "fool-the-hens" he peddled to the farmers round about. When "china" nest eggs came along along to put him out of business, he stirred up some "Kemp's Balsam, a Cure for Cough and Grippe," and later added to his line a laxative known as Laine's Tea, recommended also for skin disorders, liver and kidney complaints, and a good night's sleep. Other home remedies manufactured in Leroy were doing well, too. Celery King and Allan's Foot Ease were Leroy products, though not Woodward's.

Young Woodward found household remedies much more remunerative than nest eggs. Unlike his plaster products, "patent" medicines were fast repeat sellers. He began to expand his territory and hire help. Always a showman, he fixed his salesmen up with peddler's carts drawn by dappled gray horses. The dappled grays became his travelling trademark.

Taking advantage of the growing sentiment against coffee, Woodward developed a coffee substitute called Grain-o, concocted of roasted cereal grains. It was very little different from the beverage that early settlers and farmers had made for themselves from their own cereals in pioneer and pre-coffee days, and some were still making. He organized the Genesee Pure Food Company to promote the product, which was put out in two size packages, one retailing at 15¢ and one at 25¢.

His advertising, which it is assumed he wrote himself, was exceptionally vivid, and filled with "dreadful consequences." As late as 1902, he was belting home the same theme. One of his representative efforts appeared in that year in a "throw away" on which a reprint of Lincoln's assassination was featured—

COFFEE VS. ALCOHOL

Ask any first-grade pupil if there is anything injurious in wine and he will reply: "Yes, there is alcohol which is a poison." Ask him to tell you about coffee, and he says: "Oh, we are not taught

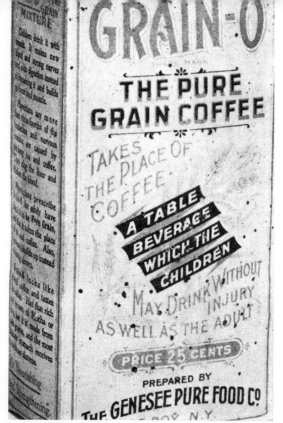

PLATE 81. Orator Frank Woodward's coffee substitute Grain-O was put out in two size packages, one retailing at 15 cents, the other at 25 cents.

anything about that." And, yet read what Prof. Savarin, of Paris, says: "Coffee is a much stronger drink than people usually suppose. A strong man can live long and drink two bottles of wine a day. If he used the same quantity of coffee for any length of time he would become an imbecile or die of consumption.
Don't allow your little ones to longer remain in ignorance of the painful effects of this insidious destroyer of health.
COFFEE PULLS DOWN, GRAIN-O BUILDS UP

To accommodate his expanding business, Woodward built a long shed where Grain-o was manufactured near the Batavia and Canandaigua branch of the New York Central Railroad. Characteristically, he decided to have painted, in largest letters possible, the full length of the roof and again on the side of the building facing the railroad, "DRINK GRAIN-O, TAKES THE PLACE OF COFFEE." He hired a relative to do the job. Whether the relative had an aversion to Grain-o, or was overly devoted to the beverage of his choice, the sight that met

Orator's eyes, as he drove out a couple of days later behind his spanking dappled grays, must have given him a jolt.

In four foot letters, the length of the building, and the length of the roof, was boldly painted, DRINK GIN, IT TAKES THE PLACE OF COFFEE. The sign was in place only a *very* short time, but long enough for the whole town to drive out to have a laugh at it.

Almost from its inception Grain-o was engaged in a linguistic battle with Graino, a rival coffee substitute, put out by the Grocer Specialty Company of Battle Creek, Michigan, who challenged Woodward's right to use the name Grain-o. Both sides were thoroughly aired in circulars and trade papers. A sample of their tactics appeared in *The Grocery World* in 1902, when Graino announced it was bringing suit "against the manufacturers of Grain-o in the U.S. Courts at Toledo, Ohio, for infringement, with similar rights of action against everyone offering Grain-o for sale." Besides threatening, the same advertisement cajoled: "Why pay $2.35 per dozen for Grain-o when you can buy the original Battle Creek Graino for 90¢ a dozen? Just as large a package and pleases your customers better."

The lawsuits, if ever filed, apparently came to nothing, for Woodward kept on selling his Grain-o, and campaigning against coffee, until he sold his Genessee Pure Food Company to the Postum Cereal interests, and Grain-o, as competitive to Postum, was dropped from the list.

Postum Cereal put in its appearance in 1895 and, through national advertising, continued to terrorize the sleepless, nervous, and undernourished coffee drinker. Though this advertising was more subtle than Woodward's vigorous compositions, it was nonetheless threatening, and because it bore the stamp of sincerity, was entirely believable. "There's a reason" became a household word, and millions of copies of "The Road to Wellville" were circulated.

This strenuous and effective advertising was written by Charles William Post, the man who invented Postum Cereal. Post was a Texan who had come, seriously ill, to Dr. John Kellogg's Sanitorium in Battle Creek, Michigan. Instead of dying as he anticipated, he recovered. Convinced by his own experience that proper diet was the solution to most human ills—and that coffee was particularly harmful—he set about to share his conviction with others by producing a healthful coffee substitute, and scaring them, if necessary, into using it.

When he began the manufacture of Postum in February 1895, he had a big idea, but little money. He laid out $11.90 for raw material, and spent $46.85 for a second-hand gasoline stove to roast bran, a hand-operated peanut roaster to roast wheat, and a coffee grinder to pulverize the mixture. He hired one man to tend the gasoline stove and stir the roasting bran, and he was in business. The payroll for his first week's operation was $12.63.

PLATE 82. Postum Cereal Food Coffee advertisement from *Munsey's Magazine*, December 1897, recommends boiling drink for 15 minutes to bring out "the phosphate and albumen which rebuild the gray matter in the nerve cells all over the human body."

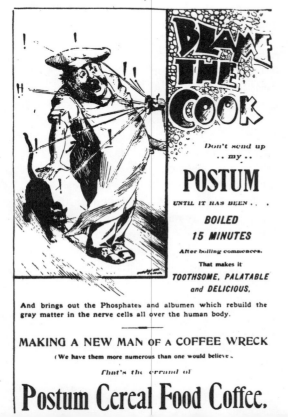

And brings out the Phosphates and albumen which rebuild the gray matter in the nerve cells all over the human body.

MAKING A NEW MAN OF A COFFEE WRECK

(We have them more numerous than one would believe.)

That's the errand of

Postum Cereal Food Coffee.

His first recorded sales of Postum Cereal, in early February, were a half dozen packages to various Battle Creek grocers; his total sales up to April 6 were $856.41. At the end of the first year he was $800 in the red. Much of his expense went to the advertising in which he believed, and which counted heavily in his eventual success.

In 1904 he began to experiment with corn flakes, and in 1911 he introduced Instant Postum. Until he died, in 1914, Mr. Post personally wrote the advertising for the "toothsome, palatable and delicious Postum Cereal Food Coffee," whose errand was to make "a new man of a coffee wreck." It incidentally made a millionaire of Mr. Post.

Puddings and Such

ABOUT 1845 Peter Cooper, who had invented the locomotive "Tom Thumb" and dabbled in all kinds of inventions, patented a gelatine dessert. Once it was patented, he did nothing more about it, nor did anyone else for nearly half a century.

Then in 1895, Mr. Pearl Wait, a cough syrup manufacturer in busy little Leroy, New York, decided to expand his business by adding a packaged food. Looking around for a product, he came up with an adaptation of the Cooper gelatine dessert. His wife, May Davis Wait, named the new product "Jell-o," and production was started in 1897.

Its sales did not come up to Mr. Wait's expectations, and two years later he was content to sell it to his neighbor, Orator Frank Woodward, for $450. Woodward immediately gave it to the Dauchy Advertising Agency to promote.

At first, no trademark was used. Then someone had the bright thought that a trademark featuring a child would convey the idea that Jell-o was easy to prepare, and a dessert children would enjoy.

Franklin King was the artist assigned to create it. King looked over hundreds of tots, trying to find the proper model. But

PLATE 83. Elizabeth King made her debut as the Jell-0 Girl in 1904.

he was hard to satisfy. One morning, wandering into his own nursery, he watched his youngest daughter, Elizabeth, playing with blocks. He took some pictures of the child, showed them at the agency—and from that day Elizabeth exchanged her blocks for empty Jell-o cartons.

Every month a new series of pictures to be used in magazine advertisements was taken on the sunporch off the King nursery. Mrs. King prepared the settings and made many of the little dresses Elizabeth wore. For four years, Elizabeth's pictures appeared in Jell-o ads. The picture taken in 1908, when Elizabeth was eight years old, served as the model for the Jell-o Girl, which appeared on Jell-o packages for years afterward. (Elizabeth is now married and living in England.)

A querulous sailor, of unremembered name, convalescing in the boarding house of Mrs. Susan Stavers in Boston in 1894, gave us another dessert. One evening Mrs. Stavers served a tapioca pudding. It was coarse, lumpy, chunky, and the sailor looked down his nose at it. He allowed he'd eaten better.

"Oh, you have!" snapped Susan, "and I suppose you can improve on it!"

"Sure can," he replied—and tossed out a million dollar idea. "Grind 'er up. Just put 'er through your coffee grinder."

Mrs. Stavers followed his suggestion; her boarders liked the result. She ground some more, packed it in paper bags, and sold it to the neighbors.

Word about Mrs. Stavers' improved dessert got around to John Whitman, then owner of the Orange, Massachusetts, *Enterprise and Journal.* He bought the rights to use her process and organized the Whitman Grocery Company. He purchased some flaked tapioca, ran it through a store-sized coffee grinder, and put it on the market as Tapioca Superlative. A year or so later, the name was changed to Minute Tapioca.

Thirty Bunches

FRESH fruit was one commodity the early American storekeeper did not have to worry with. There was none on the market. For nearly two hundred years the American settler, who had never heard of vitamins, managed with very few. What green vegetables and fruits he consumed, he raised himself. Occasionally farmers who lived near large communities peddled their surplus to city folk, but not until the late 1790s did it occur to anyone that fresh apples, pears, and peaches were a money crop to be traded in the store.

Neither were dried fruits plentiful. The few half-casks of dried prunes, raisins, currants, and grapes that trickled in with a Mediterranean cargo now and then were luxuries that seldom got beyond the seaport cities. Even local dried apples and peaches, traded at frontier stores, brought good prices. On the 1857 account books of the Graves store at South Butler, New York, Thomas Johnson was credited with $13.78 for 110½ pounds of dried peaches at a shilling a pound and $12.35 for 247 pounds of dried apples at five cents a pound. This was a substantial amount for days when farmers seldom saw $200 a year.

The earliest fresh fruit imported into New York City was the thirty bunches of bananas Captain John N. Chester brought in from the West Indies in his little schooner *Reynard,* in 1804. He worried lest thirty bunches be more than the American market could stand. Bananas continued to reach the city, but not until 1839 when John Pearsall, of J & T Pearsall, daringly chartered the schooner *Harriet Smith,* and imported the first full cargo of 1500 bunches, had so many bananas been seen there at one time. For the next twenty years, a few cargoes were imported annually. Most of these were sold in the city.

Though wealthy Colonial families had occasionally raised orange and lemon trees as greenhouse curiosities—Washington had a fine orangerie at Mount Vernon—the first commercial shipment of oranges came into this country, via the port of New York, from Sicily in 1832. Lemons followed immediately. These Italian fruits became increasingly popular, but the financial risk in importing them was considerable. Merchants had no transatlantic cable to advise them of prices in advance or of date of arrival. Often they made their transactions with local outlets before the ship put in, only to have the fruit arrive in such unsound condition that buyers refused their contracts. When this happened, as it frequently did, the importers salvaged what they could by offering the fruit at auction. To their surprise, they found it sold readily, whatever its condition, and at a fair figure. Counting their blessings, shrewd merchants opened the fruit auction house. They could not know that their "protective measure" was laying the foundation for the fruit auction warehouse through which millions of dollars worth of sound, government-inspected American fruit would pass annually.

Up until about 1870, apples, and the occasional watermelons sailed up by sloop from some southern port, were the only North American contributions to the fresh fruit counters in metropolitan centers. Lemons and sweet Messina oranges came in from Sicily; grapes, raisins, currants, and prunes, green, dried, or preserved, from Europe; pineapples, coconuts, and bananas,

from the West Indies, Cuba, and Central America. These were chiefly city treats, and limited in quantity.

But soon after the transcontinental railroad opened in 1869, Mr. N. R. Doe, a New York wholesaler, essayed a great experiment. He ordered *from California* a carload of grapes and three carloads of pears, to be shipped east in ventilated cars, attached to regular passenger trains. The fruit arrived in good condition. The pears brought from $3.50 to $5 a box, and the grapes, principally Tokays, from $10 to $15 for a 40-pound crate. Since the transportation charges on the grapes alone were $1200, this was scarcely a financial success, but it showed what could be done, and drove the first wedge of American competition into the foreign fruit trade.

Though cities became accustomed to seeing fresh fruits in the market, country stores ordered them in driblets. As late as 1889, Adams and Park of Chester, Vermont, were writing Messrs. Patch and Roberts of Boston for "2 boxes of 30 lbs. even size bright thin peel lemons, good ones at lowest price possible," and "2 bunches of good sized yellow bananas, one that will do to sell at once, and thereafter about a week later." The bill for the bananas, which was promptly paid to take advantage of the 7 cent discount, was $6.50.

To most country children of fifty years ago, oranges were something special, brought as "a present from the city," or found in the toes of Christmas stockings. Careful children were known to make a single orange, peeled and sectioned, last a week!

Grapefruit arrived too late on the scene to be carried in country stores before 1900. A Captain Shaddock, in 1696, brought from the Malay Archipelago to the Barbados, an odd fruit which he named after himself. This was coarse, bitter, and pear-shaped, growing in clusters, and weighing from ten to twenty pounds. The Spanish Colonists may have brought this East

Indian fruit into Florida as well as the bitter orange. Neither are now believed indigenous to this country.

From this shaddock, the grapefruit as we know it today was developed—in Florida.

For a long time Floridians saw no commercial possibilities in the tree. They raised it for show. Though they recognized the fruit as refreshing and tonic, they let most of it drop off the trees to rot on the ground. Northern visitors, intrigued with the taste, began asking for it back home. Between 1880 and 1885, the first shipments of grapefruit—and oranges, too—were sent from Florida to New York and Philadelphia.

In 1899, Florida produced some twelve thousand boxes, and other suitably climated states were setting out grapefruit groves in anticipation of a growing market. In 1957, 40,150,000 boxes of grapefruit added zest to American breakfasts.

Scalloped Oysters and the American Express

IN 1838, William F. Harnden, a conductor on the Boston and Worcester Railroad, conceived the idea of a package express service. He discussed the possibilities with James W. Hale, whose Reading Room in New York's Wall Street was frequented by merchants and travellers. With Hale's encouragement, he inaugurated Harnden's Express. In March 1839, advertisements appeared in New York and Boston papers announcing this means of rapid transportation for marketable goods, as well as for personal service, between the two cities.

PLATE 84.   Shucked oysters were placed in oyster barrels, (this is the 2-quart size) which were carefully nested in a flour-size barrel of cracked ice for "refrigerated" express delivery.

Similar express companies were quickly formed to serve outer points.

One man who stands out in promoting the express business is Henry Wells, whose clergyman father, Shipley Wells, had moved into central New York from Vermont while Henry was still a lad. Wells became the Albany agent for Harnden's Express between New York and Albany in 1841, when he was thirty-six years old. (He'd started his career at sixteen as an apprentice to Jessup and Palmer, tanners and shoemakers of Palmyra.)

Two years later, he established the firm of Livingston, Wells and Pomeroy to operate an express between Albany and Buffalo. He himself was a messenger, making weekly trips on five or six railroads and two or three stagecoach lines. Besides packages, he carried mail, charging 6 cents for a single letter, or $1 for twenty letters—Government charges were then two to four times higher.

Wells was one who saw possibilities in shipping perishables, and was soon soliciting business from outlying merchants, taking wild game and poultry from the country to seaboard cities, and bringing back oysters, fish, and fruits. Also about this time was inaugurated the system of collecting on delivery the amount of the invoice, and returning the cash to the shipper.

In 1850, Wells moved to Aurora, New York, where he helped merge Wells and Company, The Butterfield, Wasson and Company, and the Livingston, Fargo Company into the American Express Company, of which he was president for eighteen years. In 1852, with associates, he originated the Wells, Fargo and Company for rail and stage express to California, with Edward B. Morgan, also of Aurora, as president. In 1868, his fortune secure, he founded Wells Seminary, now Wells College, at Aurora.

The Adams Express Company, the last and strongest of the American Express

CARTHAGE,
LOWVILLE & NEW-YORK LINE.

1859

CANAL BOATS between CARTHAGE & NEW-YORK.

FREIGHT CONTRACTED

To and from New-York, at all points on the Black River Canal & River.

SHIP FROM PIER 3, EAST RIVER, NEW-YORK.

Mark Packages, " CARTHAGE, LOWVILLE & NEW-YORK LINE.

FOR FREIGHT APPLY TO

B. HARTWELL, 8 South St.. N. Y.; SHAW & THORNE. Utica; JOSLIN & SHULTZ, Boonville; G B. BEACH. Beach's Bridge; H. BLODGET. Denmark; LEWIS EATON. 95 Pier. Albany; JACOBS & ALLEN. Rome; G H. GOULD, Lyon's Falls; M. M. SMITH, Lowville; C. B RHINER. Carthage.

PROPRIETORS:

C. B. RHINER, N. WAGNER, S. P. RHINER,
D. SWEET, GEORGE SWEET, C. KHOLER.

All Goods Insured by this Line.

1858 **ROME AND NEW-YORK LINE,** 1858

IN CONNECTION WITH

WATERTOWN & ROME RAILROAD.

CULVER & CO'S UTICA LINE.

J. H. MALLORY & Co., No. 8 South Street, New-York.
CULVER & Co, Utica, N. Y.
R. C. PALMER & Co., Rome, N. Y.

AGENTS:

A. WHEDON, No. 8 SOUTH ST., Corner Moore St., N. Y. | O. N. CHAPIN, 35 QUAY ST., Albany.

Boats leave Pier 3, East River, Daily.

PLATES 85 & 86. While Express Companies served best for light, or "hurry" purchases, most heavy freight to upper New York state and the west was hauled by boat up the Erie Canal. Cards shown are those left by agents with country storekeepers when soliciting business.

Company's competitors, remained active into the 1900s, and is recalled with amusement by old timers for the once hilarious and widely circulated riddle: For what purpose was Eve made? Answer: For Adams Express Company.

The seafood introduced into the interior by the express companies was a welcome addition to country diets. Oysters, particularly, were choice treats. For shipping, the oysters were shucked, put into little half-gallon wooden kegs, and each small oyster-filled keg carefully nested in a large flour-sized barrel of cracked ice.

No one who lived in the central or western New York area fifty or sixty years ago will ever forget the scalloped oyster suppers put on by country churches. In *The Country Kitchen,* published in 1935, Della Lutes wrote nostalgically of those suppers, where the oysters, baked in huge milk pans were brought steaming hot to the long tables in the church parlors. In later years, she told, in conversation, of a letter she had subsequently received from a church in Connecticut. The ladies had read her account and decided to put on such a supper for their own church. They formed a committee, widely advertised their "Old Fashioned Milk Pan Baked Scalloped Oyster Super," ordered the oysters, sold tickets. Two nights before the event, they discovered with chagrin there wasn't a milk pan in the parish!

Canning Starts Small

FROM the most ancient of days the world had known how to dry, salt, and smoke meats, fish, and a few fruits to preserve them for future use. But not until 1765 had anyone seriously considered there might be other ways of preserving foodstuffs. An Italian abbe, named Spallanzani, became convinced that food was spoiled by invisible substances in the air, and that it could be kept indefinitely if only those unseen things, whatever they were, could be killed by heat and the food sealed in a container. Testing his theory, he heated meat extracts and other foods in enclosed glass flasks for an hour, and found they kept many weeks without spoiling.

Some time later a draper's apprentice in Amsterdam, Anton Von Leeuweenhoek, grew interested in the making of the lenses used for examining cloth, and in his work with the microscope, was one of the first to see and recognize the protozoan and bacteria—"the invisible things of the air."

For some years the idea of canning food remained only an engaging theory. Sailors on long sea voyages continued to sicken from their limited diet, and captains continued to put in at convenient islands while the men foraged for wild vegetables—sometimes they even ate grass—until their strength returned. Armies at war moved slowly, living off the land as they advanced.

Napoleon's armies, in 1795, broke the

precedent. They moved too swiftly, swooping here and there. Though they were victorious in many battles, they suffered severe losses from scurvy, starvation, and bad food. The necessity of finding a way to preserve food for transport on campaigns was pressing, and the French government offered a prize of 12,000 francs to anyone who developed something workable.

Nicholas Appert, pickler, preserver, wine-maker, confectioner, brewer, and distiller, who had been handling large quantities of food and had taken contracts for supplying armies, set out to win the prize. In the course of his experiments, he influenced glassmakers to produce specially designed bottles that could withstand heat. An apparatus was invented to put cork stoppers in tightly and wire them into place. Food was bottled and immersed in boiling water. Appert's experiments succeeded and samples of his preserved foods, carried round the world, were found fresh and wholesome after two or three years.

In 1809, fourteen years after he began his experiments, Appert was awarded the prize money, and promptly invested it in a food processing business. He soon discovered that boiling water was not always hot enough to keep foods from spoiling, and to combat this, his firm began to use an apparatus called the "autoclave," a closed vessel in which steam under pressure gave heat much greater than boiling water. This had never been used for cooking food before, but the method overcame his difficulties. The House of Appert began to grow; it still continues to operate.

One of the stipulations for the prize had been that the winner make his findings public, and Appert had written *Art of Preserving Animal and Vegetable Substances for Many Years*. Canners everywhere studied it and began to follow and improve on his methods. In 1810, a patent was granted in England to Peter Durand, a member of the firm of purveyors who had assisted Ap-

pert, for "an iron can coated with tin and cover soldered on." In 1819, Ezra Daggett, with his son-in-law, Thomas Kensett, was engaged in the packing of sealed goods in this same type can in New York City.

Durand had called his invention a "canister," which derived from the Greek word for "reed," as does "cane." Baskets woven of reed were called canisters, and people used them for tea, coffee, beans, peas, and the like. Durand's container was simply a "tin canister."

When Ezra Daggett and Thomas Kensett took out a patent in 1825 in America for an improvement in the art of preserving, they called the container a "case," and the label contained directions for opening it.

A few years later Thomas Kensett, envisioning the advantages of the Chesapeake Bay area as a canning center, moved to Baltimore. In the waters of the bay were abundant oysters, crabs, and fish. Along the shores grew peaches, apples, plums, berries, and other fruits for canning. The climate was ideal for tomatoes. Quickly it became the world's greatest canning center, and when the Civil War brought the first real demand for canned goods, Baltimore and the Chesapeake Bay region, so strategically located to war centers, prospered exceedingly.

However canning costs were high. Canners were without scientific knowledge, the tin can was still crudely made by hand

PLATE 87. This unopened 4-lb. tin of "roasted veal," packed by Donkin and Gamble, went to the Arctic with Parry as part of the *Hecla's* ship's stores in 1824, and again, on Parry's fourth voyage in 1826.

and was expensive and undependable. Tinsmiths who sealed the food in the cans were unreliable. If their demands, however unreasonable, were not met at once, they simply walked out and left the day's work to spoil.

About the time Ezra Daggett was starting his canning business in New York, William Underwood, who had served his apprenticeship in pickling and preserving in London, was operating a cannery in Boston and was shipping fruits, such as berries, in glass bottles to South America and the Orient. According to his great grandson, the late William James Underwood, the first William had come to this country in 1817, landing in New Orleans. When he found New Orleans was not the right spot for canning, he walked all the way to Boston. His establishment there was begun in 1821.

Americans, Underwood found, did not favor canned food. It was expensive, and they were suspicious of it. Those few sophisticated who *did* use canned goods wanted only those which were imported, even though they cost more. Underwood took this hurdle by printing the word "London" on his label. He also turned to more receptive foreign markets. Even there he found it best to use the magic "London" label. He sold for less than English canners, and was satisfied to take his pay in sugar and other products. It was Underwood who economically shortened the word "canisters" to "cans" in his invoices—and cans they have remained to this day. The English call them tins.

A letter from William Underwood dated January 10, 1828, addressed to Captain Sherwood of the ship *Augusta* shows the method of trade then in vogue—

Dear Sir:—

Enclosed you have invoice of pickles, sauces, mustard and preserves of first quality, most of which are labeled "London" and under which title it is best to sell them. I have invoiced them considerably less than the first quality of goods can be purchased in London, which will be some guide to you. Should you not be able to sell them for more than the cost and charges in South America, it will, I think, be best to take thm to Manila. The cranberries in bottles are preserved without sugar. I name this because should any person purchase them for sweet-meats they would be disappointed. They are to be used precisely as if purchased fresh from the market, and will keep any length of time, before the cork is drawn. Any English people will understand them, and should you fall in with any Men-of-War, they will be agreeable for ship stores for cabin use, and for any American families who wish for cranberry sauce. The Cranberry Jam is a sweet-meat and usually brings a high price; I have frequently sold it in India for $1.50 a Jar. You will use your own Judgment and invest the proceeds as you think best, but I should prefer to have Manila hemp or sugar.

Your humble servant
WILLIAM UNDERWOOD.

The captain who handled such consignments usually received half the profits for his trouble. Soy was often taken in exchange for goods sold in India, and Underwood used large quantities of it in the manufacture of his sauces and catsup. From the sections of the Orient where canned meats were most popular, he was paid in spices. To use the excess of these huge spice shipments, he began to experiment in spicing or "deviling" his canned meat products. Underwood's Deviled Ham in the can with the Little Red Devil was the result.

That Underwood was preserving milk and making shipments to South America is evident from an extract from a letter written by him in 1828—

PLATE 88. Underwood's Devilled Entrements, offered in *The American Grocer*, Nov. 9, 1872, at wholesale prices: Ham, dz. $4; Tongue, dz. $6; Lobster, dz. $3; Turkey, dz. $6; discount on 5 boxes 5%, on 25 boxes, 10%.

Among the articles which I sent to Bahia was some preserved milk, and six months later I opened a bottle from the parcel, and found that it was perfectly sweet.

Early in the 1830s, he added pie fruits to his hermetically sealed goods. Tomatoes were then considered inedible, though Phelps Compound Tomato Pills and Dr. Miles Compound Extract of Tomato were being offered as "powerful deobstruents" for billious attacks. In another few years when people had finally become convinced that tomatoes were not deadly poisonous, Underwood had tomato plants imported from England and was raising them to can. One of the old labels, of the 1835–40 era, now in the possession of the present Underwood firm reads—

Hermetically Sealed Tomatoes. This bottle contains the substance of about two dozen tomatoes and will keep good any length of time. It is prepared by straining the seeds and skins from tomatoes and evaporating the watery particles by slow heat.

English firms had early begun experimenting with the use of canned foods for army and navy. Donkin and Hall, in 1813, were sending tins of preserved foods to high authorities in the navy and army for trial. Some of their products were taken on an expedition in H.M.S. *Isabella* to Baffin's Bay in 1814. The ships were furnished with "preserved meats," "vegetable soup," and "concentrated soup," in addition to their other rations. The commander, John Ross, noted in his diary on September 8 of that year that as the store of vegetables had been expended, orders were given for serving a portion of these preserved foods in lieu of part of the salt provisions, in order to prevent scurvy.

According to Captain Basil Hall of this early period canned meats particularly appealed to the British Navy:

It is really astonishing how good the preserved milk is . . . and you must, on examining the prices, bear in mind that meat thus preserved eats nothing nor drinks . . . it is not apt to

die, does not tumble overboard or get its legs broken or its flesh worked off its bones by tumbling about the ship in stormy weather

In 1824, Captain Sir Edward Parry explored the Arctic, taking along as provision canned meats and vegetables. When a can of carrots was opened 114 years later, the carrots were described by an onlooker as appearing freshly cooked. The contents of the can smelled sweet except for a slight "metallic" odor, he said, and to the tongue, the taste was both sweet and "metallic."

Mostly Milk

ONE of the few exhibits from the United States to find favor at the International and Industrial Fair held at the Crystal Palace in London in 1851 was Gail Borden's meat biscuit. It was awarded a coveted council medal. This cake of concentrated wheat flour and beef—dry, inodorous, flat, and brittle—would keep indefinitely. "Ten pounds, mixed with sufficient water to the consistency of sago, would provide both bulk and nourishment to a healthy working man for a month."

Gail Borden, born in Norwich, Greene County, New York, on November 9, 1801, had begun his career as a schoolteacher in Indiana. Drifting down into Texas, he worked as a surveyor laying out boundary lines when that state was added to the Union in 1845. In the desert there he had watched Indian women sun-drying apricots and mixing them with jerked beef into a form of biscuit. It was this process which he adapted for his own prize winning concoction.

Though the biscuit itself was not much of a financial success, it led indirectly to important changes in the canning industry. On the slow steamer, coming back from the Fair where he had gone to receive his medal, Gail Borden was struck by the need of immigrants and their children for fresh milk. Only the rich were able to carry cows on shipboard, and even then there was no ice for keeping the milk, no methods of protecting it from contamination. If this essential, though highly perishable, food could be put into cans, he reasoned, it would have a market in cities and in wildernesses as well as at sea.

He began to work on the idea. A steaming teakettle suggested to him that milk might be condensed by boiling away the water. His first proposals for preparing milk by evaporation and putting it in sealed cans were laughed at. But then, the same people had laughed at his meat biscuit! He persisted with experiments, and in 1856 took out a patent for his process. This process is still the basis of the world's condensed milk industry.

He first tried selling his condensed milk in bulk on the streets of New York, but met with little success. Then, one day, on a train, he fell into casual conversation with Jermiah Milbank. Mr. Milbank, it developed, was a keen businessman and capitalist, and in 1858, the New York Condensed Milk Company, comprised of Borden and Milbank, opened its office in the basement of 173 Canal Street, New York City.

The new company soon outgrew its little plant at Burrville, Connecticut, and moved to the village of Wassaick, New York, which was located on the railroad and offered better chance for expansion. This condensary opened in June 1861, just two months after the outbreak of the Civil War.

Other condensaries followed, and in 1873, *The American Grocer* reported editorially—

Gail Borden has large milk condensing works in Elgin, Illinois. Though they are not as extensive as his establishment in New York, over 15,000 gallons of milk are used daily at the Illinois works, 8,000 cans of preserved and condensed milk are put up daily, fifteen barrels of refined sugar being used in the preparation.

The tin cans are made on the premises, and with the help of very ingenious machinery, invented by Mr. Borden; ten hands, mostly young girls or boys, turn out 11,000 daily.

The preserving of milk was not new, although Borden's method of packing it in hermetically sealed tin cans was.

Appert had written in his book—

They took twelve litres of fresh milk from the cows; I condensed it in the water-bath and reduced it to 2/3 of its volume, frequently skimming it. Then I strained it through a bolting cloth. When cold, I took it from the skim which had risen while it was cooling, and bottled it with the usual process, and afterwards put it in the water-bath where I let it boil for two hours; and at the end of several months, I perceived that the cream had separated itself and was swimming in the bottle in the form of flakes.

I made a second experiment on a like quantity of milk which I condensed in a water-bath, reducing it to one-half instead of one-third as I had done the former. I then added to the milk, so reduced, the yolks of eight new laid eggs, well beaten. Having left the whole thus well mingled half an hour on the fire, I completed the experiment as before. This experiment perfectly succeeded. . . . The yolk of egg had so completely combined all the particles that at the end of a year, and even of eighteen months, the milk remained as fresh as when I put it in the bottles.

An English patent for milk sugar combination was granted to De Heine in 1810. William Underwood bottled milk with sugar in 1820 which was carried on sailing vessels. Thomas Kensett of New York was

PLATE 89. Work bench in the Shaker establishment at New Lebanon, New York where Shakers claim the first condensed milk in the United States was made.

believed also to have experimented with preserving milk with sugar.

In the Shaker Museum at Old Chatham, New York, is a sign which reads: "The first condensed milk was made by the Mt. Lebanon, New York Shakers, and is said to be originally prepared on this bench." Borden himself had visited the Shakers at Mt. Lebanon, and worked with them before he put his condensed milk on the market.

A gravestone in the Middletown Cemetery, just south of Winchendon, Massachusetts, bears this inscription—

> *Stephen F. Fassett*
> *Died 1856, Aged 54*
> *I began the preserving*
> *Of Cow's milk with white*
> *Sugar for the use of steamers*
> *Crossing the Atlantic Ocean.*

Although no record of any invention or of food processing activities conducted by Stephen Fassett has been found, the claim, carved in marble, looks mighty impressive.

Borden was also interested in other canning processes. Nathaniel Amory, a friend who had visited him in Brooklyn, New York wrote in June 1853—

He [Borden] also showed us boiled milk and essence of coffee, so condensed that 1/2 teaspoonful of the salve makes a cupful of cafe au lait, or French coffee & milk. . . . He expects a patent shortly. The cup of coffee was very good.

PLATE 90. Despite the impressive claims on his gravestone in the Middleton, Mass., cemetery, Stephen Fasset appears in no record of food processing activity.

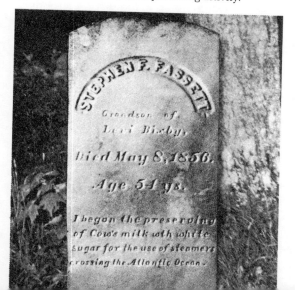

Borden's English patent for "Improvements in Concentrating Milk, and in Obtaining Concentrated Extracts from Tea, Coffee and Chocolate" was granted on August 25, 1856. A similar American patent had been issued the week previously. Borden's Extract of Coffee was actually concentrated liquid coffee combined with sugar and condensed milk. The addition of water to the extract produced coffee with milk and sugar already in it. The product proved popular and it enjoyed a wide use well into the 1890s.

In 1860, Borden patented a process for the preservation of the juices of fruits such as apples, currants, grapes, and the like, by which they were reduced to one-seventh their original bulk, and were not subject to fermentation when dissolved in water.

In 1873, a Mr. Henry Welsh was advertising in *The American Grocer*—

I am now prepared to supply my customers with Borden's Extract of Beef and Borden's Roast Beef . . . Borden's Roast Beef in chopped form is put in one pound cans. It consists of the Porterhouse and Sirloin Steaks and the Rib pieces. It is roasted, not merely par-boiled and the packers claim that one pound contains as much solid meat as an ordinary three-pound can of par-boiled ordinary desicated roasted meat.

It is cheaper than either fresh beef bought at the stalls or the canned beef heretofore sold. Sixteen-ounce tins, one dozen in a case, $4.00.

A few years later another packer hit on the idea of compressing meat so it would come out of the can in a solid piece and could be sliced. For this, cans were made in pyramid shape. The chopped meat was put in the big end, and pressure applied, so that the product, pressed against the tapering walls of the can, could be removed in a solid bulk.

Turning Point

IF the Napoleonic Wars had given initial impetus to canned products, the Civil War in the United States turned canning in America from small business to big almost overnight. With thousands of northern troops suddenly shifted to southern territory where food crops were few, everything imaginable in the way of food stuffs that could be easily transported was called into use.

The demand for canned goods was enormous, the supply infinitismal. Five to six hours was required to process the food at a temperature of 212 degrees, and the total output of the best equipped cannery was limited to about 2,000 or 2,500 cans a day. Established canneries expanded and new ones opened, but for all that, it is doubtful if the army ever had enough to issue canned foods as rations to the soldiers in the field. Canned milk was furnished for army and navy hospitals and was used in most officer's messes.

John D. Billings, in his *Hardtack and Coffee* recollected:

The army sutler played a very important part as quarter-master extraordinary to the soldiers. He was not an enlisted man, only a civilian. By an Army regulation sutlers could be appointed "at the rate of one for every regiment, corps, or separate detachment. . . ." These persons made a business of suttling, or supplying food and various collections of other articles to the troops . . . These traders pitched their tent near camp and displayed their wares most enticing to the needs of the soldiers. . . . Although he handled many other things, he made his chief reliance a stock of goods that answered the demands of the stomach. He had a line of canned goods which he sold mostly for use in officers' messes. The canning of meats, fruits and vegetables was then in its infancy, and the prices which in time of peace were high, by the demands of war were so inflated that the highest of high privates could not aspire to sample them unless he was the child of wealthy parents who kept him supplied with his stock of scrip or greenbacks . . . Here are a few of his prices as I remember them: Butter (warranted to be rancid) $1.00 a pound; cheese, 50¢ lb.; Condensed milk, 75¢ can . . . Condensed milk of two brands, the Lewis and Borden was to be had at the sutler's . . . Other than milk I do not remember any of the prices of canned goods.

To meet the increased demands of production, new processes were continually being developed. Isaac Solomon of Baltimore, about 1860, introduced the use of calcium chloride in the cooking bath to apply a higher temperature to the containers of food and so reduce cooking time. (The pressure cooker, which did the same job so much better, was invented by A.K. Shriver of Baltimore in 1874.)

In April 1862 a patent was issued to I. Winslow of Philadelphia for a new method of preserving green corn. Basically similar to Appert's process for hermatically sealing goods, this process sent a surge of canneries into central New York state where fruits and vegetables were abundant. There had been many small canneries in the area before. The Hemmingways, Olney's, and Ezra Edgett in Camden were among those already packing such provisions for the Union Army as chicken, turkeys, ducks, and army beef. The corn process simply increased the number of cannable products —and at the same time, the number of canneries.

Until Louis Pasteur's theory of fermentation was announced in 1860, canners had been working by trial-and-error methods, with no scientific knowledge as to why one method worked and another one didn't. Even after Pasteur's discovery, there was a lapse of some thirty years before scientific research was directed specifically at canning. In 1895 Samuel C. Prescott and William L. Underwood first traced spoilage to imperfect sterilization. Other individual research followed immediately, and soon the United States Department of Agriculture began organized research in canning.

There were probably no more than five million cans of food products processed annually before the Civil War. In 1870, when Army men were back home and demanding canned goods from their neighborhood grocers, the output had reached thirty million tins. Today's yearly output is estimated between 21 and 22 billion individual containers.

Not only in America are tinned foods popular. *Food Topics* reported in 1949 that canned food was once such a valuable commodity on the African Gold Coast that a handsome wife could be bought with a can of tomatoes.

Still Expanding

ONE of the men who did much to lighten the housewife's culinary burden was Gaius Lewis Merrell. Shortly after 1865, young Merrell left his father's farm in Afton, Green County, New York, and sought employment in Syracuse. According to city directories, he found it in Wilbert Bowen's grocery store at 35 South Salina Street. Later he became Bowen's partner in a canning

PLATE 91. Keuk-A Grape Catsup put up by the Keuka Grape and Fruit Co. of Rochester, N.Y. was one of dozens of fancy catsups available in the 1890's.

venture, and the 1867–68 and 1868–69 directories listed them as "Manufacturers of Canned Fruits and Vegetables of every description, Jellies, Pickles, Catsup, &c. Dealers in all kinds of Green and Dried Fruits and Nuts."

Merrell was a very inventive boy, reading everything he could find on physics and chemistry in the Syracuse Public Library, and working out formulas for his own cannery. He attracted the attention of Mr. Oscar Soule, who furnished $1,200 capital for the formation of Merrell & Soule. The Syracuse directories for 1871–2 list the firm as "packers of the Onondaga Sweet corn, vegetables and fruits." They had selected for their trademark the sculptured head of Captain George, the Onondagan chieftain who had won renown as a runner in the war of 1812, and used the brand names *Onondaga* and *Indian Canned*. They put out vegetables, potted chicken, whole roast chicken, and apples. But it was to corn that G. Lewis Merrell gave the most thought.

The usual process was to cook the corn in the can for a short time, then take it out of the boiling water, open the can, release the steam, solder the can again and recook it. Merrell wanted to find a way to cook the corn before it went into the can. Undeterred by disappointments, he kept on experimenting, and in 1873, his device, "The Merrell Gun Cooker," was patented. This was conceived of copper tubing surrounded by steam heat confined by a wooden jacket, obtaining the desired temperature for cooking the corn, and a wooden propeller on one end of the tubing to provide movement.

As others adopted this process, prices on canned corn began to drop, and it became a commonplace rather than a rarity on general store shelves. *The American Grocer* for December 15, 1869, priced a 2 lb. can of corn at $3.25 a dozen, wholesale. Four years later, it had dropped to from $2.20 to $2.90 a dozen.

Merrell never stopped experimenting and

PLATES 92 & 93. Clocks and thermometers advertising Merrell and Soule's Non-Such Mincemeat and Pumpkin-Squash, made fanciful additions to country store decor.

inventing. Of him, the *Canning Trade* wrote in 1914—

The first plan of a line of intercommunicating machines was put forward during the early '90s by G.L. Merrell of Syracuse . . . and since that time elements in the line have been improved, capacities increased and additions made as the refinements of the art developed; but there has been no real change in the general Merrell plan, to which we owe the continuous automatic, single line, trayless system of today.

Shortly after he came to Syracuse, Merrell had married Mary Antoinette Seward, who had contributed to the marriage—and the business—her grandmother Seward's recipe for mincemeat. Merrell and Soule may have made this mincemeat earlier, but not until 1885 did they really begin to push it. All kinds of fancy signs began to appear for their None-Such Mince Meat, None-Such Soups, and None-Such Pumpkin-Squash.

The company had also become interested in dietetic foods for infants and invalids. They experimented in drying milk, working with a rotating cylinder dipped into a pan of milk, allowing the milk to dry from the heat within the cylinder, but the results were unsatisfactory. Lewis C. Merrell, Gaius Merrell's son, was lying in a hospital bed when the thought of spraying the milk into a regulated current of hot air occurred to him. Even before he was back on his feet, his associates were experimenting with his idea, working in Canada lest their competitors get wind of what they were doing.

The process was so successful that Merrell & Soule disposed of their canning and canning machinery—retaining only their None-such Mincemeat—and concentrated on the new whole milk powder which they called Klim.

Merrell & Soule subsequently sold their interests to the Borden Company and today both Klim and None-such Mincemeat are put out under the Borden name.

Pork 'n' Beans

BAKED beans and brown bread are universally accepted as the New Englander's Saturday night supper. However, for Massachusetts people, until after the Revolution, salt codfish dressed with butter and hard boiled eggs was the proscribed Saturday meal the year round. This custom they had brought dutifully from England, where regular fish days were proclaimed, not as a religious observance, but to encourage and support fisheries and fishermen.

Beans took up where codfish left off—though indeed, codfish cakes are still considered a proper adjunct to a Boston baked bean supper or breakfast.

The "Boston" baked beans were prepared by soaking overnight, parboiling in the early morning, then baking in a heavy earthenware covered pot, with salt pork, molasses, mustard, salt, pepper and a pinch of soda, the long day through.

The pea bean which has long been considered the proper bean for Boston bakers, is not native to New England, but is indigenous to California. The story goes that New Englanders, shipping machinery and the like into California ports at the time of the Gold Rush, brought these small pea beans back as ballast. Thrifty New Englanders ate the ballast—and never thought much of kidney beans afterward.

As New Englanders moved west, they took their food customs with them. The sections they settled in central New York, Ohio, Indiana, Michigan, and parts farther west, still follow the Saturday night ritual, with beans baked in the same fashion.

In the late 1850s canned beans were selling well for Brother, Burnham and Morrell of Portland, Maine, who supplied them to fishing fleets, and for W.K. Lewis, who operated in Boston, and had established the name "baked" beans in the canner's glossary, but they were not so popular in other sections of the country.

In 1861, in Indianapolis, Gilbert C. Van Camp was putting up fresh fruits and vegetables in five gallon cans in the back of his Indianapolis Fruit House Grocery, along with a few incidental products in orthodox cans. Among these extras were baked navy beans, cooked with pork supplied by Homes, Paddock & Bradshaw, a nearby packing establishment. One day a fire in the

Van Camp cannery knocked everything helter-skelter, and Frank Van Camp, Gilbert's son, was rather sourly surveying the damage as he ate his frugal lunch off a sooty shelf. Mesmerized by the juxtaposition of a dented can of beans and a tomato from his lunch box, the thought flashed: "Why not dress up our baked beans with tomato sauce?"

Van Camp's drummers were soon showing—and selling in great quantity—this new taste sensation to grocers all over the country. Today, canned navy beans with tomato sauce lead in popularity in all sections but New England. There the small pea bean, baked with molasses, is still preferred. Smith & Company, present day bean processors of Marcellus, New York, estimate they ship into Maine and Boston, ten pounds of California pea beans for every pound of the slightly larger Michigan pea, or Navy, bean.

Sudden Freeze

THOUGH frozen foods may seem a recent development, the basic principle has been in use in cold countries for ages. Early settlers in America knew all about freezing meat and fish and pies.

The Pocumtuc Housewife, a book of early recipes from Old Deerfield, Massachusetts, contains the advice-to-brides—

When the team goes to Boston in the winter with a load to sell, have it bring back a fifty pound fresh codfish, and a barrel of oysters along with the molasses and sugar supply. The fish will keep frozen for weeks. A piece can be sawed off and thawed when needed. It can be salted down and is much better than store codfish.

The dried and salted "store" codfish, though edible, was not thought much of in Old Deerfield—it was a "poor folks" diet. The loafers who hung around the Old Deerfield store on Saturday nights had a little

The One Food that is Seasonable the year 'round:

Van Camp's
BOSTON BAKED
PORK AND BEANS

Sold by grocers. Sample can and booklet for 6c in stamps.

VAN CAMP PACKING CO.

PLATE 94. Van Camps 1864 can offered beans both "Boston Baked" and "Prepared with Tomato Sauce." Except in New England, the tomato sauced beans proved most popular.

song they began when the less prosperous men from the neighboring community of Wisdom came in to buy their weekly cod-fish—

Conway for beauty, Deerfield for pride
If it hadn't been for codfiish, Wisdom
    would have died.

Old Deerfield recipes also advised the freezing of pies at Thanksgiving time, echoing the common practice followed in settlements all along the Connecticut River Valley, where baked pies were stacked in cold anterooms or attics. Sausage, thinly coated with lard was another product commonly frozen. Even now, "grown-up country boys" can remember shivering up to the attic of a frosty morning to hack off a piece for breakfast. Most families butchered in late fall and hung up a quarter or a half of beef to freeze for winter eating.

Along in the mid-1850s, a brilliant young professor at the University of Glasgow, William Thompson (later elevated to the peerage and created Baron Kelvin of Largs, for his services to trans-Atlantic telegraphy), began to wonder what part morning dew played in the world. Observing that water evaporated at certain temperatures, he began to experiment with chemicals that changed to gasses with temperatures lower than the freezing point of water. From his measurements of temperature, Lord Kelvin worked out the basic law for producing refrigeration for preserving foods with artificial cold. (The *Kelvinator* is not a word without meaning!)

Though Lord Kelvin made the principle available, artificial refrigeration, as a tool for food processing, lagged until about 1890. Severe winters provided plenty of ice for even the largest packers.

Out in Sandusky, Ohio, in the early 1860s, fish were being "fast frozen" by a patent refrigerator process, which utilized natural ice. A visitor to the Sandusky plant at that time reported his impression for the *Sandusky Register*—
The first thing is pounding the ice. Ice and salt

are mixed in proportions and pounded fine for use in the new patent refrigerators. The next objects noticeable are a number of pans with covers resembling the "dripping pans" of household utility, except that each pan has a cover and is made of heavy zinc. These pans hold one large whitefish or two small ones. Fish is taken from the pile just collected from the lake, placed in the pan and the cover put on. The pans are then carried to the refrigerators, of which there are several of very large size, capable of holding many of the pans. A layer of prepared ice is placed in the bottom of the refrigerator. Then a layer of the pans containing the fish, and so on alternately, until the refrigerator is full, when it is closed and the fish left to freeze. The time occupied in freezing is generally about two hours, though with proper preparations fish can be frozen in forty minutes as hard as the "solid truth."

After two hours the fish are taken out of the pans and put away in the preserving rooms and their places supplied with others. A large force of men are constantly employed, and the fish are frozen at the rate of several tons in a day. There are preserving rooms where the fish are piled up for use when needed. Descending a ladder through a small aperture in the floor we go down into a dark room where men are dimly seen engaged in stacking fish. In front, behind, at the sides and the ends of the preserving room, they are piled up to the ceiling, and, in the center of the room we are standing six feet of the frozen swimmers. They are piled up like blocks of wood, the smaller ones being frozen in pairs, when two of them can be put into the freezing pan. There are six of these preserving rooms and the fish can be kept in them perfectly fresh and sweet until warm weather. The great merit of the process is the celerity by which the fish are frozen. In other methods the fish are frozen so slowly that quality is impaired.

It was Clarence Birdseye, recognizing the inportance of quick freezing for flavorful foods, who utilized laws already present to develop the process by which foods are frozen today.

From Bulk To Box

PACKAGED foods were few and far between until late in the 1860s. With few exceptions—Baker's cocoa was one—commodities came in bulk. Barrels of crackers, dried fruits, pickles, salt pork, chewing tobacco, cereals, and flour stood open or casually covered with an easily lifted barrel head for customer inspection. Tea was usually sold loose from the large tin counter canister, though the grocer could, if he wished, buy decorated tin or cardboard tea boxes and package it himself in small quantities. Molasses was faucetted from hogsheads into the customers' own jugs, as was kerosene. It was not an unusual occurrence for a hogshead of molasses to "explode," when the bung blew out on a hot summer's day, and shower clerks, customers, and far corners with its sweet and sticky substance.

Came the Civil War and the need for transporting food stuffs in convenient one-man quantities. Boys in service were introduced to condensed milk, fruit, and vegetables in tins, and toward the end of the war to a self-rising flour in a one or two-pound box, sold by sutlers for the making of fritters or pancakes. Sailors met up with pound-size plug tobacco.

The post war years from 1870 to 1900 exuded expansion. The percentage of the total population of the country living west of the Mississippi grew from 14 to 27 percent, concerned chiefly with farming. Eastern manufacturing increased the number of cities with a population of 200,000 or more from seven to nineteen. Newly invented machinery increased farm output, and with machinery and newly opened lands, the total value of farm property, in lands, buildings, livestock, and implements jumped from eight million dollars in 1860 to twenty billion in 1900. Manufactured products advanced from less than 2 million in 1859 to over 11 billion in 1899.

The new railroads transported foodstuffs to the cities, manufactured goods to the country. It was no longer a necessity that the farmer be self sustaining. Items once made at home could be bought at the store, and the farmer, concentrating his crops on a wider market, found it sensible to buy them.

Tempting new products were constantly showing up in the bustling crossroads stores. Tins and paper boxes were no longer made tediously by hand, but inexpensively by machine. Lest a product be lost in the anonymity of a box, art work on packages became important, advertising essential. The message of adulteration began to get through to the women, and they approved neat packages put out by firms who weren't ashamed to put their names on their labels.

Yet package pioneers met many frustrations. There was a deep core of prejudice against foods that couldn't be seen, sniffed, handled, and tasted, and years of "we never done it that way" to overcome. Early packaged goods were a curiosity to be approached with caution, and manufacturers were as cautious as their customers. Whether manufacturers discovered packaging by accident, had it forced on them by competi-

PLATE 95. Horsford's Self Raising Bread Preparation, was "something miraculous" when it was introduced during Civil War days. It has only recently ceased manufacture, being most popular in Mississippi and Northern Georgia.

PLATE 96. Events of the day were popular subjects for labels and trademarks. On May 10, 1893, old 999 of the New York Central, set a world's record for speed with steam — 11½ miles per hour between Syracuse and Buffalo, N.Y.

tion, or recognized its advantages from the start, store shelves all over the country soon burgeoned with bright red, green, blue, and yellow packages, decorated with eye appealing trademarks and fine print advertising claims. Even the die-hards couldn't resist box tops forever.

Sometimes packaging made a product. C.H. Williams, in his grand old eighties in 1942, liked to reminisce on his early store-keeping days in Jordan, New York, and expand on the ways of Fate, particularly in regard to chewing tobacco. The first he carried came in bulk, in barrels. Twist was never very popular in his section. After the Civil War when plug was called for, dozens of extravagantly named brands came on the market. Green Turtle was his most popular seller. Plug came boxed in ten to forty pound loaves, to be cut as required with a handsome tobacco cutter, furnished free by tobacco companies.

Then came a day when Bloch Brothers of Wheeling, West Virginia, one of the largest manufacturers of plug, found themselves stuck with several tons of cuttings or scraps. To unload it they mixed it up hit or miss with water, brine, molasses, licorice, salt, and sugar. The tobacco curled up prettily and "chewed pretty good." They packed it in paper bags, printed with CHEW in large letters under the name MAIL POUCH, and

PLATE 98. This Pacific Mills Allspice can was found in the ghost town of Brodie, Calif. Label shows Union Pacific Railroad train frightening buffalo from track.

took to the road themselves to dispose of it. Unexpectedly scrap became a favorite chew, and it wasn't long before barns all over the country, provided their owners were amenable to paint and cash, were emblazoned in ten-foot letters with an inspiring "Chew Mail Pouch Tobacco, Treat Yourself to the Best." Bloch Brothers are still making Mail Pouch, and Silver Cup as well. Both products are today labelled "Scrap."

The American Cereal Company, later to become Quaker Oats, was forced into packaging to survive. Oatmeal for years had been sold in kernel form, and putting it through rollers to be sold as "rolled oats" was fairly new. They were making what they thought was the best rolled oat on the market, but as for special recognition, or added sales, there was neither. When one of their salesmen wrote in that he'd seen a customer dump the new oats into a bin, set a rat trap on top of the oats, and catch two rats the first night, the company set salesmen a-spying.

Reports varied, but few were good. Said one: "Sack of oats falls from grocer's wagon into street, breaks open. Driver borrows a stable broom, sweeps up oats, puts them

PLATE 97. Boys and girls of 1890 begged mamas to buy Schepps Cocoanut for the gay tin pail, and many did.

back in bag, ties it up and drives off." Said another: "Retailer opened barrel of bulk oats. Removed barrel head, sat back comfortably on the nice soft flakes, took out a jack knife and pared his nails—into the oats!" Still another: "Retailer dumped a sack of rolled oats in window for display. Put up sign '10 lbs. for 35¢.' Nice warm sunny window. Nice soft sunny bed for Tabby Cat. (Cat hairs furnished at no extra cost!)"

The American Cereal Company shuddered, and turned hastily to packaging. Their square box was first registered with the United States Patent Office August 17, 1877.

When Proctor and Gamble got ready to bring out their white soap in cake form in 1879, they had their campaign well in hand. Ivory was the name selected, and Harley Proctor designed and patented the distinctive cake with notches on the side for cutting or breaking. For the year 1882–83, they appropriated the astounding sum of $11,000 for national advertising. (It took most manufacturers another ten years to be so daring.)

The first 1882 Ivory advertising appeared in *The Independent* on December 21. It had a selling idea and a remarkable slogan. It opened "The Ivory is a Laundry Soap with all the fine qualities of a choice Toilet Soap, and is 99 44/100% pure." That magic percent was taken direct from one of the several chemical analyses they had made by college chemistry professors and independent laboratories.

Proctor and Gamble believed in full page advertisements, and pioneered in color. Everyone who read magazines, from *Harpers Magazine* to *Babyhood,* religious weeklies or farm journals, learned about Ivory. For those less literate there were plenty of life-sized cardboard Ivory Babies crawling around on store counters to acquaint them with the new soap.

"It Floats" was first featured in a *Century Magazine* advertisement in July 1891. Five years later the idea was revived and used on a scale that made the phrase famous.

The best illustrators of the day were hired to produce their advertisements—Palmer Cox, creator of the Brownies, cover artist J. O. Leyendecker, Jessie Wilcox Smith, Maude Humphrey, celebrated painter of child life, whose young son, Humphrey Bogart, with long hair and Lord Fauntleroy suits, was her favorite model.

Large sized copies of paintings used in advertising were sent free for 10 Ivory Soap wrappers. A drawing and painting book was a premium offer for children. A watch charm in the form of a miniature cake of Ivory Soap, with a gold plated ring for attaching it to a watch chain, could be had by sending in ten cut-out center pieces from wrappers.

February 15, 1890 was a sad day for coupon savers who had done their work too well. On that day Proctor and Gamble announced to the world in full page advertisements—one appeared in *Century Magazine*—

NOTICE

As the Ivory Soap is now so thoroughly introduced we shall send NO MORE PRIZES *for wrappers after this date.*

PROCTOR & GAMBLE

FEBRUARY 15, 1890

PLATE 99. One of Maude Humphrey's celebrated paintings for which her favorite model, son Humphrey Bogart, did *not* pose!

PLATE 100. The Molasses Corn Ball man with his wagon was on hand at all public gatherings. Taylor & Fillmore were successful candidates on the Whig ticket in 1848. (Courtesy, New England Confectionary Company).

Hmmm, Candy!

NOT until the beginning of the 19th century did the thought occur in England that sugar candies might be tastier—and quite saleable—without medicinal centers. Promptly confectioners took the industry away from doctors and druggists who had been compounding sugar coated pills and medicated candy lozenges since the Middle Ages. The French had been a little beforehand with the thought, if not the separated industries. Apothecaries there had been frequently called upon for fancy pill-less comfits for special Court occasions.

Though candy was not an important item in the American country store until after the Civil War, simple stick candies, sugarplums, and molasses taffy had long been available in city stores, and were found now and then on country counters.

Local confectioners in the cities—Philadelphia listed twenty in 1816—made and sold their own goods. These were of the simplest sort. All fancy confections were imported.

French candies particularly offered exciting selections in bonbons, little candied fruits, flowers pressed from rolled candy paste, pralines, and the hard comfits or dragees, called sugarplums. Despite the "sugarplum" name, the inner core of these sugared-over candies might be other fruit or seed than raisins—almond, anise, coriander, pistachio, or slices of orange. Plain sugarplums were left with a final frosting of crystallized sugar. More luxurious "beaded" sugarplums were glaced in twice-boiled syrup, dripped on them from a funnel overhead. Candies everywhere were handmade.

In Philadelphia, Sebastian Chauveau was the candy pioneer who first manufactured gum drops, jujube paste, and marshmallows in this country. In 1845, he included in his equipment the first revolving steam pan used here.

In Boston, in 1847, Oliver Chase, who with his brother Daniel comprised Chase & Co., tired of the tedious task of cutting out lozenges by hand with a funnel shaped cutter and invented a machine to do it for him. It looked like a clothes wringer with holes in the rollers, but when he fed a sheet of candy paste into one side of the machine, a steady stream of perfectly shaped, ready-cut lozenges tumbled out the other. The Chase mint put out today by Necco still bears the Chase name and trademark.

Chase followed this invention with another—a mill for powdering sugar, patented in 1851. This, too, was a time saver, for until then the finely ground sugar, to be mixed with dissolved gum arabic for the stiff lozenge paste, had been pulverized by hand.

His brother Daniel, also an inventor, brought out the "conversation lozenge" in 1866. A candy called "cockles," made of sugar and flour, shaped like a cockle or scallop shell with a motto printed on flimsy colored paper rolled up inside, was then popular. Hawthorne mentions "these little cockles . . . much prized by children for their sweetmeats and even more for their mottoes" in *Twice Told Tales*. Daniel Chase simplified the idea by devising a machine which printed the mottoes directly on the lozenge paste, and combined it with a lozenge cutter for a one-operation machine. His lozenges were printed with couplets, conundrums, and tongue twisters, delighting both children and their elders. His "wedding lozenges" carried such cheerful predictions as "Married in satin, Love will not be lasting," "Married in pink, He will take to drink," "Married in white, You have chosen right."

The English "boiled sweet" popularized at London's Crystal Palace Exhibition in 1851, gave added impetus to the candy industry already established, and advanced it in those countries still in thrall to medicinal sweets. Candy sales everywhere took an upward turn.

In 1850, the sales of manufactured candy in this country came to little more than $3 million; by 1864, to $5½ million. With speed-up manufacturing stimulated by the Civil War, the figure reached nearly $16 million in 1870; $25½ million in 1880; and approximately $56 million in 1890—those golden days when young gentlemen were saying it with candy, and fulsome young ladies, unconcerned with diets, consumed it with pleasure. By then candy was a big item in country stores, from fancy boxed goods, selling best on Wednesday and Saturday "courting" nights, to the younger-set penny pieces.

The kinds of candy available, as of September 15, 1869, and their wholesale prices were listed in *The American Grocer's* "Prices Current" of that date—(the price given is per pound, though some types were sold only in twenty-five, thirty, or forty pound boxes, the grocer being free to box or bag in whatever quantity he liked): Assorted, 20¢ a pound; Stick candy, 20¢; Rock candy, 23¢; Arabian gum drops, 20¢; Genuine hard and soft gum drops,

40¢; Sugar almonds, smooth, burnt, and cream, at 60¢, 60¢ and 36¢ respectively; Conversation lozenges, 32¢; French mixed, 60¢; Marshmallow drops, 60¢; Cream bonbons, 75¢; Cream chocolate drops, 50¢.

In that same 1869 issue, The Editor warned lengthily of adulteration, claiming that flour, *terra-alba*—a white earth brought over from England as ballast in vessels at something less than a cent a pound, delivered and kaolin from an extensive deposit near Augusta, South Carolina, composed from 10 to 20 percent of almost all candies. Fine goods, like bonbons, suffered as much adulteration as penny stick candies. Some manufacturers adulterated their ingredients as much as 33 1/3 percent. At least 250,000 pounds of *terra-alba* were imported a year, all of which went into adulteration. He warned also of poisonous mineral coloring matter, too frequently used, mentioning especially Scheele's Green, a deadly poison, he had found in specimens he had personally examined.

He heartily recommended that honest grocers stop poisoning little girls—and big ones, too—by buying only from establishments known to make "straight goods." There were still a few candy makers left who clung to principle, one of them being the New York house of R. L. Gilbert & Co., at 16 Courtlandt Street, where about 25,000 pounds of best quality sugars (mostly Stewart's A) were converted into confections and candies each week.

Having visited the Gilbert shop and studied each department—the firm made stick candy, rock candy, sugarplums, lozenges, burnt almonds, cocoanut candies, and "as fine chocolates and bonbons as ever Paris or Berlin turned out"—he described various processes. In a room with marble slabs and furnaces, where plain sugar boiling took place, for instance:

The bright copper kettles are charged with the proper quantities of sugar, water is added, and the boiling proceeds to the proper point for pulling, which the workmen call the point of

cracking, and which they determine in a manner we would advise the uninitiated not to try. Dipping the finger first in water, they suddenly plunge it in the boiling mass, gather a small quantity between finger and thumb, and then by a practiced motion see if it will break with a cracking noise. This point reached, and it is one of great delicacy to determine accurately, the kettles are emptied on the slabs, where the now cooked sugar spreads out and cools rapidly to a temperature which admits of handling comfortably. The workman then gathers it up into a huge mass and commences to pull it by throwing it over a large iron hook and dexterously drawing it out and doubling it up, until the proper point of whiteness is reached, when it is again placed on tables, kept moderately warm by an ingenious arrangement, colored, striped, drawn out and cut up into sticks of various sizes and dimensions to suit the requirements of the trade.

For his readers inclined to wonder how rock candy, sparkling on a cotton string like a necklace of jagged diamonds, and just about as hard, was put together, he explained:—

In making rock candy a vessel is used resembling in shape a large tin pail, holding about four gallons, with holes directly opposite each other perforating the sides, through which the fine twine strings are passed and upon which the sugar crystallizes. The pail is then covered all over the sides with heavy paper, to prevent the hot liquid from wasting through the holes, and is then ready to receive a charge. Here again the nicest discrimination is needed in boiling. When the precise point is reached, the prepared pails are filled, carried to the crystallizing room, which is kept at a uniform high temperature, and in the course of a week, more or less, the entire mass is beautifully crystallized, and may be turned out in a complete piece of the size and shape of the pot.

By the 1900s, penny candies, supposedly pure, though often deliciously poisonous in appearance, were stock in trade of every country store. The variety was endless and enchanting. There were green mint leaves, 3 for 1¢; candy coated peanuts called Boston Baked Beans, and measured out in a small wooden beanpot, licorice whips, jawbreakers in awesome colors, little tin saucepans filled with a tough creamy goo and a useless tin spoon to eat it with. Imitation ice cream cones, peanuts, and bananas in unrealistic "natural" color competed with wax bottles, filled with a sweet liquid, which could be chewed after the contents were consumed, chocolate babies, Non-Pareils, and chocolate covered pink taffy brooms. For young conservatives there were 6″ strings of rock candy and coltsfoot sticks; for the more sophisticated, chocolate drops.

A few old favorites are still around, but many of the shapes best loved by youngsters fifty or sixty years ago have disappeared. Some supermarkets carry penny candies on the premise that children accustomed to buying candy for a penny will grow up to be "real" candy buyers. It is to be found, too, in "Pop and Mom" accommodation stores, and in country store restorations.

Though many penny candies cost two cents today, and stores claim the profit, considering time consumed in customer selection, is next to nothing, the 1957 output of penny candies was around $100 million. It takes a lot of hot and sticky little hands to hold that many pennies!

PLATE 101.   "The Life of the Candy Traveler," most of it spent "on the cars," was pictorially described in the *Confectioner's Journal*, in 1885.

CHAPTER FIVE

SOMETHING EXTRA

Soap Wrappers

BENJAMIN T. Babbitt was the first of the soap manufacturers to put soap in a wrapper and sell it as a "bar." Up to that time, in 1851, soap had been made in loaves for the grocer to slice off and weigh, much as he did cheese. Babbitt was also the first to give his wrappers a trade-in value and put a premium offer on the wrappers. This innovation grew out of necessity, for people did not take readily to packaged soap. It seemed to lose its identity in its new wrapping, even though the name and trademark appeared on it. The premium offer changed all this, and as his sales spurted, other soap merchants quickly followed suit.

Charles H. Williams, an old time country storekeeper in Jordan, New York, recalled the first cakes of Babbitt's packaged soap, which were wrapped in a gaudy red glazed covering. Unfortunately the wrapping was susceptible to the lye in the soap, and both soap and wrapper soon presented a sorry sight. Babbitt immediately began packing it in a light tough paper wrapper, immune to lye. Gradually the old red cakes on the market were sold, and the light papered cakes took their place.

As a young man in Utica, New York, Benjamin Babbitt was employed as a wheelwright. Deeply interested in science, he induced a professor from Hamilton College in Clinton to come over to Utica two days a week to lecture on chemistry. On those days, Babbitt arranged to go to work an hour early and quit an hour early so he could attend the lectures.

Quite likely Babbitt thought of himself as primarily an inventor. In his early life he patented a fire engine, a brush-trimming machine, and other gadgets. During the Civil War, he invented an ordnance projector and a mold for casting gun barrels. Later he turned his attention to gas engines, then to the use and control of air. Among his later inventions were an air-pump and air compressor, wind motors, pneumatic propulsion machines of various types, and an air blast for forges. However, it is by his soap products that his name is best remembered.

In the factory he established in Oneida County in 1843, he turned out potash, saleratus, and baking powder, as well as soap and soap powder. Saleratus was a leavening agent for biscuits and cakes, similar to baking soda. It was made by subjecting pearl ash to the fumes of fermenting molasses—a Nathan Read had discovered how to make it soon after the Revolution.

Babbitt also pioneered in consumer-units. He packed his saleratus in a one-pound "paper," a forerunner of the folding carton, and wholesaled them sixty to a

PLATE 102. Though Benjamin Babbitt was the first to offer premiums for soap wrappers, other soap companies were quick to follow suit. Tulip Soap, for 10 wrappers, sent a set of 4 tradecards.

case. He also put his potash in convenient tin cans, with full directions for use on each can, and advertised it "about the same price as that in casks."

His cousin Isaac Babbitt came over from Taunton, Massachusetts, to go into the expanding business with him. Isaac was also an inventor—Babbitt metal, a white antifriction alloy composed of copper, antimony, and varying proportions of tin, was one of his inventions.

Thanks to Benjamin's progressive merchandising and colorful advertising, and Isaac's capable handling of production, their factories were soon outselling all soap producers in the country. One of Benjamin's unique advertising efforts had been to picture his products on theatre curtains, but his great success lay in his soap wrapper premium idea. From the first, people went wild over premiums.

Premiums Did It

WILLIAM Wrigley, Jr. was the Town's Bad Boy. When he was eleven years old, in 1883, he ran away from home in Philadelphia and spent the summer in New York City, selling newspapers along Park Row and having a time for himself. Once in a while he sent home a post card to let the family know he was still alive. In the fall he went back home to start the school term. Unfortunately school authorities soon found a juicy pie plastered against a brown stone name plate. They chorused "William Wrigley, Jr.," and that was the end of his school days.

His exasperated father set him to work in his scouring soap factory, stirring the thick soap in the boiling pot with a wooden paddle, one of the hardest manual tasks in the factory. By the time young William was thirteen, he convinced his father he could make more money selling soap than stirring it. He proved himself right and soon the high grass towns in Pennsylvania all knew the four-horse team with jingling bells on the harness, driven by the "Boy Salesman." Years after he was an outstanding figure in the business world, a picture of those four horses hung on the wall of his office.

At nineteen, his itching foot started him toward the gold mines in the west. His journey ended at Kansas City after what must have seemed then a very ill wind had blown his hat through the open window of the train, and with it, his ticket. He had 65¢ in his pocket. A few weeks of waiting on table in a cheap restaurant gave him enough money to get home, with presents for everybody. He was soon back on the road selling scouring soap.

In the spring of 1891, when he was twenty-nine, he talked his father into opening an office in Chicago, which seemed a central spot from which the scouring soap could be shipped. He was put in charge.

He found competition growing keener in the soap business, and his soap, which retailed for 5 cents a cake was not doing well with dealers. The margin of profit

A USEFUL PRESENT GIVEN WITH EVERY POUND
R. H. STICKNEY, Agent, 207 State Street,
BOSTON, MASS.

PLATE 103. One of the few Currier & Ives prints drawn especially for advertising purposes.

was so slender they preferred to carry higher priced lines. He immediately raised the price of the 5-cent cake to a dime, and gave the dealer an umbrella as a premium with every box. From this simple beginning, Wrigley developed the premium idea until he was the largest distributor of premiums in the world.

He added baking powder to his line, and against all advice, compiled a 150-page cook book and offered it free with a 50¢ can of baking powder. Before long he was distributing 50,000 books a week, and his baking powder sales were so large he eventually dropped his soap altogether.

He had one disastrous experience with his premiums that nearly set him back to zero. He had contracted for a silver-plated filigree cologne bottle, and in his haste to turn out large orders, allowed so thin a coating of silver to be used that the bottles were tarnished by the time they were delivered. He had to make good on practically the entire contract.

His next venture proved more successful. He made a deal with a chewing gum company to use gum as a premium. He soon dropped baking powder, and made gum his product. He continued to use the premium idea—dealers would buy gum for the premium if nothing else. There followed a steady stream of articles that storekeepers could use every day—scales, coffee grinders, showcases, cheese cutters, cash registers, desks, scoops, ladders, trucks, and nail pullers. Contracting with manu-

facturers for his premiums in large quantities at rock-bottom prices, he took tremendous chances on guessing what dealers would want. Most of the time he guessed right.

He did not attempt at first to enter the large markets, but in 1902 he thought he had sufficient capital and tossed a huge campaign in New York City.

"I didn't even make a ripple on the surface," he admitted afterwards.

His next big campaign was turned loose in the New York area including Buffalo, Rochester, and Syracuse, where sales had been far from satisfactory. He purchased every square foot of available poster advertising space, every vacant space in the street cars of the three cities, and contracted for spreads in all the important papers. The campaign unloosed a flood of sales that more than paid for it.

"Now I shall tackle New York City again," he declared. "I'm going back to pick up that $200,000 I dropped in the big town."

A few years ago, Charles Wrigley, the only surviving brother of William Wrigley, Jr., in commenting on the activities of his brother, said it was nothing for Wrigley's associates to be called up in the middle of the night, disheveled and rubbing the sleep from their eyes, to find Wrigley, unable to sleep, with a big new idea, and ready to expound it.

PLATE 104. Every child of 60 years ago remembers Cream of Wheat's Uncle Rastus Dolls, Force's Sunny Jim, and the Creosote Flour boy. Dolls were printed on sturdy cloth, sent as premiums to be cut out and stuffed at home.

Something for Nothing

THERE'S magic in the word FREE. B. T. Babbitt found it out when he offered premiums for his soap wrappers; William Wrigley, Jr. knew it when he tempted storekeepers with umbrellas and cheese slicers.

Thirteen-year old Charley Thompson, up in Bridgewater, Connecticut, sensed it instinctively and parlayed seventy-five cents into a fortune by offering enough people a chance to "get something for nothing." (It is not coincidence that all these boys who succeeded so ably were thirteen-years old when they started out to seek their fortunes. A few generations ago a lad of twelve was crossing the bar of boyhood; at thirteen he was old enough to venture forth.)

With a brand new idea for a premium mail-order business, less than one dollar to lose, and no experience to trouble him, Charley Thompson set up in business. He spent his money for envelopes, large enough to hold a package of stationery, did a little shopping on credit, and borrowed some money to run an advertisement in the old New York *Tribune*. It appeared on July 4, 1866, and was headed "Trust Scheme." He offered to send to anyone by mail, on receipt of a quarter, a package of stationery with a pencil, and in addition, ABSOLUTELY FREE, a piece of jewelry. Every package was guaranteed to contain a different piece of jewelry.

Inside of two years, Charley was out of knee pants and hiring grown help. "Boys are no good," he decided, "you have to watch 'em all the time."

A better idea had followed the writing paper. Charley was now making Grandma's Wonder Healing and Complexion Cream, which others, contacting him by mail, sold for him for the rich rewards of free premiums. He advertised widely and sent twenty-four boxes of this beautifying cream—it also cured a variety of ills—to anyone who wanted such luxuries as a mandolin or set of lace curtains badly enough to sell the two dozen boxes at a quarter a box to win them ABSOLUTELY FREE. Orders came in faster than he could make up the cream!

"There was no fake about that cream," Mr. Thompson once reminisced. "There was no poison in it; you could eat it without harm. The boxes were small, about the size of a medium sized watch, and perhaps half an inch deep."

Thompson's Premium House was soon receiving an average of 10,000 letters a day. Country people liked to get mail; there wasn't much money around, and premiums were appealing; and Charley Thompson had a flair for knowing what people wanted. His catalog showed four pages of dolls alone—he shipped out thousands of them to sales-minded little girls. Boys chose rifles, magic lanterns, and watches. Housewives could win petticoats, towels, comb sets, library tables, alarm clocks, rocking chairs, sideboards, kitchen cabinets, furs, jewelry, 31-piece dinner sets, table linen, teasets, and the like.

Thompson pioneered, too, in the extension of credit. "Send No Money" was always prominent in his advertising. "Just write for two dozen boxes of salve and cream and they'll be sent *at no cost to yourself! You can't lose!*" Mr. Thompson estimated about twenty percent of merchandise mailed was never heard from. Still the business operated at a profit. His advertising cost him about two cents for each response, and in his heyday, he employed about one hundred hands.

A New York newspaper, commenting on his success wrote once: "There is not a wreck-strewn shore on the Seven Seas that does not have at least one packing case board marked *Chas. B. Thompson.*"

Mr. Thompson dropped out of the mail order business before the First World War. Rising costs, big city competition, together with the fact that Bridgewater was not on the railroad and all freight had to be carted to and from New Milford were contributing causes. He died in 1942, but his charming wife, whom he married when she was a young girl in charge of his mail room, still lives at the Bridgewater estate.

For Charley Thompson to properly find his way into this book, it should be noted that at one time he owned a general store. The exact date of purchase is hazy, but in 1899 he built a two-story brick block with his name lettered under the eaves, and moved his store from across the street into these new quarters.

One of the stories of Thompson's sales ability and showmanship—incidentally he was a good friend of P. T. Barnum, along with B. T. Babbitt, both consummate showmen—concerns a premium that went wild.

In addition to his creams, he was offering a line of garden seeds, which farmers could sell to their neighbors. One of his premiums was a lantern. This proved unexpectedly popular, and he found himself running out of lanterns at a time when he was at a financial low.

He applied to the banks for credit, but unfortunately they were in slight difficulty, too. Not quite sure where his next lantern was coming from, he sent off orders to five nationally known manufacturers asking each for a carload of lanterns, hoping that at least one of them would give him half a carload before they found out he was broke.

Charley underestimated the weight of his name. All five carloads came through. For a week every horse and ox and mule in town was busy hauling crates of lanterns over to Bridgewater from the New Milford freight yard. Charley was equal to the occasion.

The night the last lantern was delivered the sky over Bridgewater was ablaze with a rose glow. It was so bright folks four miles away claimed they could read the newspaper at midnight; and one old man started haying, thinking it was day. All over the country farmers saw the blaze and hastened to hitch up and drive over to watch the town burn down. Instead they found strings of lighted lanterns, storekeeper Charley in plug hat and white vest, and a soap box barker urging them to "step right up and get yourself a brand new lantern, with all modern improvements at HALF PRICE! Buy now! Buy now! There ain't never goin' to be no such lantern sale again!"

It took three nights, but Charley sold his lanterns.

With or Without Mustard

FIFTY years ago the Westmoreland Specialty Company of Grapeville, Pennsylvania combined two of its products in a tasty premium package. Their prepared mustard packed in their milk glass dishes shaped like hens, cows, horses, doves, owls and other barnyard creatures made a double success. The mustard, with the gift container, retailed at 10¢. The same dishes today, minus the mustard, may bring anywhere from five to fifty dollars, depending on the subject.

The Westmoreland Specialty also put out mustard in clear glass containers, and believes it is responsible for the mustard jars bearing the likenesses of William McKinley and William Jennings Bryan which appeared during the Presidential campaign of 1896, though they have no catalogs confirming this. In all, hundreds of thousands of fancy glass containers filled

PLATE 105. Westmoreland Specialty Co., made amusing glass containers for their mustard. Log cabin bank in milk glass is a rare collector's item today; a "dog dish" is harder to find now than a cat dish.

with mustard were sold between 1889 when the Westmoreland Specialty Company was founded and 1910 when the mustard business was discontinued.

In 1924, the name was changed to The Westmoreland Glass Company. It still makes milk glass animal dishes, though without mustard, and no longer for a dime.

The Flaccus Company of Wheeling, West Virginia, was another glass and mustard concern. Their milk glass container in the shape of the cruiser *The Chicago* was a big hit in the 1880s, and even more eagerly sought today. The *Chicago,* along with the *Atlanta, Boston,* and the gunboat *Dolphin,* formed the White Squadron, authorized in 1883. The *Chicago* was the largest twin cruiser in the world in her time—4500 ton, with a speed of 14 knots, and carried four 8-inch, eight 6-inch, and two 5-inch guns. Most of the Flaccus milk glass containers were marked with the Flaccus signature, a fact which adds to their value as collector pieces today.

In the 1880s, too, the Great Atlantic and Pacific Tea Company gave out as premiums with their coffees and teas a tremendous quantity of Phoenixville Majolica ware. Their given-away cups and saucers may bring $25 or more today.

When Wheaties was introduced a com-

PLATE 106. Queen City Baking Powder packaged their goods in a pressed glass container suitable for other uses when baking powder was used up.

paratively few years ago, a little blue glass "Shirley Temple" pitcher was given away with the purchase of two boxes. Already these pitchers are turning up in antique shops and second-hand stores.

Cereal give-aways and box top offers are still going strong, and the up-to-date home is well supplied with plastic toys and gadgets for children to lose, dogs to chew, and bare feet to step on.

CHAPTER SIX

A FULL LINE

Hardware

HARDWARE, in the country store, embraced all articles made of metal which were not assignable to any other specific category. Pots, pans, weapons, nails, tools, locks and bolts comprised the earliest hardware stocks and along with textiles, formed the bulk of English imports to the struggling Massachusetts colonies.

Those who had no money for imported goods relied on their own abilities to invent or make do. Many an early dwelling was built without iron, with latches and hinges of wood, shingles and clapboards of the roof held in place with "weight timbers." An uninhabited house built with nails was an invitation to arson. Certain lawless individuals figured it easier to salvage nails than to build without them.

Bog iron ore discovered near Saugus, Massachusetts, gave rise to an iron works and manufacturing establishment; under the leadership of John Winthrop, operations began in 1644. By 1650 the Saugus Iron Works was an industrial wonder, comparing in operations and equipment with the best ironworks in Europe. This rolling and slitting mill was one of the few then existing in the world. Other ironworks appeared wherever permanent settlements —and iron ore deposits—made them feasible.

The smith became increasingly important, and his presence was courted by up and coming communities. Early town records of Old Derby, Connecticut show an assenting vote—

. . . that the town grant John Smith of Milford, blacksmith, four acres of land for a house lot, to build upon, anywhere within one mile of the meeting house where he shall choose, in land not laid out, upon condition that he build a mansion house and smith's shop, and set up the trade of blacksmith, and follow it for the benefit of the inhabitants of the town for the space of seven years.

After the Revolution, when it was possible for Americans to trade with countries other than England, they began to buy their imported hardware from Germany. As a rule, German goods were crude and poorly made, and offered little competition to the well-crafted articles turned out by local blacksmiths.

Immigrants to farming districts brought their hoes, rakes, and forks with them from the old countries, and turned to local blacksmiths for replacement and repair. People were quite content with the iron tools and implements fashioned for them to order; few manufactured items were imported; and the manufacture of hardware in the United States proceeded slowly.

But from 1863 when Henry Disston built and operated the first crucible steel melting plant for saw steel in the United

States, the picture changed rapidly For a hundred years there had been very little change in imported hardware. It was still crude, poorly made, and not specifically adapted to New World needs. When the Americans began manufacturing their own steel, they sought all manner of means to woo the customer to American manufactured goods. A simple change in packaging won many converts. The English and Germans wrapped their hardware in paper. Wide-awake American manufacturers soon discovered the customer liked them delivered in wooden dove-tailed boxes with slide lids.

A "hardware" item which prospered the country store was the bicycle. The cycling craze, which had started in England with the advent of the high-wheel bicycle in 1873, hit this country about five years later. Previously Pierre Lallement's velocipede, the "bone shaker," patented in the United States in 1866, had figured as a popular sport among the fashionable set. The wheels of this velocipede had wooden spokes, wooden felloes, and iron tires of equal size, with pedals on the front wheels. Schools had been established to teach the art of riding, and everyone who had aspirations "to be somebody" owned one. Though some were sold through country

stores, it was the two-wheeler that made marketing history.

Bicycles, with a very large front wheel to which the pedals were attached, and a small rear wheel, were first made in America in 1878.

The Columbia high-wheeled bicycle, advertised in *The American Grocer* in 1880, at wholesale prices from $80 to $100 according to size, had wire spokes on the wheels and hard rubber tires.

The craze reached its crest around the turn of the century when over ten million were then in use and another million being sold each year. By 1904, so quickly do fads pass, interest in cycling had declined and the annual production had fallen from 1880s $31,000,000 to a mere $5,000,000, a figure which has remained more or less stationary.

Keep It Light

THE means of producing artificial light—candles, lamps and the illuminants used in them, matches to produce fire—were always standard items in the general store.

For the first Colonists, light after sundown was furnished by a floating wick in

PLATE 107. Advertising card for the "new" removable "cold handle" flatiron. The Euterprise Mfg. Co, relied heavily on humorous advertising.

PLATE 108. Nutmeg graters, common to all hardware shelves 50 to 100 years ago are "whatever for?" objects to today's housewife who seldom sees a whole nutmeg.

The "Daisy" Glass Oil Can.

The "Daisy" consists of a heavy glass jar, encased in a deeply-ribbed tin jacket, with a tin bottom below the glass bottom of the jar. The glass is thoroughly protected, and is not easily broken.

The contents can always be seen.

The TIN BOTTOM of the jacket fully protects the bottom of the glass jar, and it cannot be broken by a fall.

The only can that is washed and papered before being packed.

PRICES.

½ gallon	per doz	$3 00
1 gallon	per doz	3 50
2 gallon	per doz	8 00

PLATE 109. Early kerosene cans for home use were of glass set in tin jackets. Ball & Ball, in Buffalo, N.Y. did such a business in glass oil cans, they enlarged their plant, then had to look for additional glass products.

a dish of oil, pine knot torches, or candles, imported at fourpence each, for those who could afford them. Until domestic animals were brought over, there was no tallow for candlemaking, and housewives in those first years experimented with candles of deer suet, moose fat, and bear's grease as well as bayberries and beeswax. Later, whaling introduced candles made from spermaceti, which gave nearly three times the light of tallow. These were manufactured and sold in quantity.

Betty lamps, shallow saucer-like receptacles of iron with a projecting nose or spout, usually equipped with hook and chain by which they could be suspended, were first imported, then made by local blacksmiths. In these the wick floated in oil or grease.

In 1784 Aime Argand in France made lamp history with his circular wick, double wick-tube, and chimney, but his advances were not at once universally adopted. The popular whale oil lamp in early America was of pewter, fitted with a tin burner—a thin cap with one or two wickholders passing through a short cork into the font. It was chimneyless. When glass pressing machinery, developed in the late 1820s, brought mass production, glass lamps of the same type took the place of pewter.

By mid-nineteenth century, as the whaling industry declined, whale oil grew scarce and expensive. People turned either to cheap, but unsatisfactory, lard oil, or to the newly introduced camphene and other "burning fluids." Lamps for such fluids had two round wick tubes with small caps attached which went over the tops to prevent evaporation when the lamp was not in use. Still no chimneys.

In 1856 petroleum was discovered in Pennsylvania. Kerosene seemed the ideal illuminant—bright-flamed, cheap, safe. But it smelled and smoked and customers kept right on asking for neat explosive Camphene. Came the Civil War, and turpentine used in burning fluids could no longer be easily and cheaply obtained from North Carolina. Kerosene was, of necessity, the order of the day. Lamp chimneys came soon to take care of its disadvantages. By 1875 there were thirty-one concerns engaged in making glass chimneys, with Pittsburgh the center of the industry. Thousands upon thousands of lamps, in various styles and sizes, and kerosene to fill them, were distributed through country stores before twentieth century electricity put the modern light bulb on the counter.

The friction match invented by Alonzo D. Philips of Springfield, Massachusetts, and patented October 25, 1836, was the first outstanding improvement in the picking of fire the world had seen since the making of fire with lint and steel had been developed in the Dark Ages.

PLATE 110. Fancy lamps with decorated base and hand painted 7" dome shades were offered in the *American Drug Trade* for May 1886.

ASSORTMENT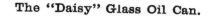

12 Decorated Vase Lamps, assorted Hand Decorations with Decorated 7 inch Dome Shades to match. Vases and Shades Tinted Pink, Blue, Buff, Green, etc.

These Lamps are artistic and beautiful enough to adorn any parlor. The SHADES are decorated to match the VASES of the LAMPS, making the Lamp complete very attractive. The lamps, as shown in the cut, stand 21 inches high, and are elegantly proportioned and beautifully mounted.

Price, complete, 12 Lamps, assorted, as per above description, $12.00 per dozen.

Assortment ⟨E⟩

Hunters and trappers in the New World had learned to use the fire drill from the Indians. The hunter who would spare the powder, could fill the powder pan of his flintlock, pull the trigger, and send a flash into dry tinder. Inside the house, fire was carefully conserved. If a new hearth fire was to be started, coals were borrowed from neighbors, or carried from one location to another in a blacksmith-forged "ember contrivance." Spills of thin wood or rolled paper carried fire from hearth to candle.

The first matches were splits of wood dipped in sulphur which would ignite with tinder or shavings when struck by a spark from the flint.

R. and N. S. Allison of Burlington, Vermont, in 1814, took out a patent on a "match light box." This consisted of a bottle containing sulphuric acid on asbestos and wood splints, tipped with a paste of chlorate of potash, powdered sugar, and gum arabic. The English "Congreves" matches of 1827 were similar—thin strips of wood or cardboard coated with sulphur and tipped with a mixture of mucilage, chlorate of potash, and sulphate of antimony. A box of 84, with a piece of "glass paper" through which the match could be drawn for striking, sold for 25 cents.

Of Philips, whose match was a major invention in all time, the New England Historical and Genealogical Register, 1857, noted:

The inventor of friction matches was the shoemaker, Alonzo Dwight Philips. He worked in a powder mill in East Hartford in 1831 and there, by mixing the ingredients of powder, conceived the idea of igniting a compound by friction. He succeeded, peddled matches, made money, spent it as he made it, and died poor.

Many match manufacturers sprang up throughout the country. One who did not "die poor," was William Gates. A miller, surveyor, and general storekeeper at Ballston, Saratoga County, New York, Gates was wiped out by the panic of 1837. To

PLATE 111. Gates matches, 9 packs to a box, at 25¢, were sold under the Gates name for some years after the company had been sold to the Diamond Match Company.

make a living for his family, he moved them to Frankfort, New York, where he began repairing watches and clocks. In the winters of 1843 and 1844 he travelled for a clock firm in Westfield, Massachusetts, and it was in New England the thought occurred to him there was money in matches.

Back in Frankfort, he experimented until he obtained a suitable head. Then he planed five gross of match sticks by hand, cut them into match lengths, dipped them in his composition, dried them, packed them in boxes, and left them around at various stores in Utica to be "paid for when sold." None were sold. The next matches he made, he more wisely traded for merchandise. Once the matches were their own, storekeepers encouraged customers to give them a try. Soon, according to his son Fred, Gates was loading the Democrat wagon with twenty or twenty-five gross of matches every week, and driving over to Utica to sell or trade them.

Before long he had erected a factory on Mayer Creek, fifty rods from the Erie Canal, with machinery driven by water power from the creek, and was selling matches like mad through all the northern states from Maine to Iowa. Between 1864 and 1877, when a revenue of one cent on every box of 100 matches was assessed toward the war debt, nearly $3,000,000 was paid on Gates matches alone. When Gates died in 1877, the firm organized as William Gates & Sons, Inc. In 1881, it joined the Diamond Match Company.

Since friction matches occasionally exploded, and insurance rates were high, not all transportation companies would ship them, and many wholesale firms refused to stock them. H. K. Thurber & Co., for one, noted in their advertisement in *The American Grocer,* Nov. 8, 1877—

We do not keep matches, and ask our friends to order them from wooden warehouses which keep them in stock and have shipping permits from the leading transportation companies.

A block of sulphur split matches—the Diamond Match Company made millions of them—looked much like a comb, and was as handy to carry in the pocket. Conveniently the matches could be struck crosswise on the match sticks. Another safety match, registered in 1864, "The Universal," was accompanied by a sheet of emery paper for striking.

Even after the advent of the "parlor" or "strike anywhere" match, old timers continued to favor the sulphur split match. As late as 1890 Adams & Park of Chester, Vermont, wrote to the Diamond Match Company of Boston—

We have jobbed matches for years to the trade, and yours as long as 10 years ago, as you will see by your books and not a bill over 10 days have we had or do we wish. We never had much success with parlor matches and have enough of them to last 2 or 3 years.
If you want us to handle your matches, we must have your very bottom figure. Our sales will probably be principally the split match. Please quote Diamond Painted Split Card matches, North American Diamond Painted Card matches. Also any other match that sells well. We can see by your sample cards rec'd of 16 matches in a card what they are & we remember that the North American & Diamond Painted were of the same length, painted . . . and all the difference between Diamond & North American was in wrappers. Are we correct?

Book matches were invented and patented by Joshua Pusey, an attorney, in 1892. Three years later he sold his patent to the Diamond Match Company. In 1896, an order for ten million "books" to be used in advertising by a well known brewery, established their success.

A Peck Of Flies

HOW doth the fatal little fly?" was "Very well indeed, thank you," until along in the 1860s when some effete Victorian became fed up with insects in the house and invented wire mesh screeening. Until then, no place had been sacred to the fly. He was everywhere at home—in the ashery, the abattoir, the barnyard, dunghill, kitchen, sickroom, privy, and parlor. He dealt typhoid with a free foot, while his mosquito relations concentrated on malaria, sometimes designated as Genessee fever, ague, chills and fever, or simply "the shakes." Between them they caused more fatalities among early settlers than Indians and wild beasts together.

But once the screens were up at window and door and the aesthetic pleasure of a flyless house was recognized, the war of People vs. Flies was on. Though the Fly went along in his usual direct, disinterested, and disastrous fashion, People became devious. They began building traps and snares, and extremely elaborate ones, too.

Patent papers taken out on October 7, 1856 read in part—

PLATE 112. Gilbert Fly Trap, Patent #15,848, dated Oct. 7, 1856.

PLATE 113. Fly Trap patented by David S. Kidder, Turners Falls, Mass., (#204, 053), and manufactured by Alonzo Burnham, Montague City, Mass.

Be it known that I, George Gilbert of Westville, in the County of New Haven and State of Connecticut have invented a new and useful Improvement in Fly-Traps . . . My improvement consists in using a revolving cylinder on which I took the bait (as molasses) to attract the flies, and while they are feeding, the revolving motion of the cylinder will carry them quietly into a dark chamber, from which they will naturally pass up, through a screen, and to a light chamber, which is enclosed by wire gauze, and will thus be securely caged, to be dealt with at pleasure.

One summer afternoon, a few years back, a researcher who remains modestly anonymous obtained one of these Gilbert

traps, and set it near the rear door of a restaurant. In the hour and a half it stood in the sun, he had to wind the clockwork in the trap three times. Wagering with an equally earnest student on the number of flies to fall for this tomfoolery, our researcher unfortunately underestimated the intelligence of his adversary. Only seventy-five succumbed to the lure.

Another wind-up fly trap, invented by David S. Kidder and patented in 1878, was manufactured by Alonzo Burnham in Montague City, Massachusetts. Under the cover over the clock, he posted these directions, with word or two of sales talk thrown in—

Directions

Wind up; saturate with molasses, water and a little vinegar the fluted edge of the cylinder, leaving a space dry between, as flies will light on a dry surface and while eating will be stealthily drawn into their prison. If wetting should swell the cylinder it might hit the guard in front and stop the trap; ascertain this by turning the cylinder over end for end, turn to see if it hits, if it should, use a bit of sandpaper until it passes clear. For killing the flies remove the cage from the trap, pour hot water over the screen and empty from the bottom. Oil spiral screw that stand perpendicular with a drop of sewing machine oil, when necessary.

This little trap brings joy and gladness to the household, ease and comfort to the husbandry, as

PLATE 114. Fly Fan, Patent #321, 352, granted W.R. Fowler, June 30, 1885.

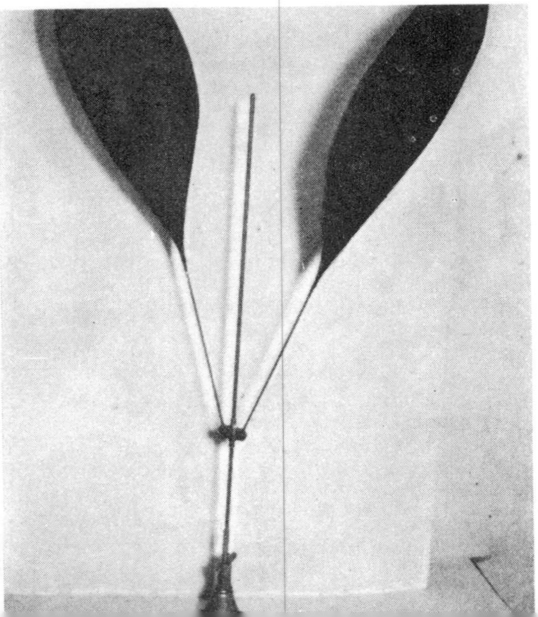

PLATE 115. Automatic Fly Fan, Patent #266,774, of Oct. 31, 1882. Fans, suspended and held by wire rod, whirl as well as oscillate.

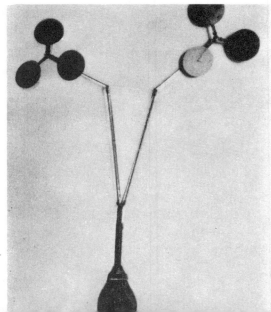

a peck of flies are worth a bushel of corn to the poultry yard.

It is assumed that such mechanical devices of destruction were first peddled from door to door, but they were soon to be seen on the shelves of the country store, along with screen covers in assorted sizes to be used over foods on tables in kitchens and dining rooms.

In the elegant eighties, and into the nineties, a popular patented device was the fly fan, whose outstretched cloth fans, revolving slowly, cast shadows all around —and everyone knew that a shadow over a fly would cause him to decamp quickly. Such fans were as frequently found above cheese and food counters in country stores as over restaurant or family dinner tables. These, too, were wound manually, usually by a built-in key on the top of the case.

The National Enameling and Stamping Company of Baltimore, Maryland, patented, in 1885, what they called the "Twentieth Century Fly Fan." William Cofer's patent, in 1882, was for a fan with two arms carrying three discs each which rotated against the wind as well as by keywind.

For the less mechanically minded, poison flypaper was evolved. Since its poison was as harmful to humans as to flies, the Seibert's Poison Flypaper—a type floated in a shallow dish of water—had its antidote printed on the bottom of each package—

Should this poison be taken by mistake give whites of raw eggs and luke-warm water, or drinks of warm water and mustard. Induce vomiting by tickling the throat with finger or feather, send for a physician immediately.

Unfortunately small children, like flies, could not read, and Seibert's sinister attempt at fly massacre never became truly popular with parents. The same held true of the tempting Shoo-Fly Pie, patented by

PLATE 116. Advertisement from the *Grocer's Criterion,* published in Chicago, August 25, 1879.

William R. Craun of Butler, Indiana, in 1908, whose object was to—

. . . provide a receptacle simulating a pie or other pastry having an absorbent filling designed to hold a suitable poisonous fluid, access to which can be had by the flies through minute openings or kerf formed within a top or "crust" of the device.

The *Grocer's Criterion,* Chicago, in August 1879 offered—

Allen's Fly Brick
The Little Giant
Fly Killer
Ten cents worth kills more flies than ten dollars worth of flypaper. Wholesale for five cents, retail at ten.

Just how these fly brick lured their prey is not now known, but Mr. J. D. Simpson, the enterprising manufacturer, offered to furnish advertising trade cards to any dealer who would—

. . . hurry, hurry—send your orders at once as later it may be impossible to put your imprint on the advertising cards.

Tanglewood sticky fly papers, not child-proof but, at least, free from poison, are of fairly recent usage, superseded only by insect sprays and D.D.T.

Rats and mice were other annoyances to be dealt with, and country stores sold a great many patented mouse traps. The same *Grocer's Criterion* that furthered the Fly Brick, advertised the still familiar circular mousetrap, with back-breaking spring, in various sizes, at $1.50 per hole.

The directions which came with the cheaper, more popular wire trap which encaged the monster live, read:

Put as large a piece of cheese or cake as you can crowd into the bait box; shut and fasten the lid. Place the trap in a desirable place and it never fails. To kill the mice let them out in a pail of water.

Indicating that stores were as much in need of traps as their customers, the directions conclude—

Traps on sale should be inverted when placed on

the shelves otherwise mice will be caught and may die in the trap.

Better Than A Doctor

Little deeds of Kindness
Little words of Love
Make our earth an Eden
Like the Heaven Above.

Pierce's Little Pellets
Easy things to Take
Ward off Bilious Fevers
And the Ague Shakes.

SICKNESS, death, and the frailness of human life were perennial subjects of conversation and correspondence," wrote Charles W. Andrews in his *Old Medicines in Colonial Folk Ways,* "and few family letters of those days were free from allusions to them. From infancy to old age, death took ample toll, so great was the Colonial disregard for the laws of sanitation, so little the attention

PLATE 117   Carter Spanish Mixture promised a permanent cure for "all Diseases arising from an impure state of the Blood, or habit of the System."

paid to drainage and disinfection. The human system was dosed and physicked until it could hold no more. Governor Ogle of Maryland said of his predecessor that he took more physic than anyone he had ever known in his life, and Maria Byrd was accustomed to swallow 'an abundance of phynite,' whatever that was. Every home had its medicine chest whether made up in England at Apothecaries Hall or supplied by some nearby druggist, who furnished the necessary 'chymical and Galenical medicines.' "

Joseph Cuthbert of Savannah, Georgia, was one who fitted up boxes of medicines, with directions for dosage, for use on plantations. Indian doctors dispensed medicinal herbs, and ambitious peddlers put up popular concoctions which they sold in vast quantities to credulous people.

Even the earliest trading posts carried books on home remedies. *The Poor Man's Physician and the Sick Man's Friend,* printed in the early 1800s by Josiah Burlingame of Madison County, New York, contained some three hundred pages of sure cures for every disease known to man. For bilious colic he recommended:

Give a spoonful of sweet oil each hour, for this has cured one who was thought to be at the point of death . . . In case the complaint is obstinate and will not yield to mollifying and gentle medicine, give an injection of strong tobacco, specked with flaxseed, and I never knew it failed. This method must be resorted to before the strength of the patient is too far exhausted.

Patent medicines, mixed up by anyone with enterprise and a basic recipe, appeared early on country store shelves. Dr. Hans Kierstad in New Amsterdam was using a secret family recipe for his Kierstad Ointment in 1638. (It's still being made and sold.) In 1788, a poetic storekeeper in Massachusetts was listing his medicines in the Springfield *Hampshire Chronicle—*

MARCUS MARBLE

Has lately receiv'd, and is now very willing
On terms which are easy, quite soon to be selling,
An assortment of medicines, all genuine

And Drugs which are us'd in the medical line;
Doctor Bateman's Grand Cordial Elixer, for cure
Of disorders of body, so notedly sure;
With his Pectoral Drops, which are very well known
To people residing in country and town;
Doctor Turlington's Balsam of Life, and the best,
Has been proved, and found to be probatum est;
Hooper's, Anderson's, Locker's, and other fine pills
Which often have cur'd the most dangerous ills;
Oleum Rinini, six shillings per bottle,
And British Oil, cheap, if your purses will rattle.

Marble continued to offer—in rhyme—brandy, New England and West India rum, Lisbon and Malaga wine, molasses, loaf sugar, tea, coffee, and chocolate, and ended:

All these will be sold very cheap; but no trust
Is allow'd to the best any more than the worst;
In payment is taken Gold, Silver and Cents,
Good country produce, and final settlements.

With the years, the general health of the public became even more precarious if one can judge from the amount of patent medicines sold by peddlers and through general stores. In June 1841, The New York *Tribune* printed a testimonial from Jane Bemee of Utica, New York, a young woman of thirty-two, who, in the two years she had been bedridden with a disease that was "eating away her face," had consumed: 14 bottles of Phoenix Bitters, 20 Boxes of Life Pills, 100 boxes of Brandreth's Life Pills, 3 bottles of Phelps Arcanum, 4 Bottles Smith's Anti-Mercurial Syrup, 5 Bottles Swaim's Panacea, 3 Bottles Indian Panacea, six dollars worth of Conway's Boston Medicine, a large quantity of Fowler's Solution of Arsenic, and different preparations of mercury prepared by doctors. Blissfully, she concluded her testimonial, which was witnessed and corroborated by a Justice of the Peace at Utica—

I am satisfied that my life has been preserved and my health entirely restored by the blessing of God and the use of Bristol's Fluid Extract of Sarsaparilla.

There was never a decline in the patent medicine business, and from the mid-eighties, when temperance was an issue, and many states were "voting dry," these nostrums became even more popular. Teetotalers who had never "touched a drop" found stimulation in such recommended cure-alls as Hostetters Stomach Bitters (44.3. per cent pure alcohol), Gensonica, Kidney Specific, and the like. Those accustomed to their little nips, sought knowing solace in Dr. S. B. Hartman's Peruna. In West Virginia and other southern sections "Peruna jags" were so prevelant that advertisements offered cures for "the Peruna habit"—with cures even more alcoholically potent than Peruna.

In 1905, Samuel Hopkins Adams, exposing the patent medicine racket in a a reverberating article in *Collier's,* wrote of testimonial hunter for the Peruna Company who was referred by a Minnesota druggist to a prosperous farmer in the neighborhood. The farmer gave Peruna a rousing and enthusiastic send off, even showed the agent a heap of seventy-four empty bottles. When the agent showed the druggist the testimonial, the dispenser merely shrugged, "That old boy has had a 'still' on all the time since he discovered Peruna.

PLATE 118. Warner's Log Cabin Syrup was both liniment and cordial, rubbed on for pain and inflamation, rheumatism, burns, scalds, stings, and bites, taken internally for cramps, cholera, dysentery, summer complaints, pleurisy, asthma, croup, and almost any other ailment.

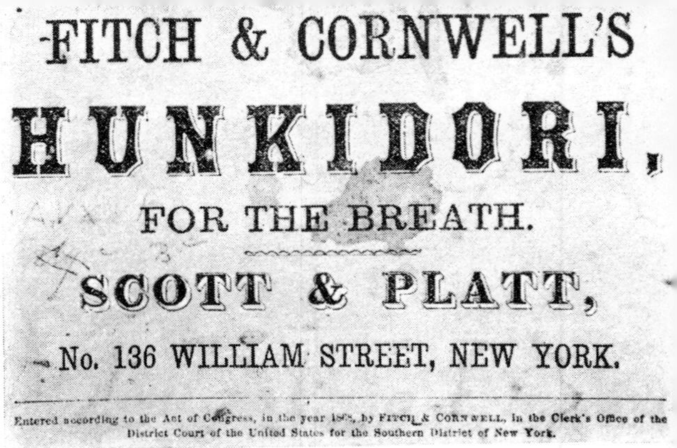

He's my star customer." (The druggist's testimonial was not printed.)

Mr. Hopkins' expose brought at least one libel suit against *Collier's*. Dr. Williams' Pink Pills, advertised to cure paralysis were, according to Mr. Hopkins, nothing more than green vitriols, starch, and sugar. The Pink Pill people brought suit for $100,000. The *Ladies Home Journal* was outspoken, too, about proprietary medicines, shedding light on Mrs. Winslow's Soothing Syrup for teething babies. Its principal ingredient was morphine.

Of the fortunes made in patent medicine, one-third to one-half of the receipts were turned into the lusty, "anything goes" advertising of the day. People were so deeply impressed with advertising claims that they ignored warnings of experts, disapproval of doctors, and even the open attempts by a few conscientious storekeepers to dissuade them from spending money on such "worthless medicine."

Testimonials with real names, real pictures, were greatly fancied, and medicine manufacturers strewed them lavishly in every newspaper in the country. Nor was it difficult to find substantial citizens to "testify." One patent medicine manufacturer used the simple device of offering an elegant white onyx mantel clock, with the name of his remedy painted on the dial, to anyone who purchased a bottle of his medicine, wrote a letter attesting his cure from one or more symptoms printed on the box, and supplied a picture of himself. This could all be handled through the dealer who sold the medicine.

Stronger measures were applied to large city newspapers who were occasionally bribed with full page advertisements to furnish testimonials of local bigwigs. Politicians were especially sought, and few were averse to having their pictures appear in print in whatever fashion.

Since some twenty-thousand newspapers in the land were making more money advertising these nostrums than the manu-

PLATE 119. "Everything is hunkidory" may have sprung from the 1868 sweetener of the breath; it was also the refrain from a Broadway musical hit.

facturers themselves, there was little effort by the press to investigate too carefully into the claims of these proprietary medicines or start any crusade against them. Even in 1839, the New York *Herald* was devoting almost half of its advertising space to medicinal panaceas. In fact the proprietary medicine advertisers toward the end of the century protected themselves with a clause in their contracts, called the "contract of silence," which helped muzzle the press. Advertising contracts of the J. C. Ayers Company of Lowell, Mass., in 1905, included the paragraph—

It is agreed in case any law or laws are enacted, either state or national, harmful to the interests of the J. C. Ayers Company, this contract may be canceled by them from the date of such enactment.

This was the same John C. Ayer, who through his benefits to the town of Groton Junction, Massachusetts, effected the change in the name of the town to Ayer.

An old story persists that Asa T. Soule, whose fortune was made with Doyle Bitters, was driving up to his country estate with a friend when he was asked: "Now confidentially, Asa, do those bitters really do any good?"

Mr. Soule stopped his horses, waved his arm toward his magnificent buildings surrounded by beautiful meadows and acres of crops, and drawled: "Well, you can see what they've done for me."

Continued attacks against proprietary medicines in *Collier's* and *Ladies Home Journal,* the appearance of Upton Sinclair's best seller, *The Jungle*, combined with President Theodore Roosevelt's personal determination that Congress take action, resulted in pure food regulations. In 1907, when the new laws went into effect, the patent medicine business changed somewhat in character. The "honest statement of contents" that was called for on the label forced many of the bitters, tonics, and cordials with high alcoholic content from the market.

"Quack medicine," alas, is not a thing of the past, nor is the mania for dosing oneself confined to an earlier century. In September 1958, *Redbook Magazine* points out to present-day self-doctorers that even "honest" words can be misleading. The Post Office Department, it noted, in a recent 12-month period had closed down 152 fraudulent mail order promotions of medical products —schemes known to be taking in at least $225,000 daily.

Teach Your Horse To Spit

MacGREGOR Jenkins, writing in the September issue of the *Atlantic Monthly* in 1904, put his finger on the pulse of the American attitude toward the lusty and highly equivocal advertising of the day:

The Americans have a curious indolence and toleration of a fraud or an injustice. Nowhere is this seen more plainly than in the average man's attitude toward the ingenious humbug and adroit swindler. To be good-naturedly imposed upon is a positive pleasure provided the cost of it is not too great. This explains the vast number of trifling frauds carried on year after year in the advertising columns of magazines and newspapers.

The adroit rascal who announced in countless agricultural papers that for the sum of ten cents he would supply an unfailing Potato Bug Eradicator—he sent two neatly whittled pieces of pine with direction to "place the potato bug between them and press together"—knew the sheer audacity of the proceeding would tickle innumerable funny bones, and that he could count on orders from those to whom the original purchaser would recommend his "marvelous eradicator."

A humorless Post Office Department caught up with him eventually, but many more, perhaps because they were less successful, slipped through legal fingers.

The *Lakeshore News*, Wolcott, New York, in 1896, reported on an advertisement then going the rounds, which offered a recipe to prevent any type worms from destroying crops. For one dollar, the purchaser would receive a slip of paper, with the printed message: "Don't plant any crops."

A Savannah, New York, farmer was fooled when he sent fifty cents to a man in Portland, Maine, for a sure way to cure his horse from slobbering. His printed slip read, "Teach your horse to spit."

This type of goings-on was nothing new. Back in 1870, *The American Grocer* had run a story, purportedly based on fact.

A German peddler sold a man a liquid for the extermination of insects.

"And how do you use it?" inquired the man after he had bought it.

"Ketch te insect un drop von little drop into his mouth," answered the peddler.

PLATE 120. Universal pattern #7924 for this "Simple Ladies house Dress," 1886, required only 7½ yds. of 27" material, came in sizes from 32 to 42 inch bust measure, cost 30¢.

"The deuce you do!" exclaimed the purchaser. "I could kill it in half the time by stamping on it."

"Vell," said the German "dot is a good vay, too."

Dressed To The Nines

THOUGH foods sold in country stores were of basic concern, certain manufactured necessities, which could not be made at home, were always carried in stock.

Dry goods:—For the first hundred and fifty years of American storekeeping, dry goods were imported. For Colonists of wealth, determined to keep up with English fashion, silks and other fine goods were available in seaport cities. Boston in 1774 was an especially lush market for the latest London modes. Merchants in the back country met the requirements of their clientele with a limited stock of the coarser woolens, linens and cottons, buttons, thread, and an occasional "ribband." A silk dress was so great a luxury for most pioneer women that one might be bequeathed by will to as many as three generations.

Most of the material used for clothing, for both men and women, was made from flax or wool raised at home, carded, spun, and woven by the women of the family. When the Continental Congress in 1775 appealed for 13,000 winter coats for their armies, thousands of Colonial housewives responded with hand tailored homespun garments of highest order. Still preserved in occasional New England villages is the "Coat Roll," listing the names of the troops and the makers of their coats.

The homespun picture changed rapidly after 1790, when Samuel Slater, with the financial backing of Moses Brown, began to spin cotton by machine in Pawtucket, Rhode Island. Young Slater, as a mechanically gifted apprentice in the Arkwright factory system in England, had, in learning his trade, committed to memory the secret and closely guarded processes patented by Arkwright and Hargreaves. Without funds to pursue his ambition of becoming a mill owner at home, he was lured to the industry-hungry New World by a mention in a Philadelphia paper of a £100 bounty to be paid by the Pennsylvania legislature to the man who designed a successful textile machine. Circumstance led him to Rhode Island instead of southward to Philadelphia. His astounding memory for machinery served America well.

New England, with water power aplenty, proved agreeably situated for cotton mills. By the end of the War of 1812, the combined states of Rhode Island, Massachusetts, and Connecticut boasted 165 cotton mills, most of them owned and operated by men who had learned the processes from Slater, and to whom he had supplied machinery. Slater himself owned, wholly

PLATE 121.   Something for everyone at the country store: lisle hose embroidered above the shoe tops for the ladies, paper collars for the gents, games and puzzles for the young fry.

or in part, at least seven mills. By 1834, some 80,000,000 pounds of cotton were being spun annually into cotton manufactured goods, valued at over $7,000,000.

Spinning and weaving in the home soon become an occupation of the past. The Industrial Revolution in America, fathered by Samuel Slater, was under way, quietly nosing out the meticulous time-consuming home manufacture of one item after another, and adding day by day new products for country-wide consumption.

Ready Mades:—There was little demand for ready made clothing in early days, and the clothing industry got off to an unprepossessing start. The first ready made clothes for men seem to have been made in New Bedford, Massachusetts, about 1830, to supply the immediate needs of sailors returning from whaling voyages, or stocking their chests for new trips at sea. These clothes were of coarsest material.

In 1849 the trade was stimulated by calls for ready-mades from adventurers taking off in haste for the California gold fields, and by an influx of immigrants who brought few items of wearing apparel with them. During the Civil War the industry expanded under government demands for clothing for soldiers in the field. After the War, the opening of new lands in the west, brought another market.

One of the early shirt manufacturers was Oliver Winchester. As a carpenter in Baltimore, he had invested in a furnishing goods store there. The proprietor failed in business in the early 1840s, and Mr. Winchester took the stock in security for his investment. He went to New York for advice as to whether he should attempt to continue the business himself. As a result of his conferences with men important in the

clothing world, he decided a shirt factory of his own was worth a try. He opened his shop in New Haven, and with one assistant began to cut out shirts. Before long his factory was turning out two hundred dozen a week. But Mr. Winchester was a restless genius, and at the outbreak of the Civil War, he turned his attention to firearms, producing in 1860, the repeating rifle that made his name famous.

Collars & Cuffs:—By the middle of the 19th century, ready made clothing for men was an established industry, and all sorts of little niceties were being added. Back in 1819, Ebenezer Brown, had invented the first detachable collars made in the United States and manufactured them in his textile factory in Troy, New York. Then in 1854, Walter Hunt, another York Stater, came along with a detachable paper collar. This paper collar had "the elasticity to bend to the motions of the head, possessed a beauty in whiteness of the most carefully-dressed linen collar, and preserved itself unsoiled for a much greater length of time." In its manufacture, a paste was spread over thin white paper, then coated on both sides with thin cotton muslin. It was then varnished with a colorless shellac, which helped make it proof against perspiration and allowed it to be wiped clean with a damp cloth.

Paper collars, at first considered "dudish," were soon popular items in country stores, and were offered for sale coiled up in little round boxes. For some thirteen years after the Civil War, each paper collar box bore a revenue stamp affixed to the bottom, indicating the Government's "sales tax on luxuries," used to help defray the expense of the war.

The later celluloid collars proved even more durable than paper collars. Fancier, too, as they came in color. Peddlers, as well as country stores, did well with this innovation. Scarcely more than sixty years ago, in South Butler, New York, Pete, the Johnson hired man, was called away from his work at cutting and stringing tobacco to talk

PLATE 122. "The paper collar dude" just in from the recruiting station, as pictured in John Billing's *Hard Tack and Coffee,* wore enamelled long-legged boots, and custom-made suit, but "often proved a surprisingly fine soldier"

with a "celluloid peddler," a Mr. Howe from Port Bryon. The next Sunday afternoon when Pete started out to call on his girl, sitting stiff and straight in his buggy behind his little trotting mare, a festoon on his buggy whip, he was resplendent in celluloid collar, celluloid tie, celluloid shirt bosom, and celluloid cuffs, all in brilliant pink. His cuff links, also celluloid, had been "thrown in to boot" by the enterprising Mr. Howe.

Women's Wear:—Women in the meantime were still making their own clothes, or seeking out capable dressmakers. Paper dress patterns, invented by Ebenezer Butterick of Sterling, Massachusetts, and patented in 1864, were an overnight success. Sewing machines, once scorned by the women they would benefit, had proved their worth in Civil War days when demand for military apparel was heavy. Peace time ensconced both sewing machine and the paper dress pattern. In 1871, over six million patterns were sold. Country storee keepers profited also from yard goods and trimmings.

About 1852, "lingerie" became the more elegant word for the usual "white work," "white sewing," or "under wardrobe." Modesty was the perogative of the lady, and as late as 1880, a shopkeeper in Brownville, Nebraska, still remembered by his grandchild—Mrs. Della Owens of Villa Park, Illinois, would delicately call his wife to take charge, and *leave the store completely* while the purchase of such an unmentionable as a corset was in progress.

Shoes:—The shoemaker was among the earliest craftsmen to be sought by American colonies. One Thomas Beard with "hides, both upper and lower, was shipped out" to the Massachusetts Bay Colony from England with the recommendation that he be given his "lodging and diet." The governor gave him, in addition, fifty acres of land.

During the Revolution most of the shoes worn by Continental soldiers, as well as all ready-made shoes sold throughout the Colonies, were produced in Massachusetts. It is recorded that "for quality and service, they are quite as good as those imported from England."

Many boots and shoes were made alike for each foot, and were called "straights."

PLATES 123 & 124.   In 1898 the Lewis Knitting Co., Janesville, Wisc., offered men's union suits, high neck, ankle length, and choice of long or short sleeves. Their ladies version daringly pictured high neck, short sleeves, ankle length for conservative winter wear, low neck, no sleeves, knee length for summer, or evening, wear.

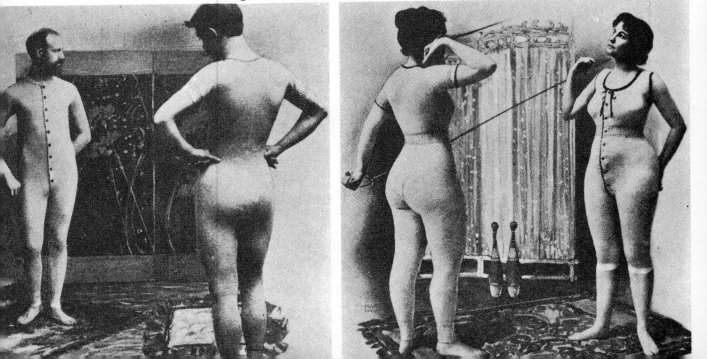

The purchaser marked them himself in his own fashion, and by always wearing them on the proper feet, watched them assume the shape of "lefts" and "rights." Mr. John Miles of New Haven, Connecticut, is credited with leading a crusade for shoes conforming to the foot. Though some shoemakers fell in with his ideas and began to turn out "lefts" and "rights," country people for a long time scoffed, and called them "crooked shoes."

Boots and shoes were always volume items for the country storekeeper. Men and boys of sixty years or more ago, who did a lot of teaming or logging, found felt boots with rubber lowers a good combination for heavy wear. A somewhat lighter boot was in all wool knit, with the overshoe of heavy duck covered with fine quality pure gum rubber. For dress-up, Congress gaiters were long popular, and country stores sold thousands of them.

Mittens & Gloves:—The Indian knew the mitten, and had introduced the early settler to rude hand-covers made from the skins of wild animals. The making of gloves followed in the next century. A Vermonter named Burr was among the earliest to establish a factory near Gloversville, New York, and Sir William Johnson of Johnston Hall, in 1760, is credited with bringing over from Scotland a whole settlement of glovers for the twin cities of Gloversville and Johnstown. Deer or buckskin was considered the only leather suitable for work or driving gloves, and the neighboring forests provided raw material in plenty.

Hats:—Men's headgear was another popular country store item. After the three-cornered hat of the Revolutionary period, the beaver held sway for many years. During the middle of the 19th century, white cassimere high hats had a long run. When Hungarian patriot Kossuth visited the United States in 1851–52, he wore a soft hat trimmed with a black ostrich feather—a style which became immediately fashionable in America.

PLATE 125. For years boots and shoes were sold direct from wooden shipping boxes or "shoe bins," where they were tumbled helter skelter, though the various sizes were accorded separate bins.

Hatmaking was established in Danbury, Connecticut, as early as 1734, and in nearby Bethel, and Norwalk soon after. Around 1817, the Shakers in and around Albany were making beaver hats which retailed at $7.50.

The first straw hats produced in the United States, about 1800, were of the palm leaf variety. The material was imported from the West Indies, parcelled out by storekeepers to capable customers who braided the hats at home and turned them back for merchandise.

Then came Hunton Leghorns, made from imported Italian material. It is said that the sharp-pointed Italian-type hats came into this country as wrapping for loaf or cone sugar, saving boxage and at the same time cushioning the sugar loaf.

For the ladies, who trimmed and retrimmed their own bonnets, were "artificals" of feathers and flowers. Some of these were listed in the invoices of the George K. Graves store in South Butler from 1840 to 1846, and were apparently used as hair ornaments, and decoration for the home, as well as on hats. The making of these artificials seem to trace to French colonials from Haiti, who fled the various uprisings there and sought a means of livelihood in the States.

It was customary to unite the flower and the feather industries in the same shop, and in 1840, in New York City alone, there were ten such manufacturers listed in City directories, with P. Chagot, head of all the operations.

May the Best Man Win

FROM earliest days the country store was head over heels in political discussion. Around the cracker barrel, presidential campaigns were won or lost, and the grass roots of the nation, a phrase coined in later years, called the turn.

The storekeeper himself was a man of consequence, his opinions respected, if not always agreed with. Though he often lacked formal education, he was almost always exceptionally well informed. As postmaster he kept up with the times through the periodicals and newspapers that passed through the office. Yearly buying trips to Philadelphia, New York, Boston, or New Orleans introduced him to a wider world. Slack time in winter could be improved by reading and meditating on the books he carried in stock. Not at all unusual was the book selection of a merchant in a small Missouri town in 1829, who advertised volumes by Josephus, Byron, Shakespeare, Cervantes, Scott, Fielding, Herodotus, Hume, Smollett, Milton, Defoe, Homer, and Bunyan. No wonder, in an age of flowery harangue, the storekeeper was capable of Fourth of July speeches full of classical reference, and holiday toasts second to none. In his political beliefs, he seldom hesitated to stand up and be counted.

Political campaigns brought excitement to the crossroads and novelties to the corner store. Campaign souvenirs reached a high peak during the 1890s. Political posters appeared wherever there was a store wall to paste them on. Japanese lanterns printed with political advertising, American flags with the names of candidates stamped across the bars hung from the rafters. Anything large enough to hold a candidate's name or his picture was made up for sale—handkerchiefs, crockery, lamp chimneys, match safes.

In the busy 1896 campaign a mustard company packed their product in glass mugs picturing Bryan or McKinley. These were wholesaled in cases of forty-eight, two dozen for each candidate in each case, and retailed at 10 cents each. An "unbiased" sofa pillow cover showed McKinley's picture on one side, Bryan's on the other.

In 1951, on the wall of the empty store room of Wilson Brothers in South Butler, was found a thick bunch of posters. A 1916 Hughes and Fairbanks topped Taft and Butler (1912); Taft and Sherman (1908); Roosevelt and Fairbanks (1904); McKinley and Roosevelt (1900); McKinley and Hobart (1896); and a very brittle Benjamin Harrison and Whitelaw Reid (1892). Folded Japanese balloons were found there, too. An ingenious wire apparatus when inserted into the balloon, formed it into a ball on which the candidates' portraits appeared. The Republican Wilsons had staunchly blocked out the pictures of Hendricks and Thurman on Democratic

PLATE 126.   Homemade Harrison and Morton flag hung in front of Constant Pattet's general store in Little France, Oswego Co., N.Y in 1888 campaign.

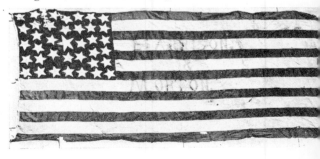

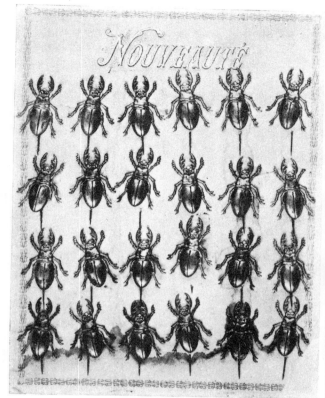

PLATE 127. Made in France, "Gold Bug" pins for the McKinley campaign of 1896, indicated McKinley's stand for the "sound money, gold standard," as against Bryan's plank for the silver standard.

PLATE 128. On flags printed with campaign sentiments, stars and candidates' portraits were arranged to suit individual tastes. Large bunting flags hung outside on store porches; paper flags and posters indoors.

balloons, and used them as decoration only. A Harrison and Morton (1888) lantern bore in addition to the candidates' pictures, a log cabin, and the slogan "Tippecanoe and Morton, too," an advertisement for Law's Bluing. (This bluing, made in South Butler by Arthur Law who supplied the lanterns to his customers, was later manufactured in Syracuse and sold as Merchant's Bluing.)

The Wilsons must have over-ordered on goldbug pins for the 1896 McKinley campaign for several untouched cards still remain. These were made in France and wholesaled at $6 a gross for the smaller size, $8 a gross for the larger.

The American Flag was always a "best seller" in country stores. The earliest offered for sale were made with the stars

PLATE 129. Elaborate embossed tin store sign in red, white and blue, distributed to wholesale customers by Campbell Soup in 1902 advertised the 21 varieties then made. Campbell policy decreed against using the American flag for advertising.

and stripes cut separately and sewn together by hand to form the design. The American Flag in various sizes was also frequently used as a background for advertising or messages.

President Taft, in 1912, put an end to outsize flags by establishing flag proportions, but it remained permissible to print messages on the flag until 1917. At times of gubernatorial and national elections, as well as for commemorative events like the opening of the Erie canal, many flags were struck off with advertising or souvenir sentiment. Though these had tremendous sale in country stores, examples are difficult to find today.

CHAPTER SEVEN

SUPERMARKETS

Help Yourself

BY 1930, the country general store had slipped into the past. Chain food stores, with low prices, wider selection, made possible by quantity buying, were solidly entrenched in even the smallest towns. F. W. Woolworth's Five and Tens, mushrooming like mad during the 1920s— there were already 1,000 of them in 1911— took over the market in gadgets and incidentals. Automobiles and improved roads had shortened the country miles—the fifteenth million T Model Ford had been turned out and the Model A was new in 1927. Some fourteen other firms were engaged in making automobiles for the one out of five Americans who owned them. Rural Free Delivery was dropping off bulky bargain-filled catalogs from Sears Roebuck and "Monkey Ward" at back country mail boxes and picking up postal orders for "citified" merchandise. National advertising had made the housewife brand-conscious. She no longer asked for "soap, flour, cornflakes, coffee;" she requested brand named goods.

The store at the crossroads, pushed too hard, settled down to an accommodation —a handy spot to pick up a last minute loaf of bread or quart of milk when other stores were closed. The general store in town turned to Fancy Groceries which the chain did not carry, or gasped along with a few old regular customers who abhorred change.

Practically all foodstuffs once handled in bulk were packaged. Occasionally an independent storekeeper arranged packaged goods so that the customer could make his own selection, carry it to the counter for payment, and avoid a long wait for service. Though this practice worked well for the few who tried it, it was generally considered a pretty slipshod way of doing business.

Even the Great Atlantic and Pacific Tea Company, when approached by Patrick Aloysius Cullen, head of their Syracuse Division, with a carefully worked out plan for a self-service store, saw no future in it, and turned thumbs down on such a revolutionary idea.

Mr. Cullen, on his own, went ahead to rent a mammoth garage in Jamaica, New York, and convert it into the self-service food store he had envisioned. His sign— KING KULLEN—proclaimed the first self-service supermarket.

Three interested Syracusans, including the writer, visited the Cullen operation and returned home to organize the Associated Foods, Inc. In the first week of December 1931, they opened in Syracuse, the second large self-service market in the East. [Mr. Johnson, who was president, part-owner of the company and manager of the Associated Foods market, resigned shortly to open the

first of his own Johnson Supermarkets.]
The Big Bear, located at Jersey City, was
the first supermarket to open in New
Jersey.

Self-service presented its own problems.
One, for which there seems no remedy,
is the lack of contact between customer
and those who work in stores. Another was
the total discovery that self-service customers selected advertised brands, ignoring
nationally unknown merchandise of quality and value on which stores had formerly
made a good profit. The latter challenge
was met successfully with new techniques
—low pressure selling, planned display,
and "talking" sales signs.

While the manager of a self-service chain
store, whose buying is all done for him,
may receive a bonus on increased volume,
the independent operator, knowing his
costs and in a position to put extra effort
on merchandise where profits are high,
has opportunity to make more money on
the same volume. By keeping in mind that
the average woman shopper notices no
more than thirty-one items on a trip to the
self-service store, he soon learns to display
the merchandise to be featured in a "stand-
out" fashion. For instance, if an 8 oz. tin

PLATE 130. Central shopping centers are nothing new.
Renaissance market place shows stalls of optician, shoemaker, tailor, and incidental sidewalk vendors. (Print
file of N.Y. Public Library)

of canned goods is to be pushed, he is
never guilty of minimizing its size by
placing it beside a larger can.

The story is told that Sir Thomas Lipton, as a boy in his parent's little grocery
in England, watching his father count out
eggs and put them in the customer's basket,
remarked sagely, "Let Mother serve the
eggs. Her hands are smaller—the eggs will
look larger." The same positive approach
had been long a precept to country store
clerks, weighing commodities in front of
a customer: "Always put a short quantity
in the hopper and add to it to reach the
required weight. If you pour in too much,
then take some out, the customer is bound
to feel cheated."

In self-service, the importance of the
placard was early learned. Once in the
Johnson market, a quantity of Old Trusty
Dog Biscuits, shaped like a dog bone, were
purchased in bulk, weighed out in two-
pound cellophane bags, and placed for sale
under a "2 lbs. for 25¢" sign. Next day a
belligerent matron slapped a package of
dog biscuits on the counter, "We can't
eat these cookies. They're stale. They won't
even dissolve in coffee." The identifying
"Dog Biscuits" appeared immediately
thereafter on the sign.

In another instance, when some ten
tons of Venezuelan sugar, bought at a price,
were placed on sale, an opened package
and explanatory placard anticipated complaints on the darkish color, and sold the
lot: "This is Venezuelan sugar. Though not
refined as white as ours, it is just as sweet,
just as pure, and is served on the tables
of the best Venezuelan families."

Frankness and "under-sell" were found
assets on "talking signs." A special Johnson sale of standard grade peas offered
"2 cans for 15¢." The can had a particularly
attractive label and unfortunately people
took their cue from the label, not the price.
They expected fancy peas. As complaints
came in, and the problem was recognized,
a printed explanation averted further dis-

appointment: "These peas are NOT fancy, mostly standard grade. Some are over-cooked, and some are hard." Curiosity sold the peas fast. Nothing could be quite as bad as the sign indicated!

Pilfering in self-service? No more than existed before—always a minute percent. Country store sagas are filled with men trying to conceal long-tailed codfish under short-tailed coats, and women, secreting butter in their bloomers, forced by all-seeing storekeepers to long uncomfortable conversations near stoves or over hot air registers. A sheepish good nature—and another story to tell—emerged as each help-yourselfer was caught. A constant offender, confronted with a can of sardines taken from his pocket and the question, "Now Henry, what have you got to say?" was content to gulp plaintively, "Shucks, Mr. Johnson, I thought I was going to have sardines for supper."

Second World War rationing offered special temptations. In the Johnson store a display of " Seven Day" coffee in the bean was placed on a counter in the center of the store. An attendant stood near to assist in the grinding, and to pick up the ration stamp. Payment was made at the regular checkout counter. Rather than change the counter display each week, a dummy display of bags filled with sawdust and shavings was made up. In the first week of coffee rationing, twenty-two dum-my bags, dexterously removed from the display, were paid for at coffee prices. There were no complaints from the ration stamp cheaters, and the Red Cross received from the store a check for the full amount of "sawdust" profits.

Gradually the self-service food store began to add related merchandise—not a wide selection but enough to give the specialty stores a twinge of competition. Today's supermarket, like the old country store, may carry stockings, shirts, baskets, flowers, seeds, bathing caps, infants wear, drug sundries, bedding, magazines, china and glassware, encyclopedias, and every-thing needed in the hardware line to furnish a kitchen. Some even handle heavy equip-ment stoves and refrigerators, purchasable on time.

Other departments of the country store —shoes, men's and women's clothing, millinery, knit goods, baked goods, chil-dren's toys, fabrics, trinkets, and odds and ends are to be found in specialty shops clustered about the supermarket core of today's Shopping Center.

Today and Tomorrow

TODAY'S food distribution business, tot-alling almost fifty billion dollars annually, is the nation's largest. In 1958, seven hun-dred and ninety chains operated some 180,-000 supermarkets with 2,000 more planned for 1959. The country's 360,000 independ-ent food stores meet the competition of arena size supers with their own additions and improvements.

While bigger supermarkets are being planned, other grocery operators are lean-ing to smaller "accommodation" stores. *Changing Times* reports a planned chain of seven-sided pagoda-like "Automats" in Denver, octagonal-shaped "Time Saver" stores in California, hexagonal-shaped "Del-amarts" in Los Angeles, and similar space-saving stores in New Mexico, Texas, and Arizona. Here last minute shoppers can drive up to the store, park, and pick up fast-moving staples, vegetables, and meats in a trice. Already in Yakima, Washington, an "all-day, all-night" vending machine on the front of a market conveniently dispenses about 100 different items.

As to technical innovations and speed-up services now in use or in the planning stage, there's a machine to bag purchases; another that wraps 32 packages of meat per minute; specially designed racks to replace packaged goods the minute they are removed, and a device that automatically carries away bottle empties and furnishes a receipt for them! The latest cash registers show the amount of change due.

As for the wonderful tomorrow, *Changing Times,* with its ear to the ground and its fingers on business statistics and movement writes glowingly—

Well within the realm of possibility in another ten years are the punch-card shopping, where electronic machines select and collect your groceries; motorized and electronic push carts; constantly changing lighting patterns inside the stores; moving sidewalks from parking lot to store door; automatic check-out counters that add your bill, pack your groceries and deliver your change— all without human guidance.

BIBLIOGRAPHY

ABELL, MRS. L. G. *The Skillful Housewife's Book, Complete Guide to Domestic Cookery*. D. Newell, New York, 1846.

ADAMS, JAMES TRUSLOW. *Provincial Society*. The Macmillan Company, New York, 1927.

ADAMS, SAMUEL HOPKINS. "The Great American Fraud." *Collier's Weekly*, October 7, 1905.

"Albany Bicentennial, 1686–1886," *Albany Journal*. Edited by Thurlow Weed Barnes. 1886.

The American Joe Miller, American Wit and Humor. Carey and Hart, Philadelphia, 1840.

ANDREWS, EDWARD D. *The Community Industries of the Shakers*. University of the State of New York, 1933.

ATHERTON, LEWIS ELDON. *A Quarterly of Research*. University of Missouri Studies. Columbia Mo. April 1, 1939.

AVERY, GILES B. *Sketches of Shakers and Shakerism*. Weed, Parsons & Co., Albany, N. Y., 1884.

BAILYN, BERNARD. *The New England Merchants in the Seventeenth Century*. Cambridge University Press, Cambridge, Mass. 1955.

BARBER, JOHN W. and HOWE, HENRY. *Historical Collections of the State of New York*. Publ. for the authors by S. Tuttle, 1841.

BEERS, F. W. *Atlas of Cayuga County, N. Y.* Walker and Jewett, 1875.

BEAUCHAMP, WILLIAM M. "History of the New York Iroquois," *N. Y. State Museum Bulletin*, #78.

BOTKIN, B. A. *Treasury of American Folklore*. Crown Publishers, New York, 1944.

BOTKIN, B. A. *A Treasury of New England Folklore*. Crown Publishers, New York, 1947.

BREMER, FREDRIKA. *Homes of the New World, Impressions of America*. Translated by Mary Howitt. Harper & Bros., New York, 1853.

BRIDENBAUGH, CARL. *Cities in the Wilderness*. Donald Press, New York, 1938.

BRISBIN, GEN. JAMES S. *Brisbin's Stories of the Plains*. Anchor Publishing Co., 1884.

BURGH, NICHOLAS PROCTOR. *A Treatise on Sugar Machinery*. E. and F. N. Spon, London, England.

CARSON, GERALD. *The Country Store*. Oxford University Press, New York, 1954.

CAULKINS, FRANCES MANWARING. *History of New London, Conn*. Press of Chase, Tiffany & Co., Hartford, Ct., 1852.

A Century of Service, 1815–1915. Silas Peirce & Co., Ltd., Boston, Mass., 1915.

CHAMBERLAIN, SAMUEL AND FLYNT, HENRY N. *Frontier of Freedom*. Hastings House, New York, 1952.

CHURCH, HIRAM AND BROWN, EDWARD T. "Pioneer Days of Wolcott, N. Y.," *Lakeside News*, Wolcott, N. Y., 1953.

CLAYTON, W. WOODFORD. *History of Onondaga County, New York*. D. Mason & Co., Syracuse, N. Y., 1878.

The Clockmaker, or the Sayings and Doings of Samuel Slick of Slickville, Carey, Lea and Blanchard, Philadelphia, Pa., 1837.

COLDEN, CADWALLADER. *History of the Five Indian Nations of Canada*. London, England, 1747.

COLLINS, JAMES H. *The Story of Canned Foods*. E. P. Dutton & Co., New York, 1924.

CONOVER, GEORGE STILWELL, Lewis Carr Aldrich, complr. *History of Ontario County, N. Y.* D. Mason & Co., Syracuse, N. Y., 1893.

CURRIER, JOHN J. *"Ould Newbury."* Vol. I. Damrell & Upham, Boston, Mass., 1896.

DABOLL, NATHAN. *Schoolmaster's Assistant*. Printed by E. P. Cady for S. Green, New London, Conn., 1808 (?).

DEPEW, CHAUNCEY M. *One Hundred Years of American Commerce*. D. O. Haynes & Co., New York, 1895.

DEVANS, RICHARD, MILLER. *Cyclopaedia of Commercial & Business Anecdotes*, D. Appleton &

Co., New York, 1864.

EARLE, ALICE MORSE. *Home Life in Colonial Days*. The Macmillan Company, New York, 1899.

EDMONDS, WALTER D. *The First Hundred Years*. Oneida, Ltd., Oneida, New York, 1948.

EVERETT & ENSIGN. *History of Tioga, Chumung, Tompkins and Schuyler Counties, New York*. D. Ensign & Co., Philadelphia, 1878.

FELKER, M. S. *The Grocer's Manual*. Grocer Publishing Co., St. Louis, Mo., 1879.

FOX, DIXON RYAN. *Yankees and Yorkers*. New York University Press, New York, 1940.

FRANTZ, JOE E. *Gail Borden, Dairyman to a Nation*. University of Oklahoma Press, Norman Okla., 1957.

FURNAS, C. C. AND FURNAS, S.M. *The Story of Man and His Food*. New Home Library, New York, 1937.

The Galleon. Bulletin for the Society of Colonial History, No. 14. Edited by John J. Vrooman, Schenectady, N. Y., 1954.

GOULD, MARY EARLE. *The Early American House*. M. McBride Co., New York, 1949.

GOULD, MARY EARLE. *Early American Wooden Ware*. Pond-Ekberg Co., Springfield, Mass., 1942.

Grocer's Companion and Merchant's Hand-Book. Benjamin Johnson, Boston, Mass., 1883.

HISLOP, CODMAN. *The Mohawk*. Rhinehart & Company, Inc., New York, 1948.

HALSEY, FRANCIS WHITING. *The Old New York Frontier*. Charles Scribner's & Sons, New York, 1901.

Harper's New Monthly Magazine. August 1851; February 1852; June 1861.

HEDRICK, ULYSSES PRENTICE. *A History of Agriculture in the State of New York*. J. B. Lyon Co., Albany, N. Y. (Printed for the N. Y. State Agricultural Society) 1933.

HEDRICK, ULYSSES PRENTICE. *A History of Horticulture in America to 1860*. Oxford University Press, New York, 1950.

HEDRICK, ULYSSES PRENTICE. *The Land of the Crooked Tree*. Oxford University Press, New York, 1948.

STIMSON, ALEXANDER LOVETT. *History of Express Business*. Baker & Godwin, printers, New York, 1881.

History of the Mohawk Valley, Gateway to the West, 1614–1925. 4 vols. Edited by Nelson Greene. S. J. Clarke Publishing Co., Chicago, Ill., 1925.

History of Newburyport, Massachusetts. Vol. 2. 1909.

HOTCHKIN, REV. JAMES H. *Religious History of Western New York*, (1848?).

HOUSE, ALBERT V. "Two Yankee Traders in New York." *New England Quarterly*, September 1938.

HOWE, HERBERT BARBER. *Jedediah Barber, 1787–1876*. Columbia University Press, New York, 1939.

HOWE, HERBERT BARBER. *John Meeker, 1787–1840*. mms, Syracuse Public Library, Syracuse, N. Y.

HOWELL & TENNEY. *History of the County of Albany, New York, 1609–1886*.

IRVING, WASHINGTON. *Knickerbocker History of New York*.

"Journal of Madam Knight," *Museum of Foreign Literature in Science*.

"Journal of William Block, 1744," *Magazine of History & Biography*. Vol. 1.

KEIR, R. MALCOLM. "The Unappreciated Tin Peddler." *Annals of American Academy of Political and Social Science*. Vol. 46. 1913.

LAWSON, HARVEY M. *History and Geneology of the Descendants of Clement Corbin*. Hartford Press, Hartford, Conn., 1905.

LESLIE, MISS. *The House Book, or a Manual of Domestic Economy*. Carey & Hart, Philadelphia, Pa., 1840.

LOMBARD, PERCIVAL HALL. *The Aptucxet Trading Post*. 1953.

MCCAFFERTY, E. D. *Henry J. Heinz, A Biography*. Bartlett Orr Press, New York, 1923.

MCINTOSH, PROF. W. H. *History of Wayne County, New York*. 1877.

Merrell-Soule Products. Merrell-Soule Company, Syracuse, N. Y., 1919.

MERRIAM, HILDA DOYLE. *North of the Mohawk*. University of Chicago Press, Chicago, Ill., 1950.

MOORE, R. *Everybody's Guide, or Things Worth Knowing*. Copyright New York World. J. C. Ogilvie & Co., 1889.

Narratives of New England, 1609–1664. John Franklin Jameson, Editor. Charles Scribner's & Sons, New York, 1909.

NORTON, REV. JOHN FOOTE, *The History of Fitzwilliam, New Hampshire from 1752 to 1887*. Burr Printing House, New York, 1888.

Pompey Reunion and History. 1875.

BREWSTER, CHARLES WARREN. *Rambles about Portsmouth, Sketches of Persons, Localities and Incidents of Two Centuries*. First Series. L. H. Brewster, Portsmouth, N. H., 1873.

RAWSON, MARION NICHOLL. *Of the Earth Earthy*. E. P. Dutton & Co., Inc., New York, 1937.

Rex Et Regina Vs. Lutherland. Will Bradley, Philadelphia, Pa., 1692. Lenox Collection, New York Public Library.

ROBINSON, JAMES HARVEY. *Our World Today*

and Yesterday. Ginn & Company, Boston, Mass., 1934.

ROE, ALFRED SEELYE. *Ninth New York Heavy Artillery*. Published by author, Worcester, Mass., 1899.

SCOVILLE, JOSEPH A. *The Old Merchants of New York City*. Charleton, New York, 1863.

SEMPLE, ELLEN CHURCHILL. *American History and Its Geographic Conditions*. Riverside Press, Cambridge, Mass., 1933.

SHERWOOD, UNCLE BOB. *Hold Your Horses, the Elephants Are Coming*. The Macmillan Company, New York, 1932.

SINCLAIR, UPTON. *The Jungle*. Viking Press, New York,

Somerset Quarterly. New Jersey, July 1913.

STANTON, WILLIAM ALONZO. *Geneological and biographical statistic record of Thomas Stanton of Connecticut and his descendants*. J. Munsell's Sons, Albany, 1891.

STIMSON, A. L. *Wells College, Its Founders*. 1901.

The Story of a Pantry Shelf. Butterick Publishing Co., 1925.

BARNUM, P. T. *Struggles and Triumph, or Forty Years' Recollections of P. T. Barnum*. J. B. Burr & Company, Hartford, Ct., 1869.

TAUSSIG, CHARLES WILLIAM. *Rum, Romance and Rebellion*. Minton, Balch & Co., New York, 1928.

THORNTON, HARRISON JOHN. *The History of the Quaker Oats Company*. University of Chicago Press, Chicago, Ill., 1933.

THURMES, E. S. *The Shocking History of Advertising*. E. P. Dutton Co., Inc., New York, 1953.

VAN WAGENEN, JARED, JR. *The Golden Age of Homespun*. Cornell University Press, Ithaca, N.Y., 1953.

WAUGH, ALEC. *The Lipton Story*. Doubleday & Co., New York, 1950.

WHEELER, GRACE DENISON. *Homes of Our Ancestors in Stonington, Conn.* Newcomb & Gauss, printers, Salem, Mass., 1903.

William Wrigley, Jr. manuscript. Outdoor Advertising Association of America, Chicago. 1939.

WILLIAMS, MAJOR WILLIAM. *History of Early Fort Dodge and Webster County, Iowa*. Edited by Edward Breen. Copyright by KVFD-KFMY, Fort Dodge, Iowa, 1950.

WILLIAMSON, JEFFERSON. *The American Hotel*. Alfred A. Knopf, Inc., New York, 1930.

INDEX